DEMYSTIFYING SYRIA

Other Titles in the Series

British-Egyptian Relations from Suez to the Present Day

The Gulf Family: Kinship Policies and Modernity

Higher Education in the Gulf States: Shaping Economies, Politics and Culture

Oil and Democracy in Iraq

Popular Culture and Political Identity in the Arab Gulf States

Translating Libya: The Modern Libyan Short Story

Turkey, the US and Iraq

SOAS MIDDLE EAST ISSUES

Demystifying Syria

Edited by
Fred H. Lawson

SAQI
in association with

**LONDON
MIDDLE EAST
INSTITUTE
SOAS**

ISBN: 978-0-86356-654-7

A full CIP record for this book is available from the British Library.

A full CIP record for this book is available from the Library of Congress.

Manufactured in Lebanon

SAQI

26 Westbourne Grove, London W2 5RH
Tabet Building, Mneimneh Street, Hamra, Beirut
www.saqibooks.com

in association with

The London Middle East Institute
School of Oriental and African Studies, Russell Square, London WC1H 0XG
www.lmei.soas.ac.uk

Contents

Acknowledgements

Julie Gauthier's essay originally appeared as 'Les evenements de Qamichlo: irruption de la question kurde en Syrie' in the May 2005 issue of *Études Kurdes: Revue Semestrielle de Recherches*, published by Editions L'Harmattan in Paris. It is translated and republished here by permission of the editor of that journal.

Louise Hosking of the London Middle East Institute copyedited the manuscript with exceptional skill and insight, and with persistent good humour. The editor and contributors are deeply in her debt.

Introduction

Fred H. Lawson

Syria's political, economic, social and diplomatic affairs are often described as 'mysterious', 'puzzling' or 'strange'. Sometimes, the descriptions seem apt. At least for now, the October 2005 death of Minister of the Interior Ghazi Kan'an remains a mystery, as does the killing of General Muhammad Sulaiman at his beachfront chalet in early August 2008.[1] Equally mysterious at this point is the rapid and unexpected eclipse of General 'Asif Shawkat, the brother-in-law of the president and head of one of the country's powerful security services.[2] And it is fair to say that 'mystery surrounded a powerful car bomb explosion that ripped through a residential neighbourhood on the outskirts of Damascus [at the end of September 2008], killing at least seventeen people and injuring fourteen in the deadliest terrorist attack in Syria in more than two decades'.[3] The location of the blast, just outside the headquarters of one of the security services, and at a busy crossroads leading to the Shi'i pilgrimage site of the tomb of al-Sayyidah Zainab, leaves one wondering whether the intended target was the military post or the Lebanese, Iraqi and Iranian pilgrims who frequent the area.

Other so-called mysteries reflect a lack of information or superficial analysis. It is probably not helpful to conclude, for instance, that an armed skirmish between Islamist militants and security personnel that erupted in the heart of the capital in June 2006 'remains shrouded in mystery', despite a flood of rumours surrounding the episode.[4] It is almost certainly misleading to think of the alliance of Syria, Iran, Hizbullah and Hamas as 'strange [and] unnatural',[5] simply because it brings together unlikely bedfellows. And asserting that Syria's reluctance to engage in public discussions with Israel after an eight-year hiatus, which Damascus blames on inflexibility and high-handedness on the part of the Israeli and the United States leaderships, illustrates 'the political and military murkiness' of Syrian diplomacy is patently unfair.[6]

Perhaps there are underlying reasons why unsympathetic observers would characterise any given country as mysterious, puzzling or strange. Western liberal thought exhibits a tendency to interpret actions and platforms that do not conform to its own basic tenets as irrational or inexplicable, and this inclination lies at the heart of a good deal of United States foreign policy.[7] There may even be good reasons for astute players to shroud their actions and platforms in a cloak of mysteriousness: one of the more intriguing social movements in contemporary Syria actually calls itself 'The Strange Ones' (*ghuraba al-sham*), perhaps in order to keep the authorities guessing about its true intentions and programme.

But for anyone who wishes to understand today's Syria, referring to developments in domestic and foreign affairs as mysterious and puzzling is a clarion call to exert greater effort to unravel the mysteries and solve the puzzles. The contributors to this collection of essays have been energised, rather than confounded, by the complexities, uncertainties and paradoxes that characterise Syria's internal and external affairs. They offer insight into a wide range of current trends, sometimes by analysing this particular case in terms of broader theories and debates in the social sciences and sometimes by presenting information that is generally overlooked or unreported. Readers will come away knowing much more about this pivotal country than they did when they first opened the book and can be expected to gain a clearer understanding of the political, economic, social and diplomatic dynamics that shape one of the few countries that continues to resist the 'end of history'.

Notes

1. 'Syrian Interior Minister "Commits Suicide"', *The Times* (London), 12 October 2005; Nicholas Blanford, 'The Mystery Behind a Syrian Murder', *Time*, 7 August 2008.
2. 'The Mysterious Downfall of Assef Shawkat', *Mideast Monitor*, vol. 3, August 2008.
3. 'Car Bombing in Damascus Kills at least 17', *Los Angeles Times*, 28 September 2008.
4. Chris Zambelis, 'Violence in Syria Points to Growing Radical Islamist Unrest', *Terrorism Focus*, vol. 3, 13 June 2006.
5. Ely Karmon, *Iran-Syria-Hizbullah-Hamas: A Coalition Against Nature: Why Does It Work?*, United States Army War College, Proteus Monograph Series, vol. 1, no. 3, May 2008.
6. 'A Recent Assassination Makes Syrian Politics Look as Mysterious as Ever', *The Economist*, 14 August 2008.
7. Michael H. Hunt, *Ideology and U.S. Foreign Policy*, New Haven, Conn., 1988.

ONE

Changing Social Structure, Shifting Alliances and Authoritarianism in Syria

Salwa Ismail

Since the 1960s Syrian politics have been dominated by authoritarian forms of political rule that have concentrated governmental power in the hands of a few. Using repression, and resting on an elaborate security apparatus, the military officer class that rose to power in the 1960s entrenched itself and banished all contending forces. Following his assumption of power in July 2000, President Bashar al-Asad expressed support for political liberalisation and pluralism. Seizing the opportunity, segments of society began to organise in the public sphere under the rubric of the movement for the revival of civil society (*harakah 'ihya' al-mujtama'ah al-madani*).[1] However, the promise of this political opening was short-lived, as the regime soon moved to close down the civil society forums, arrest activists and restrain all forms of societal organisation.

This retreat into repression notwithstanding, the Syrian regime exhibits signs of weakness and appears to be faltering. Further, there are indications that splits inside the military–political elite are developing, as evidenced by numerous episodes of rivalry and squabbling. Among the questions that arise in this context are: what are the internal forces of change and who are the actors that might press for a transition away from authoritarianism?

To answer these questions, I suggest that we examine the structural foundations of authoritarianism in Syria and the transformations that these are undergoing as the result of a reconfiguration of political forces and alliances. By bringing into focus the structural conditions that allow for the consolidation of authoritarianism, and by tracing changes in these conditions, this article contributes to understanding how authoritarian regimes persist.[2] Recent political developments in Syria present us with a good case for the study of authoritarianism in crisis.

With the ongoing process of elite differentiation that has accompanied economic liberalisation, a realignment of socio-political forces is taking place in contemporary Syria. On one hand, the historical alliance between the 'Alawi-dominated military regime and the Sunni merchants is under increasing strain and may be dissolving. On the other, the alliances of earlier eras – for instance, the alliance between shaikhs and merchants – are being resurrected. I contend that we are witnessing the reproduction of a religio-mercantile complex that may contribute to further disintegration of the regime.

Changing Class Foundations

As a military-led regime in which key positions are held by individuals from the 'Alawi minority, the Syrian system has often been referred to as one of 'Alawi rule. However, this formulation is simplistic and lacks nuance. 'Alawi political dominance takes such forms as the control of security positions – intelligence services and key army divisions, for instance. However, there is a civilian decision-making group in which Sunnis, with a strong Damascene component, are well represented. During the era of President Hafiz al-Asad, two of the most trusted politicians were Sunnis, namely Mustafa Tlas and 'Abd al-Halim Khaddam. Both men are credited with having prepared the grounds for Bashar al-Asad's accession to the presidency. All the same, some Syrian intellectuals include Tlas and Khaddam as members of a regime of political 'Alawism (*al-'alawiyyah al-siyasiyyah*). Political 'Alawism refers to a form of rule that consecrates sectarianism and rests on a certain alliance and intersection of interests. The concept is meant to capture the idea that authority and rule (*al-sultah wal-hukm*) are 'Alawi, but that the 'Alawis do not rule. This situation can also be described as the sectarianism of authority (*ta'ifiyyah al-sultah*) but not the authority of the 'Alawis (*sultah al-'alawiyyah*) or the authority of the sect (*sultah al-ta'ifah*).[3]

The military–sectarian power configuration is tied to a particular economic order that rests on alliances and exchanges with certain socio-economic forces. These, in turn, broaden the ruling coalition and bring in strata that have a vested interest in the continuation of the ruling elite's monopoly over state power. Thus, in considering opportunities and con-straints in the process of transition, we should take sufficient note of the political–economic alliances that support the regime and, importantly, outline certain features of the wider configuration. The al-Asad regime was consolidated through a historic alliance between the predominantly 'Alawi military officer corps and the Sunni merchant-business class, in particular its Damascene component. We should consider briefly the terms of this historical alliance, the context in which it was fostered and how it has unfolded over the last three decades.

The Ba'th Party, from its more radical days in the mid-1960s, under-took to liquidate Syria's landed elite and small group of large industrial-ists. Through land-reform laws and nationalisation, these two strata were effectively marginalised. It should be recalled that these social forces had taken the form of notable families and clans that had dominated not only Syria's economy but also its polity. Thus, the families who engaged in what Albert Hourani called 'the politics of the notables' virtually disappeared from Syria's political scene.

During its revolutionary phase (1963–70), the Ba'th Party in government embarked on policies of economic redistribution and welfare provision that reshaped society and contributed to the rise of new social forces that provided the party with widespread support. As Raymond Hinnebusch[4] shows, peasants and workers were major beneficiaries of these policies. In return, they gave their allegiance to the regime and constituted its social base. These forces were absorbed through corporatist structures organised and managed by the party.

As the radical phase came to an end with the rise of Hafiz al-Asad, a slow move towards a mixed economy began and measures of economic liberalisation were introduced. Studies of the political economy of Syria under Hafiz al-Asad point out that the Ba'thi regime engaged once again in the restructuring of economic forces, helping to engender the rise of strata whose vested interests were intimately tied to the ruling group.[5] As such, it helped create commercial–business interests that worked in conjunction with the state monopoly of most sectors of the economy and that benefited from the 'socialist' principles guiding economic policy. The liberalising turn set the ground for the development of new social and political alliances that consolidated the regime. Over the years, differentiated economic elites grew in power and extended support for the ruling group.

With the regime's move towards a mixed economic system, certain private sector actors were allowed to resurface, namely segments of the middle merchant class. Thus, after a period of contraction, there was a resurgence of the middle-level merchant families of the 1930s and 1940s – for example, al-Shallah, al-Qalla', al-Qabban, al-Habbal, al-'Aqqad, al-Farra, al-Haffar, al-Jallad and al-Sabbagh – whom the state sought to incorporate while continuing to shun the remaining 'aristocratic' families of the Ottoman period. Central to the incorporation of this stratum was its role as a junior partner to the state in the economic field. In this partnership, the middle merchants dominated the chambers of commerce and were given privileged entry into the mixed sector. In that role, they functioned as subcontractors on deals managed by the state. For instance, the middle merchant class was party to the barter agreements with East European countries. To repay its military debt, the Syrian government entered into numerous such agreements, using its local manufacturing industries to supply products in return for monies owed on purchases of arms. Trade in textiles, chemicals and foodstuffs flourished under these arrangements.

The co-optation of the representatives of the middle merchants was central to the regime's consolidation of power. The most notable event that cemented this alliance took place in 1980 when the regime faced one of its most serious crises – a possible nationwide uprising. At the forefront of this uprising stood the established merchants of Aleppo. Having called for a nationwide strike that included the closing of shops in the *suqs* (marketplaces), the merchants signalled their public opposition to the regime and their willingness to join other forces contesting it, mainly the Muslim Brothers and the banned leftist parties. Damascene merchants were expected to join the strike, and it was thought that their participation would bring down the regime. However, while the merchants of Aleppo closed their shops, their Damascene counterparts kept theirs open. To this day, many local observers believe that the Damascene merchants could have brought down the regime but chose not to do so. By all accounts, elements of the traditional merchant class co-operated with the regime at this crucial moment. The role of the Damascus Chamber of Commerce and its resident, Badr al-Din al-Shallah, was particularly important. According to some accounts, al-Shallah and his aides called other merchants and advised them not to participate in the strike.[6] A warning was given that shop shutters would be forcibly opened and that no protection would be provided. There are also indications that intimidation tactics were used and rumours circulated to the effect that some merchants who opposed the decision not to strike had been murdered. The decision by the Damascene merchants not to join the strike was shaped by their earlier experience of a national strike in 1964, when their locked shops were forcibly opened and their stores looted. Further, there was a fear of a bloody confrontation with the special military forces of Rif 'at al-Asad, which were thought to have encircled the city.

From that moment on, Damascene merchants became partners of the regime and continued to express their public allegiance. The close relationship between al-Shallah and President al-Asad attained legendary status when, during a national election, the latter chose to cast his vote in al-Shallah's precinct. This was more than a photo opportunity. Rather, the symbolism of an allegiance declaration (*bay'a*) was realised when al-Shallah took off his cloak (*'abaya*) and placed it on the president's shoulders.

The National Bourgeoisie and the Rise of Awlad al-Sultah

Along with the re-emergent merchant strata of the 1930s and 1940s, a commercial bourgeoisie – whose main figures, as noted by Volker Perthes,[7] were al-'A'idi, al-Nahhas and al-'Attar – was engineered by the regime in the 1970s. During this period, the principal areas of state–business partnership were in tourism and transport. Perthes's classification of the Syrian bourgeoisie into four groups highlights an early process of elite differentiation. His schema captures similarities among the various strata, as well as divisions and fissures. One line of division that remains important and has now been accentuated is that between what Perthes calls the 'industrial bourgeoisie' and the 'new class of contractors and middlemen'. At the heart of the division lies the distinction between productive and unproductive economic activities and between national capital and crony capitalism. These distinctions are important in the context of liberalisation and privatisation, as rent-seeking activities undermine trust and weaken interest in long-term investments in favour of quick-profit-making ventures.

Lines of division and fissure among the economic elites have been accentuated. The rise of new actors, known as *awlad al-sultah* (the children of authority), as key players in the new sectors of the economy has exacerbated elite divisions. These new players have joined the commercial stratum engineered by the regime in the 1970s. We can now speak of a new class that has distinctive features, best captured under the descriptor 'oligarchy' (whose economic activities are concentrated in areas such as car dealerships and information technology). These features and characteristics have implications for the period of transition. Of these, the flight of capital, the illegal appropriation of public resources, the usurious nature of investment and the web of connections represent important challenges. The conditions outlined here enter into the scenario of a breakdown of the historical alliance between the national bourgeoisie (traditional merchants and industrialists) and the state.[8]

These developments constitute key variables in understanding the process of reform and the course of transition. For present purposes, I want to highlight the implications of two interrelated developments: first, the rise of *awlad al-sultah* and second, the apparent loosening of the alliance between the ruling group and the traditional bourgeoisie. The economic opening pursued by the regime since the 1980s and consolidated in the 1990s saw the rise and integration of what some Syrian analysts call a new oligarchy, composed of high-ranking officials and their offspring. Members of this new class profited from the spoils of the economic opening: car dealerships, travel agencies, monopoly rights over the provision of certain goods and services. Certain features of their activities confirm the monopolistic character of their economic engagement. For example, some areas of production and commercial distribution are in the hands of a few – in the area of food imports, the al-Jud, al-Tun and Tlas family names stand out. It should be noted, further, that these same families are present in a multitude of commercial sectors.

Families and clans tied to the regime have become major economic actors. Today, Rami Makhluf, the president's maternal cousin, is held to be the most representative figure of this development. Makhluf has a virtual monopoly over mobile phone services, given through a sweet deal in which tendering rules were manipulated. He also enjoys a monopoly in the running of duty-free markets on Syria's borders. His diversified business portfolio includes a number of other ventures, such as the country's top private English-language school, sole representation of Schindler elevators and various restaurant chains. Makhluf is the most high-profiled member of *awlad al-sultah* but there are others: the sons of Mustafa Tlas, who own MAS Group, have real-estate interests, restaurants and an unspecified number of companies including a meat-processing factory with sole rights to supply processed meat to the army; the sons of 'Abd al-Halim Khaddam, whose profile is similar to that of the Tlases; the son of Bahjat Sulaiman (the head of internal security until June 2005) controls some significant businesses, including United Group, a major advertising and publishing company; the Shalishes (cousins of the president), who are prominent figures in real-estate development and in the oil service sector. Counted among the *awlad al-sultah* are the immediate members of the al-Asad family ('Asif Shawkat, Bushra al-Asad, Mahir al-Asad) as well as members of the extended clan.

What is the importance of the *awlad al-sultah*? It may be argued that its economic activities are parasitic and unproductive, and that it carries little weight in Syrian politics and society. However, this stratum has a stake in the regime and in the preservation of its economic interests. Many of its figures are tied to the security apparatus. Thus, the members of *awlad al-sultah* are likely to use their connections to influence the direction of change.[9] Indeed, today some members of this stratum have chosen to support reform. For example, Firas Tlas has been working to assume a public role, engaging through the media on issues of reform and corruption. Similarly, Bilal al-Turkmani, the son of the current minister of defence, publishes *Abyad wa Aswad*, Syria's only privately owned weekly magazine dealing with political issues. Debating reform and setting the frame for political engagement are modes pursued by the *awlad al-sultah* with the purpose of laundering their families' pasts and becoming integrated. Such strategies, if successful, may help to ease the transition by reducing the financial and political costs that these economic elites might otherwise incur.

In contrast to the *awlad al-sultah*, whose members are newcomers, the other important economic force is the national bourgeoisie, composed of traditional merchants and industrialists, some of whom compromised with the Ba'thi regime or managed to reach a *modus vivendi* with it. The position of this stratum relative to the regime appears to be changing at present. In some sense, it can be argued that its alliance with the regime has loosened, if not broken. According to one merchant, the alliance broke apart 'when they began to put their hands into our pockets'.[10] The reference here is to *awlad al-sultah* trying to muscle in on established merchants' businesses. Emblematic of this struggle between *awlad al-sultah* and the established merchants is the conflict over the Mercedes-Benz automobile dealership. In this incident, Rami Makluf tried to take the dealership away from Sanqar Sons, who have been Mercedes-Benz's official representative since the 1960s. When Sanqar Sons refused to relinquish the dealership, state intervention in the form of a legal loophole was used to obstruct the company's ability to import spare parts. As a result of the conflict, Mercedes-Benz suspended operations until the matter was internally resolved and the dealership was returned to Sanqar Sons.

Fissures inside the economic elite stratum run along various lines. The episode of conflict between Makhluf and Sanqar could be read as the expression of economic rivalries between new business-class entrants and older ones. It can also be read in sectarian and clan terms, since one side belongs to *awlad al-sultah* and the 'Alawi political elite and the other to the Sunni merchant class. This second motif is deployed in the narrative of preferential treatment in the distribution of business deals, as well as in the implementation of new regulations governing privatisation and the expansion of private sector activities.

Differential access to new distributional opportunities and the preferential treatment accorded to various economic players point to the narrowing of circles of beneficiaries in favour of the *awlad al-sultah* and its partners. This is illustrated in an instance of controversy and conflict surrounding the implementation of new directives issued to encourage private companies to sell shares to the public. Seeking to capitalise on the opportunity for capital growth, two companies took steps to advertise share sales, converting their limited liability companies to shareholding companies: one is Syriatel owned by Rami Makhluf and the other is al-Nama' owned by industrialist Ahmad Da'bul.[11] The timing of the sale of shares of the two companies coincided. Syriatel's sale proceeded smoothly, despite many objections on questions of legality. Da'bul's venture was questioned as well, but ended up being suspended.[12]

The setting-up of shareholding companies crystallises certain problems in the transition to a market economy. The controversy surrounding the conversion of these two companies highlights some of the problems. First, the Ministry of the Economy did not intervene to oversee the financial and technical evaluation of either company. In the case of al-Nama', doubts were raised about the veracity of the evaluations that were presented. In particular, it was thought that the depreciation of the company's fixed assets was not calculated correctly, inflating the value of company holdings. Concerns about Syriatel were manifold. Syriatel's status as build, operate and transfer (BOT) means that the company would revert to state owner-ship after fifteen years of operation.[13] Additionally, Syriatel is registered as a communications company with mobile telephone services being only one of its activities; some of its other activities are potentially loss making. Yet, critics point out that in floating shares on the market, Syriatel did not list all of its activities and buyers were led to believe that they were purchasing shares in mobile telephone services exclusively.[14]

The Makhluf and Da'bul episodes and others like them are usually seen as part of a wider process of monopolisation of business opportunities and concentration of wealth on the part of the *awlad al-sultah*. Traditional merchants and industrialists are concerned that state monopolies will move into the hands of the new stratum and entrench the polarisation of society. To ensure that this does not happen, they point out that laws governing the ownership and operation of shareholding companies should apply to privatised companies. These laws put a ceiling on the percentage of shares that can be held by any single shareholder.

In interviews, merchants and industrialists noted that they were never in the forefront of political action. They admitted weakness and lack of will to get involved directly in politics. In this respect, Riyad Saif and Ma'mun al-Homsi are exceptions in terms of businesspeople's active participation in the civil society movement. Some leading and noted industrialists explain their reluctance to engage in the movement as a function of their concern with its leftist orientation and the connections that link some of its players to foreign actors.[15] Indeed, some have opined that certain actors maintain close links with American and European embassies and ministries of foreign affairs in European countries. These ties are seen as dangerous and are construed as a foreign plot not only against the regime, but also against national interests and independence. Thus, a nationalist discourse is used by traditional merchants and businesspeople to justify their reluctance to play an active role in politics.

The absence of the merchants and industrialists from the political fray continues to characterise the Syrian domestic arena. However, behind the scenes, there are developments that help to explain their public posture. Industrialists like Khalid Mahjub, the owner of a modern glass factory, and Sa'id al-Hafiz, a leading figure in household appliances production and sales, whose companies date back to the pre-nationalisation period, are consulted by the regime on matters of policy that directly affect their sectors. Further, they have been co-opted into the wider power structure by informal means.[16] This strategy of co-optation ensures their support.

Despite its reluctance to take a public role, Syria's traditional merchant and industrial class has assets at its disposal that it can deploy to increase pressure for change. Also, if it were to enter an alliance with constituents of the civil society movement, it could bring much needed support to the intellectuals and professionals who are battling the regime and its security services. Syria's national bourgeoisie commands a significant part of the economy – in fact, the majority of industries, if oil is left out, are in the private sector. It also controls a significant percentage of the national product and employs a growing percentage of the labour force. Moreover, its businesses are among the main sources of the foreign currency that is so greatly in need to stabilise the economy. A further flight of Syrian capital might well paralyse industry and trade. The regime has been betting on the return of Syrian capital invested abroad, which is calculated to be somewhere in the range of $800 million to $10 billion. Attracting any of this capital back to Syria requires a greater incorporation of the national bourgeoisie.

So, despite their present timidity, the members of the national bourgeoisie are actors to be reckoned with and their actions and strategies could well shape the direction of future change.

Middle Merchants as a Re-Emergent Socio-Political Force

The historic alliance between the Damascene Sunni merchants and the 'Alawi-led military regime is the foundation of the Syrian regime. This, however, should not be understood to mean that the merchant class has joined this alliance wholesale, nor that it is fully incorporated. The regime enlisted a fair number of middle-level merchant families in the service of the state-controlled economy during the 1960s and later on allowed them to expand as part of the liberalisation programme. However, Sunni merchants at the middle level maintained a substantial degree of autonomy in various respects. Therefore, in evaluating the possible dissolution of the ruling alliance, we should pay close attention to the middle merchants and to their modes of organisation.

The economic, social and, potentially, political weight of the 'traditional' social strata of middle merchants and workshop owners becomes clear when we consider that small and medium-sized enterprises represent the majority of private businesses and employ the bulk of the labour force engaged in private sector, non-agricultural economic activity. In addition to their economic weight, traditional merchants and workshop proprietors have maintained a degree of independence from state institutions, in particular in the financial sphere. The links that have been forged between merchants, workshop owners and workers represent one feature of disengagement from the state that carries a potential for political transformation if, for example, middle merchants enter into an alliance with actors in the civil society movement or if they make an alliance with the religious establishment.

Greater insight into the middle merchants' forms of organisation can be gained by looking closely at the economic and social roles that they occupy in the Damascus *suq*s of Hamidiyyah and al-Hariqah. It should be pointed out that the *suq* is still dominated by 'Old Damascenes', many from established families of the old city. These families control many of the medium and small enterprises in key areas of production and sales, primarily textiles, foodstuffs and chemicals. Only migrants from Mnin, a village outside Damascus, have penetrated the textile manufacturing businesses located in the *suq*. This carefully guarded cohesion is furthered by the use of networks of finance and credit that are independent of the state. Middle-level merchants avoid the use of bank loans for religious reasons, as well as for practical reasons. For example, until 2003 it was not possible to hold foreign currency accounts in Syria, so many merchants had to rely on accounts in Lebanese banks. They therefore tended to carry out transfers of foreign currency and exchange among themselves, beyond the purview of the state-controlled banks.

Additionally, credit networks organise the manufacturing and commercial cycles. Merchants and workshop owners rely on instalment payments and advance payments to purchase supplies or sell their merchandise. A mode of accounting referred to as the circular account (*al-hisab al-dawwar*) structures dealings among merchants and manufacturers. The credit networks link up the workshops and the market by providing both credit and supply. For example, merchants may offer an advance to workshops to buy material to be used in the production of the finished goods that they order. When the workshops deliver the goods, the credit is deducted from the purchase price, which is paid in instalments, thereby allowing the merchants to sell the merchandise over a period of time. Instalments are usually paid out on a weekly basis. An examination of the production and circulation process suggests that the relations between merchants and workshops are complex and layered and embody social hierarchies of power.

In this set-up, the chamber of commerce plays a limited role in representing the interests of the wider merchant class. It could be argued that control of the *suqs* is maintained more through the use of state-imposed local committees which survey relations among merchants, monitor daily happenings and work to ensure compliance with the regime. However, the forms of organisation sketched here point to the continued autonomy of the middle-merchant class and to the existence of informal networks and institutions that diminish its dependence on the regime and state.

The Religio-Mercantile Complex: an Islamist alternative?

There is an important cultural dimension to the relative independence of the middle merchants. This has to do with the strong links that they maintain with the religious establishment. Merchants and shaikhs have preserved a long-standing alliance which may be identified as a religio-mercantile complex. The connections between these social forces manifest themselves in important areas of social life and have political implications. For example, religious leaders continue to be the favoured arbiters in disputes among merchants, including rich merchants. A number of my interviewees narrated incidents of dispute arbitration among higher-echelon merchants that drew on the authority of the religious establishment for resolution, rather than on state institutions. The most notable of these incidents was the business conflict in the chemical industry between Da'bul and al-Hafi.

The positioning of the various forces that constitute themselves in Islamist terms is important to discern in order to understand the kinds of alliances and pacts that may well be in the making. First, in the words of one of my interviewees, 'the turban [the shaikhs] and the tarbush [the merchants] preserved the ruling powers'. However, this alliance is under growing strain, and some merchants state that it has already been dissolved. In this context, the question that arises is what the position of the various religious forces – including the religious establishment – will be if the alliance with the merchants breaks apart.

The co-optation of the religious elite ('ulama) is best illustrated by the 'Kaftaru group' comprising the late mufti, Shaikh Ahmad Kaftaru, and the Centre for Islamic Studies in Damascus, which he founded. Under Hafiz al-Asad, conservative figures like Shaikh Kaftaru flourished. The regime continues to rely on the support of 'ulama like Shaikh Sa'id Ramadan al-Buti and the current mufti, Ahmad Hassun. Through the co-optation of its representatives, official Islam has served as a source of support and legitimisation for the regime. This veneer of religious legitimacy is also garnered from the representative of the enlightened trend, namely Dr Muhammad Habash, an independent member of the People's Assembly who is married to the granddaughter of Shaikh Kaftaru. Habash's political positions are very much aligned with those of the regime.

There are also conservative Islamist groups that are closely tied to official Islam, but whose politics are difficult to pin down. A good example is the Qubaisiyyah, the female followers of Shaikha Munira al-Qubaisi. They are said to number somewhere between 25,000 and 75,000 women in Damascus and its environs. One journalist who looked into the phenomenon closely reports that the Qubaisiyyah is active in recruiting the wives and daughters of high-ranking officials and well-off merchants and businesspeople. The potential recruits attend home-based lessons by disciples of Shaikha Munira and, if they join, become members of a highly structured and regimented piety group. The women wear dark blue coats and colour-coded scarves that represent their rank within the group, from novice to learned member. The Qubaisiyyah represents the conservative trend in Sunni Islam in Syria. This trend has no political project as such. However, it may be in search of a leader and it could possibly be politicised.

Leaving aside the issue of radicalisation, the signs and symbols of re-Islamisation enter into the reproduction of the religio-mercantile complex. In addition to the conventional signs of re-Islamisation, such as the increased adoption of the veil and the proliferation of bookstores selling Islamist books and pamphlets, we should note the spread of religious practices that are oriented towards the production of distinct socio-cultural identities. Among the merchant and business class, reproduction of Islamic rituals has become a means to express both religious and class identity. Thus, *mulid* parties organised by wealthy merchant and business families have become common social activities. These parties are held not only on the occasion of the Prophet's birth, but also to mark family festivities. Invitees come from the families' social circles. Women and men congregate in separate rooms, shaikhs are present, and there are collective readings of the Qur'an. These activities express a Sunni social and cultural identity that is articulated in distinction from others, primarily the 'Alawi identity. The presence of shaikhs at these events confirms their continued links to the business elite. One of my informants, a member of a wealthy Sunni family, remarked that 'every merchant has a shaikh' (*li kulli tajir shaikh*).

Historically, merchants have deployed religious references in their discourse and framed their activities using religious idioms.[17] Politically, they allied with the Muslim Brothers and only the Damascene merchants broke that alliance. In my view, there are good reasons that make them, along with the small workshop owners and traders, a latent constituency for the Muslim Brothers.[18] First, they have no affiliations with the Ba'th Party and would support regime change. Additionally, they have shown an affinity for the Muslim Brothers in cities like Aleppo, Hama, Homs and Damascus. Expansion of their ranks owing to the informalisation of economic activities, in addition to the fear of heightened foreign competition resulting from the European–Mediterranean Partnership Agreement, may foster some kind of common platform.

Conclusion

The reconfiguration of political alliances that accompanied successive phases of economic liberalisation represents an important transformation in the foundations of Syrian authoritarianism. The emergence of new economic strata favoured by state-sponsored economic networks has hastened the differentiation of economic elites. The Ba'thi regime's ability to navigate its way among competing economic contenders may be limited due to its close links to segments of these elites. Additionally, without an alternative formula that can bring in the private sector as a partner in creating economic growth and jobs, it may not be possible for the authorities to maintain the distributive policies that are necessary to preserve social peace. Thus, the regime faces the loss of its broad social base and its key strategic alliances with the national bourgeoisie and the traditional merchant class. A dissolution of this alliance, along with the abandonment of the broad social base, would undermine the structural foundations of authoritarianism in Syria. The existing political elites, despite being divided, are attempting to forge new alliances and refashion institutional networks, while at the same time holding on to the corporatist frames of yesteryear. This task is increasingly difficult.

Notes

1. This short-lived revival is usually referred to as the Damascus Spring.
2. The debate on authoritarianism in the Arab world is being revisited in some recent scholarly works. For a discussion of contending accounts of authoritarianism in the Arab world, see Eva Bellin, 'The Robustness of Authoritarianism in the Arab World', *Comparative Politics*, vol. 36, no. 2, 2004, pp. 139–57.
3. In interviews, some Syrian intellectuals used the idea of political sectarianism to describe the regime and its allies.
4. Raymond Hinnebusch, *Authoritarian Power and State Formation in Ba'thist Syria*, Boulder, Colo. 1990.
5. See Volker Perthes, *The Political Economy of Syria under Asad*, London 1995.

6. Author's interviews with merchants in Damascus, April and May 2005.

7. Volker Perthes, 'The Bourgeoisie and the Ba'th', *Middle East Report*, no. 170, 1991, pp. 31–7.

8. Author's interview with merchants and industrialists, Damascus 2005.

9. Bassam Haddad argues that hardliners within the regime are tied to the old business community and that 'softliners' are connected to the new entrepreneurs. Such a clear-cut division is difficult to ascertain and the lines of division appear more blurred. Some new entrepreneurs like Tlas and al-Turkmani take a reformist posture, but they are none the less tied to the military and security apparatuses. Further, figures of the old business community favour greater political opening and accountability and are thus more aligned with 'softliners'. See Haddad, 'The Formation and Development of Economic Networks in Syria', in Steven Heydemann, ed. *Networks of Privilege in the Middle East*, New York 2004.

10. Author's interview, Damascus 2005.

11. This account of the contentions surrounding the establishment of Syriatel and al-Nama' as shareholding companies draws on media accounts and interviews with journalists in Damascus.

12. The official newspaper *Tishrin* published many articles putting into question the soundness of the financial evaluations of al-Nama'. See the economic pages of *Tishrin*, 21 and 26 Ayloul 2004.

13. See *al-Nur*, 29 September 2004 and *al-Hiwar al-Mutamaddan*, 27 September 2004.

14. Ibid.

15. Author's interviews in Damascus, April and May 2005.

16. Haddad identifies the institutional set-up that facilitates this kind of access and incorporation.

17. Fred Lawson, 'Social Bases for the Hamah Revolt', *MERIP Reports*, no. 110, 1982, pp. 24–8; Hanna Batatu, 'Syria's Muslim Brothers', *MERIP Reports*, no. 110, 1982, pp. 12–20.

18. The Muslim Brothers does not have a tangible, organised presence in Syria. However, from its headquarters in London, the organisation has been active in building alliances with Syrian forces. It has begun to reappear on the political scene and engage in debates through proxies and public declarations from its headquarters. For example, the Muslim Brothers' leadership joined the Damascus Declaration of November 2005, thus entering an alliance with factions of the secular political opposition.

TWO

Enduring Legacies:
The politics of private sector development in Syria

Bassam Haddad

There has been no 'private sector proper' in Syria since 1963.

Muhammad Ghassan al-Qalla', Syrian industrialist and chief
academic consultant to the Damascus Chamber of Commerce

Our regime is unable to tolerate a strong private sector, a giant. Either it must remain a dwarf, or it may grow in the shadow of the state, but it must not operate in the open, under the sun ... it must operate only through [committing] collective violations and chaos, so as it can be taken out at any moment.

Riyad Saif, Syrian industrialist and member of parliament

There is no conflict of interest between the state and the private sector.

Ratib Badr al-Din al-Shallah, president of the
Syrian Union of Chambers of Commerce

In Syria itself, as well as in the academic literature on Syria, it is often said that former President Hafiz al-Asad was an enigma. This may have some truth in it. But there is another broader enigma – Syria's 'private' sector.[1] If an enigma is something that is not easily understood, then the private sector fits such a definition, notwithstanding the work of various analysts who take the private sector at face value.[2] The absence of fruitful field research opportunities, even during the less restrictive Bashar al-Asad era, continues to be the single greatest obstacle to examining the complexities and subtleties of Syria's private sector and the behaviour, preferences and mentality of the actors within it. Another obstacle is that the constitution continues to speak of Syria as a socialist republic and to accord little importance to the private sector or privately owned assets. Despite a gradual loosening of discursive controls since 1998, and the evolution of the term 'social market' under Bashar al-Asad, Syria's relatively muted public discourse and powerful security apparatuses, by creating an atmosphere of pervasive suspicion, hinder the kind of information-gathering that researchers require.

That the private sector is too small, too weak, too divided; that no single private firm's closure would be consequential to the economy; that not everyone in the private sector supports economic reforms; and that the state remains largely in command of the economy – these are perhaps the most often stated conclusions of researchers on the Syrian private sector, and for good reason. Still, even a cursory look at the figures of the Central Bureau of Statistics, or a visit to Syria, would yield a very different view. Since 2005, the private sector has made rhetorical and actual advances, although the gains are part of a regime survival strategy rather than ones that empower the private sector as whole. What need further elaboration are the political conditions under which the Syrian private sector has developed, the trade-offs that the Syrian regime has made in the process, and the institutional context that frames the stunted development of the private sector.

The Private Sector[3] Versus the New Bourgeoisie

The Syrian private sector is a heterogeneous amalgam of social components that are brought together nominally under the umbrella of the word 'private', defined largely by the juridical separation between property owned by private individuals and property owned by the state. In reality, the larger segments of private sector assets and capital are those of individuals under the umbrella of the regime; they were accumulated in the shadow of the state, often directly through state authority and using the state's own mechanisms and agencies. This gives a peculiar meaning to the phrase 'private sector'.

Such policies have led to an increase in the size of the private sector in nearly all cases, invariably at the expense of the public sector's share of the economy. Such shifts in ownership are usually associated with expectations of a growing demand for more accountable government, if not in fact a democratic system, on the part of private business. But as in most late-developing countries, the most powerful elements within the private sector favour the status quo, and the reason lies beyond the customary explanation proposed long ago by Jean Leca,[4] that such businessmen prefer to seek rents in the shadow of the state rather than compete in an open market. This is certainly a part of the explanation in the Syrian case, but the rest lies in the kinds of economic networks that have developed between the regime and the new bourgeoisie, itself largely a creation of the state; in the fact that the largest parts of the private economy in Syria are operated or owned by a state bourgeoisie; and, finally, in the continuing mistrust between the regime and the larger business community that has further altered the preferences of the new bourgeoisie in favour of the status quo. In practice, the tilt of the 'new' state-created bourgeoisie towards a status quo that dwarfs the business community as whole, while doling out special privileges to some, puts the new bourgeoisie – especially its most powerful segments – at odds with the remainder of the private sector.

While the new bourgeoisie is content with proximity to the state and membership in the networks where rents are distributed and laws openly transgressed, the rest of the business community has had to play by the rules, contend with endless bureaucratic procedures and negotiate a contradictory legal environment. More significant is the fact that privileges and rents have been doled out by regime potentates to select business partners without any expectation of good economic performance. The state bourgeoisie and its offspring have been in the forefront of those on the receiving end of special privileges, often being the same individuals who were distributing them, making rent-seeking extremely efficient. The result was massive investment in the early 1990s, most of which turned out to be either in non-productive activities or in one way or another protected from competition by tailored policies.[5]

Since 1991, and more recently since 2001, the lion's share of new opportunities and markets has gone to a small group of individuals associated in one way or another with the regime, either through familial ties or through public or governmental positions or posts in the military and security services. Thus Syria has a private sector that is not 'private' at all, since most assets are owned by individuals who occupy state positions. Hence, an opposition develops between the interests of the new bourgeoisie (including the state bourgeoisie) and others in the business community who comprise the true private sector.

Nowhere is the opposition between the new bourgeoisie and the private sector proper more evident than in the inconsequential pattern of distribution of assets between the private and the public sectors during the 1990s. Whereas the public sector had claimed the upper hand in terms of fixed capital formation since 1963, relegating the private sector to small and medium business ventures, the situation was reversed in the early 1990s.[6] The immediate cause was Investment Law Number 10 of 1990–1, which encouraged private domestic and foreign investment by providing tax breaks and other incentives.[7] The contrast between the shares of public and private assets over time becomes stark when one considers the dramatic reversal in fixed capital formation figures that occurred between 1985 and 1992 (see Table 2.1). Whereas the public sector's share in 1985 was nearly twice that of the private sector, at 66 per cent and 34 per cent respectively, the opposite prevailed in 1992, leaving the public sector with a 33 per cent share of fixed capital formation and the private sector with more than double that figure. Similarly, private sector investments increased by 62 per cent between 1991 and 1994, amounting to nearly two-thirds of gross investment in both 1992 and 1993,[8] with economic correlates following suit in the commerce, agriculture, service, construction and transportation sectors,[9] but less so in the manufacturing sector. Private sector imports and exports also increased significantly after 1991: by 1992, the amount of imports doubled and continued to increase until 1996, and by 1994, exports had risen by 85 per cent and continued to rise until 1995.[10]

In contrast to the spate of optimistic reports and articles published in the mid-1990s, projecting a decisive victory for private sector enthusiasts, these numbers proved to be quite misleading, both in themselves and in terms of the changes they portended. Furthermore, with few exceptions, most observers discounted the fact that private sector growth was not unrelated to the weakened, some say embattled, public sector at the time.[11] We thus witnessed a decrease in the role of the state, but not necessarily a change in the identity of those who make policy decisions regarding the sectors in which the state had presumably ceded control to the 'private sector'. This state of affairs reflects a regime-survival strategy that eschews the broadening of the role of the private sector. One must turn to Syria's history to find explanations for such a choice.

Table 2.1: Gross Fixed Capital Formation by Type of Ownership[12]

Year	Public Sector Share	Private Sector Share
1963	51	49
1970	67	33
1975	70	30
1980	63	37
1985	66	34
1990	43	57
1991	42	58
1992	33	67
1993	35	65
1994	42	58
1995	44	56
1996	48	52
1997	58	42
1998	59	41
1999	59	41
2000	64	36
2001	65	35
2002	62	38
2003	63	37
2004	48	52
2005	48	52
2006	46	54

The State and the Private Sector

Relations between the state and the business community in Syria have historically been quite strained. Despite ebbs and flows, usually associated with economic booms and busts, the general sense in structural terms and at the level of individual officials and businesspeople is that the two forces are at odds. Some analysts, certainly most hardliners inside the regime of Hafiz al-Asad, viewed the relationship in zero-sum terms: the rise of the private sector must occur at the expense of the Ba'thi regime. Conversely, it is no puzzle that the rise of the regime itself after 1963 occurred at the expense of the traditional private sector, symbolised by what is called the 'traditional' or 'old' bourgeoisie.

The reasons for state–business antagonism and mistrust are complex and constitute a focal point of this study. The bitter legacy between state and business has its roots in both political and social factors stemming from the emergence and development of a radical populist authoritarian regime. Such regimes are common in post-colonial settings and emerge as a solution to both international and domestic challenges associated with the incorporation of states into the global capitalist economy. A populist authoritarian regime 'seeks to establish the authority of a strong state autonomous of the dominant classes and external powers and to launch national economy development aimed at easing dependence and subordinating capitalist forces to populist goals'.[13]

The challenges that these regimes face during their emergence and consolidation phases shape their alliance preferences, their institutional preferences and the larger trade-offs or social pacts they make.[14] One such dimension is of direct relevance to understanding state–business relations in modern Syria. Confronted with a resilient business community that was both urban and Sunni in character, the nascent rural minoritarian Ba'thi regime had a limited set of choices. Having lost or marginalised other secular allies such as the Nasserists or communists, the Ba'th Party had by 1964 become a lone star, largely isolated from a conflictual society in which the only significant social force was the tenacious bourgeoisie, in its commercial and landed varieties. Both the United Arab Republic (UAR) experience and the conservative secessionist coup of 1961 were instructive to the increasingly minoritarian and radicalised Ba'th: the first gave the party a good reason to regard external interference in a country like Syria with supreme suspicion; the second convinced the Ba'th that a soft approach in dealing with political opposition does not work. Thus, the Ba'thi regime adopted hardline populist strategies that did not permit the participation of non-populist forces and subordinated the state and the army to the needs and requirements of the party. The wave of nationalisation of private assets that took shape in 1964–5 complemented the land-reform policies that the UAR started. Subsequent land reforms further eroded the vestiges of the traditional landowning class and perhaps went so far as to alienate some of the middle peasants, who saw their own property rights compromised by radical measures.

Exacerbating this political antagonism was the social antagonism that characterised the differences between the rural minoritarian Ba'this who had historically been subordinated to 'masters' who belonged to the urban Sunni elite. This coincidence of political and social factors pitted the two social forces against one another more intensely than in similarly structured settings, such as 1960s Egypt. This divide made the eventual reincorporation of the business community a more risky affair than similar attempts elsewhere. The regime had to find alternatives, even after the 'correctivist' Ba'thi coup of November 1970 that narrowed the divide between urban conservative forces and rural radical ones. In short, and in contrast to the case of Egypt, when the time came and the need arose, the business community or the private sector 'had to be let [back] in through the back door'. According to Nabil Sukkar, this means that the private sector had to be brought back into the economic equation, but that it was not welcome.[15] The underlying dilemma, which plagued the beleaguered regime of the late 1970s and the early 1980s, still characterises state–business relations today.

The Secondary Role of Private Business in the 1970s and 1980s

While its strategy shifted slightly in 1970, the Ba'thi leadership has related to the private sector as a whole through the prism of security since its initial assumption of power in March 1963. All along, the regime would give only moderate concessions to the private sector as a whole or dole out 'magnanimous' privileges to a select few for the purpose of preserving its macroeconomic autonomy. Such tactics occurred, and still occur, at the expense of the overall health of the local economy. Another notable but less visible expense, and one which the regime incurs in the first degree, is that with the economic price that the regime must pay to preserve its decisional autonomy, and ultimately its security, comes another administrative cost: a sharply decreased capacity to run the economy which diminishes its punitive power. Though they can be averted in the short and medium term by increasing oppressive measures and raising dependence on external sources of income, administrative costs eventually come back to haunt regimes when the rents dry up, a prospect with which the Syrian regime will have to contend in less than a decade.[16] Until then, it is unlikely that the regime will voluntarily change its strategy towards the private sector, a strategy that is now nearly four decades old.

Directly after the 'Corrective Movement' of November 1970, the Ba'thi leadership of Hafiz al-Asad was less ideologically inclined, more pragmatic politically, far more careerist and, most important, fundamentally outward looking. The new regime recognised its social and political vulnerabilities: it was a radical rural minoritarian regime, which was largely cut off from the rest of Syrian society by virtue of a radicalism that had polarised the country for half a dozen years; it was in charge of an embattled state that had suffered a grave defeat only three years earlier at the hands of Israel; it ran an ailing economy that was not likely to receive support from conservative Arab states; and, most significantly for the purposes of this study, it had arisen at the expense of the party apparatus[17] and, to a great extent, the army, supported primarily by the security services and 'special forces' that rival regime strongmen had busily been setting up since the late 1960s.

By turning to the conservative Arab states for external support, as well as to the equally embattled but still threatening remnants of the traditional bourgeoisie at home, the al-Asad regime sought not to create new dependencies, but rather to become independent of all domestic social forces at once. Shortly after the 1970 coup, it reduced its reliance on the labour movement, cultivating a rapprochement with parts of the private sector; it pushed the party apparatus aside as the leading authority within the public sector and replaced it (unofficially) with a refurbished security hierarchy; and it moderated its regional stance by re-establishing relations with the Arab Gulf states, particularly Saudi Arabia, and the post-Nasser regime in Egypt, while at the same time sending signals to both the Soviet

Union and the United States that Syria was open to new opportunities and allies.

The domestic aspect of this shift is of immediate concern here, but should not be studied in isolation. Turning to the oil-rich Arab states was not intended to heal the wounds that had been inflicted by the Salah Jadid regime's fiery rhetoric towards conservative Arab governments. Rather, it was intended to capitalise on much-needed aid in the form of direct financial assistance, oil deals and/or investments.[18] As both the contemporary history of Syria and the available statistics make abundantly clear, such aid and investment soon became Syria's lifeblood, and the engine of development for its politically charged public sector and, thus, its economic autonomy. It was a mixture of the regime's external sources of income or rents and the legacy of mistrust vis-à-vis the business community that determined to a large extent the nature of its relationship with the private sector as a whole.

Given its long-standing animosity towards private capital and its preoccupation with security and decisional autonomy, the al-Asad regime was disinclined to offer the private sector any legitimate representation or allow it to erect expressive institutions independent of state control and scrutiny. Instead, until 1973, when foreign aid finally swamped Syria in the aftermath of the October war against Israel, the state preferred to keep the once-thriving private sector under tight control. In addition, the regime attempted to create a new bourgeoisie in its own image, but was encumbered by the turbulent events of the 1970s and early 1980s.[19] The first twelve years after the Corrective Movement were largely consumed by war – in 1973 with Israel, from 1976 to 1982 with the militant Islamists, from 1976 onwards with various factions in Lebanon, in 1982 with Israel – and thus internal social alliances remained fluid and ad hoc. Social forces did not really begin to coalesce until the end of that period, when, ironically, Syrian civil society was dealt a decisive blow.[20]

In the meantime, the regime continued to toy with the idea of creating 'real' allies in the private sector. Proponents of such an attempt were drawn from circles close to, and including, the president's brother, Rif'at al-Asad, rather than those close to the leader himself, who was preoccupied with Lebanon, Israel and a host of other regional issues.[21] The regime embarked on what Volker Perthes calls the 'first *infitah*',[22] by moderately liberalising imports on the one hand and granting special privileges on the other, but only to a select few whose loyalty was either purchased or guaranteed through mutual deals that bound them to the state. Such deals were either in mixed sector ventures that split capital and management between the state and private businesspeople, or in under-the-table schemes that, retrospectively, could hold private business interests accountable.

Strategically, the domestic situation persisted through the 1970s and early 1980s, but the inflow of capital after the 1973 war, combined with a general lack of economic expertise and entrepreneurship among both regime personnel and their allies in the countryside and the labour movement, necessitated an escalation of rapprochement with the private sector. State–business relations that had existed from 1970 to the mid-1980s remained largely informal, with the exception of some notorious cases that have been overemphasised by analysts because they are among the few businessmen who were visible and accessible.[23] The 'troika', as they are often labelled, included 'Uthman 'A'idi, the tourism mogul, Sa'ib Nahhas, the transportation mogul, and 'Abd al-Rahman al-'Attar, a businessman of a somewhat lower order.

Though these cases were salient, the majority of businesspeople working with, or in the shadow of, the state and its personnel remained faceless for more than a decade. Only in the late 1980s did we witness the emergence of more visible relations between the regime and individuals in the private sector, usually through patronage relations associated with the chambers of commerce and industry and the rejuvenated People's Assembly elections. Even then, it was difficult to link state officials and businesspeople, especially for 'outsiders', that is, those who must take what is observable from afar at face value. The protégés of security service strongmen in the chambers, for instance, are quick to condemn the hold the state has on the economy,[24] naturally leading the 'uninitiated' to conclude erroneously that they are rivals.

Creeping Ambivalence towards the Private Sector in the Late 1990s

In the 1990s, the strategic situation changed, if only because of the growing state–business alliance. While in the 1970s the only conspicuous 'representative' of the private sector, a man by the name of Tahsin al-Safadi, would gather the courage to ask for a reduction in inspection campaigns by the Ministry of Supply, by the 1990s, business 'representatives'[25] were members of parliament and board members of the various chambers of commerce and industry, able to make policy recommendations at high-level institutions that connected the state to the business community.[26] While this image accords best with particular individuals connected to regime strongmen through established economic networks, it does not apply to the interactions and strategic relations between the state and the private sector as a whole. What is important in this regard is that, despite the regime's suspicion of the private sector in general, it could no longer reverse the growth of the private sector and became far more dependent on it for investment, job generation and foreign exchange procurement. However, the regime could still do much to prevent the conversion of the private sector's new-found economic power into political influence. Besides establishing relations with select businessmen in the form of networks that undercut collective action among private sector businesspeople, the regime was able to create a structure of incentives that made it irrational for private sector members to come together either to do business in large groups or to organise against the state.

In addition to the regime's low or, most often, zero tolerance for independent organisation, it has at its disposal the law as a tool that could incriminate virtually anyone doing business in Syria with any substantial amount of capital. The fact that laws, decrees, rules and regulations have been piled on top of one another for more than half a century – with the nullification of only a few – has rendered most mundane business practices subject to prosecution. Says one industrialist: 'In Syria today, we are working under the commercial law of 1949!'[27] A prominent Syrian lawyer observes that 'all the modernising [reform] decisions are in tension with the [Ba'th] party's rules ... the reforms they've announced since 1991 are subject to the same restrictive economic regulations that existed before.'[28] Despite some changes in the regulatory and legal environments between 2001 and 2008, this state of affairs continues to weaken the resolve of investors. Those who invest despite such restrictions, especially those whose businesses require dealing in foreign exchange and other prohibited or sensitive activities, often do so alone or with family members whom they can trust. Many such ventures must operate underground, or must under-report profits:

'Two medium-size merchants may be working in the same commodity side-by-side [as distributors] but they do not know that they distribute the same product because the signs at the entrance of their shop do not reveal that.'[29]

The general effect of the state's strategy in dealing with social forces generally since the 1970s has led to the kind of atomisation that is hardly conducive to collective action, even if the will and the means are within sight. Though this grim picture started to change in the late 1990s, especially after Hafiz al-Asad's death in 2000, private businesspeople who deal with substantial capital prefer to 'work alone', so long as the state is 'leaving an area of freedom to do some business', which it is increasingly doing.[30] Nonetheless, according to insiders who are privy to intra-regime discourse, there is a creeping ambivalence among some regime strongmen towards those parts of the private sector that might become truly independent of the state.

The Ba'thi regime's long-standing ambivalence towards the private sector, let alone that sector's revived prosperity, is evident in the snail's pace at which the government moves in formulating and implementing liberalising policies of any sort and magnitude. This constitutes basic politics in Syria: if the regime does not want to give up or share its political control, its preferences shrink dramatically, especially when paranoia is fed by deteriorating economic conditions. After the presidential succession in 2000, the reconsolidation process that lasted until 2005 also contracted preferences and made the regime increasingly risk-averse.

The regime finds itself caught in a dilemma governed by three bitter facts: it needs the private sector to generate foreign exchange and jobs; it is unwilling and unable to share power; and the private sector's economic clout – for instance, its share of gross domestic produce, investment, employment generation, exports, international connections and expertise – continues to grow as a direct result of the government's slow retreat from the economic sphere. Thus, the optimal outcome for the regime, given its security preferences, is to have the private sector grow enough to save the economy but not enough to threaten the distribution of power between state and business.

Many analysts have observed that the Ba'thi regime wants to have the upper hand in the economy in order to retain decision-making power in all spheres. Against this rather intuitive approach to understanding the regime's preferences, some Syrian observers have posited a more nuanced view. According to one such proponent, 'What the regime is trying to do is in fact quite clever: it brings businesspeople into its circle, does business with them and implicates them with its own problems. If and when it lets them go freely, they remain tied to the state by virtue of their past action. In the meantime, they do much of the dirty work, take the blame for the regime's economic foul-ups and the men of the regime make money off them.'[31] Granted, the regime is concerned with simple arithmetic – that is, how big is the private sector compared to the public and mixed sectors? – but it is far more interested in how to prevent the private sector, irrespective of its current growth, from converting its economic power into political power, whether collectively or individually.

To do so, the regime has been gradually and selectively networking with the most economically significant individuals in the private sector, individuals whose initial rise was a result of the patronage and blessing of the state. Since 1973, the regime has adopted first informal and then formal methods to develop such networks. Informally, the state has created and recreated an incentive structure that renders rational and/or necessary voluntary co-operation on the part of a select group of businesspeople. Formally, the state began in the late 1980s to mobilise particular members in the private sector into the formal political process through participation in the People's Assembly, through election onto the boards of the chambers of commerce and industry and through representation in the Guidance Committee that links the private sector to the state. Essentially, money is left in private hands so long as it does not encroach upon the regime's domain, that is, politics. Otherwise it becomes 'public' money and is seized by the regime through the selective invocation of laws and regulations that 'must' have been transgressed by big business practices in a context of a contradictory legal environment.

Private sector members are not unaware of the regime's calculations, but have no intention of giving off signals that might cause the regime strongmen's eyebrows to rise. They act and speak timidly. The behaviour of business candidates during the campaigns for the People's Assembly reflects such caution. So does their intentionally submissive attitude in dealing with government officials and the media. Somewhere deep inside – which can be inferred from extended conversations with prominent individuals – many businesspeople in Syria belittle the regime's intelligence; some assume that their public statements in praise of the regime's policies are taken by the regime to be genuine expressions of support. In fact, both parties are aware of the political game that the other is playing, even if they are not cognisant of the fact that their own opportunism is transparent. The regime, however, finds itself at an increasing strategic disadvantage, since it is playing a positive-sum game with the private sector at a time when the opportunity costs facing the private sector are very low. In this regard, one close observer stated the following: 'Regime officials think along the following lines: If you get ten businessmen like Riyad Saif [who is both independent and politicised], they could form a formidable front. Such a business-financial bloc, even without a unified and stable base of organisation, may increase the leverage of the business community and ultimately shift the balance in favour of the private sector in terms of economic policy-making. For the regime, this is unthinkable under the current arrangements.'[32]

The problematic for the regime is to benefit from private economic initiative without paying a political cost. If the state succeeds, both sides benefit economically and the state benefits politically in the short run. In the longer run, calculations are likely to change. For big business, the opportunity costs of co-operation are likely to increase at the same time that the regime's opportunity costs approach zero, thereby giving leverage to big business. For the time being, however, we remain in the short term, where observable gains remain within the state's orbit.

'Private Sector Institutions'

An important characteristic of the Syrian private sector is that it has no genuine representation. Existing institutions such as the chambers of commerce and industry represent only portions of the business community, despite appearances to the contrary. The chambers' role ceased to be effective in March 1963, when the Ba'th Party took power. Their rejuvenation after the Corrective Movement of November 1970 left much to be desired by the business community. It was not until 1982 that the Chamber of Commerce in Damascus acquired an elevated political, not economic, status as a direct result of its members' decision to side with the regime in its confrontation with the Islamists.[33] Nonetheless, the chambers seem to be more popular within regime circles than among the traders they claim to represent. Though they attend special chamber lectures and meetings from time to time, many merchants are aware that their voices or interests are 'heard', but usually no more than that. Some say that this is why 'we say nothing. I'd rather work on my next shipment than to plead for the fiftieth time for the most simple and rational of requests.'[34]

The situation is similar in kind, though much worse in degree, in the chambers of industry. Even board members at the Chamber of Industry in Damascus bemoan their ineffectual role: 'We are not decision-makers even regarding chamber issues; we are neither an executive nor a consultative party ... we examine economic matters and forward them to the "decision-maker". We do not make any decisions.'[35] According to Riyad Saif, '[t]he chambers are akin to "populist organisations" that the government creates and they do not possess any power to actualise their demands. Membership in the chambers began in the late 1980s because it was a necessary prerequisite for acquiring a commercial or industrial record and a variety of licences to do business.'[36]

Economists concur. Rizqallah Hilan, a respected Syrian economist, related increases in chamber membership partly to the satisfaction of everyday needs that are independent of business: 'Products in general were very expensive in the early 1990s because of high custom duties irrespective of who was benefiting from higher custom duties or whether they went into the state's treasury. The result was that people would try to get around such duties. For instance, people would sign up with the chambers of commerce so they could get a pick-up truck with reduced custom duties, supposedly for business use.'[37] This is a prevalent view in the business community in Syria, from Aleppo to Hama and Damascus, and it applies to both the chambers of industry and the chambers of commerce, though industrialists' complaints and disillusionment are far deeper in nature. After a lengthy discussion on the state of the Damascus Chamber of Industry, Muhammad Saraqbi, a former vice president of the chamber, stated that the objective of chamber members was for the chamber to attain the status of the Damascus Chamber of Commerce,[38] by repute an ineffectual and scarcely representative organisation.

What many in the private sector look to as an institution that is far more effective, but far less accessible, is the Guidance Committee, the only institution that officially links the business community to the state. But the picture is just as cloudy there. According to independent Syrian economists and former public sector officials working in economic affairs, the Guidance Committee has effectively taken over the role of the legislative and executive authority with respect to a wide range of policies spanning tax exemptions and selective licences for import and export commodities.[39] Some businesspeople accord it supreme importance: 'The Guidance Committee is the most important economic institution in the country because, as opposed to the governmental Economic Committee, its decisions acquire a legal form. Its decisions are intended to be general and strategic.'[40]

The Guidance Committee became effectual at a particular juncture, shortly after the 1986 crisis, when the state needed to mobilise investments to compensate for dramatic reductions in public sector access to foreign exchange and, hence, investments. For the regime, the caveat was to do so without empowering the private sector as a whole. In practice, this translated into efforts to mobilise investment capital either without relinquishing any more economic levers than necessary, even to ostensible private sector allies, or, to worse effect, without creating new winners from outside the networks on which the regime has depended since the late 1970s. The result was the effective supplanting of the Economic Committee – which nonetheless persists as an organisational shell dealing mostly with ideological issues that are far removed from daily economic operations – by the Guidance Committee, which represents the formalisation of hitherto informal relations between the regime and its select partners and protégés in the private sector. Though it was created in 1981 for the purpose of 'encouraging exports and designing more rationalised import policies',[41] the Guidance Committee – officially entitled the Committee for the Guidance of Imports, Exports and Consumption – became the hub for the distribution of rents after 1991, especially in the form of selective liberalisation of import commodities associated for the most part with existing or new businesses owned by regime officials and their private sector partners.

The Guidance Committee is officially headed by the prime minister and his deputy for economic affairs, and is presented as the only government institution in which private sector representatives are full participants and have the opportunity to address their grievances in a context that includes representatives from other social groups, including the economic office of the Ba'th Party, the General Federation of Trade Unions, the Peasants' Union and the presidents of the Damascus Chambers of Commerce and Industry.[42] Among the larger business community and its proponents, the Guidance Committee is understood to be the institutional arm of the informal economic networks[43] where 'corridor policies' take shape.[44] According to Khalid 'Abd al-Nur, among others, 'though the Guidance Committee was created to serve a macro-function, its behaviour [*sulukuha*] serves a micro-function by tailoring policies ... In the end, the Guidance Committee is concerned with simple matters, and even these simple matters reflect the interests of power centres that are in harmony with the interests of the beneficiaries.'[45]

Thus, independent businesspeople in the private sector do not consider the available institutions to be representative, nor are they allowed – much less willing – to erect their own for fear of reprisal. Many are indeed waiting for a time in the not too distant future when these institutions assume their intended role. In the meantime, however, businesspeople look for alternatives to build support. Better-connected businesspeople have found expression in the two relatively recent holding companies (Sham Holding and Syria Holding), which were created after 2005. According to Haitham Jud, perhaps the leading figure of the former, 'We felt that existing institutions are out of step with the economy ... there are entire sectors, such as information technology, that are wholly unrepresented.'[46] Jud and many of his partners and colleagues consider the recently formed holding companies to be the new face of the private sector. While it is true that these bodies are relatively up to date and 'modernised', private sector observers remain doubtful on two counts: first, they do not deem holding companies to be real institutions, at least not 'representative' ones, since most businesspeople are not likely to be associated with them.[47] Thus they view this development more as a club than as an institution. Second, it is public knowledge that both holding companies are wholly dominated either by regime officials or by individuals beholden to the regime 'in the final analysis'. However, yet another brand of economists does see the potential for such endeavours to assume a more productive role, if circumstances change.[48]

Two general outcomes result from the lack of representation. First, the larger business community remains fragmented – sectorally, politically and geographically. Businesspeople with capital work in different sectors simultaneously in order to avoid complete collapse in the event that one of their businesses fails due to a government crackdown or an inability to compete in a market due to excess supply. Such excess supply results from a lack of effective institutions to channel information between the government and the private sector and among various private companies. Politically, there is a great divide between the regime's supporters and its detractors. In the Syrian political context, economic rationality does not always make for productive partnership or fruitful collaboration, even among regime detractors. By the same token, regime supporters who belong to the same networks that allow them to transgress laws and regulations are themselves competing for rents and protection, making collaboration far less likely. Finally, the private sector in Damascus is generally more beholden to the state than its counterparts in Aleppo, Homs, Hama and the rest of the country (precluding the coast generally and Latakia in particular). At the same time, the private sector enjoys an uneven presence in both Damascus and Aleppo as compared with the rest of the country.[49]

A second outcome of the lack of representative institutions for the private sector is that it remains as a whole, large and small, family oriented. More than religion, sect or region, the extended family – and increasingly the nuclear family – represents the most trustworthy social framework for a business community that operates under grave conditions that force or compel the pursuit of illegal or semi-legal business operations (see Table 2.2).

Table 2.2: Private Sector Firms[50]
Total Number: 24,753 Firms

Number of Workers Per Firm	Number of Firms	Percentage
1–5 workers	20,047	80.99
6–9 workers	2,810	11.35
10–50 workers	1,824	7.37
51–100 workers	47	0.19
101 + workers	25	0.1

This situation is certainly not unique to Syria, but the lack of trust between regime and the business community is an additional factor that reinforces family patterns of business development. 'Economically speaking,' as *al-Hayat* entitled one of its articles on Syria, 'the dependence of the [Syrian] private sector limits its ability to expand its investments and its capacity to absorb labour.'[51] Thus, the expansion that the private sector witnessed in the early to mid-1990s was not accompanied by a proportionate reduction in unemployment. While the number of private sector firms increased 245 per cent and investments 492 per cent during the 1990s, 90 per cent of firms remained family-run businesses.[52] Besides the fact that most of the expansion occurred in non-labour-intensive sectors, the new businesses that did emerge tended to rely first and foremost on family members, many of whom already had a job in the public sector that left their afternoons free for a second job.

Two immediate conclusions can be drawn from the above discussion. Economically, the private sector is indeed chained. It is unable to invest properly, unable to employ its credentials and unable to articulate its collective demands in a prioritised manner. It is therefore unable to become a viable 'economic sector' under conditions that Saif describes accurately from personal experience: 'The private sector is an abnormal [*ghair tabi'i*] sector that grew and developed under abnormal conditions and under abnormal circumstances.'[53] Politically, a remarkably weak organisational capacity results, leaving private sector independents isolated from one another, atomised. Attempts to reverse this situation have left the initiators in jail, as in the case of Riyad Saif, who was arrested and has remained in jail since September 2001.[54]

New Leader in a New Century:
Ideology Versus Security under Bashar al-Asad

Given the country's long-standing economic stagnation, the regime's way out of its strategic dilemma becomes a valuable indicator of its overall resilience. Bashar al-Asad's succession to power after his father's death in 2000 appeared to mark a significant shift and, more importantly, represent a hope that Syria would truly liberalise its political system and modernise its economy. Ideologically, the regime had been firmly against the dominance of foreign capital in the domestic market. This view remains entrenched among state sector managers, bureaucrats, most army strongmen and the majority of civil servants, including top officials outside the regime's core. Politically, the leadership wanted to maintain the status quo – that is, state control over business – against private sector development and growth.[55]

After the mid-1990s, even before the transition to Bashar, regime preferences no longer coincided. The bottom line for the top echelons was to retain the favourable distribution of power between the state and private capital. Foreign investments do not endanger sovereignty in a real and direct manner, nor do foreign investors have aspirations to hold political power. Still, such investments might alter the dispersion of domestic resources away from the regime. Under Bashar al-Asad, the ideological markers shifted, allowing some flexibility in the regime's stance regarding a market-driven versus a state-controlled economy. However, the regime's security concerns have not shifted. In other words, regime strongmen have become more willing to move ideologically than their proclaimed stance allows, except that such a move is likely to collide with the goal of retaining a favourable balance of economic power. Still, something had to be done to deal with economic stagnation.

The 'historical' compromise has come in spurts and culminated in the announcement of a 'social market economy', a term that addresses what needs to be done but without completely abandoning the regime's socialist pretensions. Thus, under Bashar al-Asad, and after the famous Tenth Regional Ba'th Party Congress in 2005, when the new leader's power was consolidated in both the party and the army–security apparatuses, we see a proliferation of private banks, the legalisation of dealing with hard currency and the establishment of holding companies that represent 'new' and more specialised private interests.[56] More importantly, the economic bureaucracy has become more 'economist' in nature: it has been pruned of elements that represent the era of central planning and a new economic team has been ushered in, symbolised by the youthful and energetic new deputy prime minister for economic affairs, 'Abdullah al-Dardari. In an interview conducted in the summer of 2007, al-Dardari spoke of a new era, in which 'the regime is now aware of the globalised nature of the economy: we either work to compete in it, or it will forever leave us behind.'[57] He explained that this thinking now proliferates among the new leadership and is evidenced by its recruitment pattern of putting the right person in the right place: 'In the past, economic posts were occupied by political figures; today, these posts are occupied by economic experts.'[58]

It might seem that, under these conditions, one can be hopeful that the private sector will bloom. After all, we are witnessing progress in the bureaucratic, financial and policy environments that bode well for private capital accumulation. We are also witnessing an effort by the top leadership to enter into the world economic market, even if only for purposes of regime survival. Nonetheless, there are two immediate obstacles to the expansion of the private sector. First, there are questions regarding the authority possessed by this new economic team, legally, institutionally and, most important, politically. What incentives does this team have to push against long-established red lines involving wealth and its potential political effect? Why should the new team take risks and tackle age-old taboos that might in fact be the most formidable hurdles to exercising an economic rationality that collides with regime logic? These are basic but not simple questions.

Second, assuming that the will to liberalise and rationalise the economy is indeed a regime priority, how does it conflict with entrenched economic networks that, for the time being, will certainly block rational policies that undermine their standing and practices? The power of such economic networks should not be underestimated and cannot be considered subordinate to *dirigiste* or mundane administrative influence. Elsewhere, I have detailed the emergence and impact of these networks and described their organic relations with the regime and their elusive nature.[59] It remains a challenge to rein in these networks, while maintaining a favourable balance in economic and security terms.

Notes

1. Although the private sector proper includes all economic assets and activities outside the state sector, this article is primarily concerned with what can be called 'big business' within the private sector, that is, the portion of the private sector that is potentially capable of influencing the state on issues of economic policy or of gaining political leverage in state–society relations. In practice, this means that the petite bourgeoisie – the moderately propertied artisans, traders and shopkeepers and farmers – are

not part of this study, though the new bourgeoisie and the old bourgeoisie are, in all their varieties described herein.

2.   Many Syria analysts of the contemporary period have discussed the private sector in a problematic manner, precisely because the private sector was not analysed properly. With the possible exception of some of Perthes's indirect writing on the subject and Joseph Bahout's study on the Syrian business community, Syria analysts have rarely deconstructed this category to reflect realities on the ground as opposed to what is expected of the private sector based on its 'historic' role elsewhere. It is true that some mention divisions within the private sector, however, such delineations usually have two problems. First, they divide the private sector along categories that are not politically or economically significant in practice (for example, according to sectoral divisions, commercial versus industrial divisions, old versus new bourgeoisie, exporters versus everyone else, those integrated into the national market versus those whose business activities bypass the intricacies of this market and so on). Second, although each such division carries a grain of practical relevance, they are not sufficient to explain the behaviour of actors that are found in these categories.

3.   The best-informed work on the economics of Syria's private commercial and industrial sectors in the 1980s so far is Volker Perthes, 'The Syrian Private Industrial and Commercial Sectors and the State', *International Journal of Middle East Studies*, vol. 24, no. 1, 1992.

4.   See Jean Leca, 'Democratization in the Arab World: Uncertainty, Vulnerability and Legitimacy. A Tentative Conceptualization and Some Hypotheses', in Ghassan Salameh, ed., *Democracy without Democrats: the Renewal of Politics in the Muslim World*, London 1994.

5.   For more details on the nature of investments by the private sector in the early 1990s, including the protection of private manufacturing firms, see Khalid 'Abd al-Nur, 'The Private Sector in the Shadow of Protection', (*al-Qita' al-Khass fi Thill al-Himaya*), paper no. 13, 2000 Conference Series, Economic Sciences Association, Damascus 2000.

6.   For the best-informed account and nuanced narrative of private sector growth during that period, consult Volker Perthes, *The Political Economy of Syria under Asad*, chapter 2, London 1999.

7.   See Sylvia Polling, 'What Future for the Private Sector?', in Eberhard Kienle, ed., *Contemporary Syria: Liberalization between Cold War and Cold Peace*, London 1994.

8.   See 'Abd al-Nur, 'The Private Sector', p. 337.

9.   See Perthes, *The Political Economy*, p. 59.

10. See 'Abd al-Nur, 'The Private Sector', p. 338.

11. Critical economists in Syria forward the argument that the deterioration of the public sector was not entirely an accident. The evidence put forth

is not uncompelling: various public sector firms were losing business to emerging private firms or, in fact, semi-legal operations, owned by powerful members of the state bourgeoisie who often worked in the same business domain. Examples abound, including the decline of public sector firms that manufacture cigarettes (for example, Gota) and refrigerators (for example, Barada), both replaced by privately procured versions of the same products.

12. For figures up to 1999 (at constant prices of 1995), see Statistical Abstract 1998, published by the Central Bureau of Statistics, Syrian Arab Republic, Chapter 16, 'National Accounts', pp. 546. Figure for 1999 is an estimate. For figures after 1999, see Statistical Abstract 2007, published by the Central Bureau of Statistics, Syrian Arab Republic, Chapter 16, 'National Accounts, table 16/38, p. 565.

13. See Raymond Hinnebusch, *Authoritarian Power and State Formation in Ba'thist Syria*, Boulder, Colo. 1990, p. 2.

14. For more on the intricacies of such challenges and their influence on resultant social pacts, see Steven Heydemann, *Authoritarianism in Syria: Institutions and Social Conflict, 1946–1970*, Ithaca, New York 1999, chapters 1 and 7.

15. Interview with Syrian economist Nabil Sukkar, Damascus, 9 January 1999.

16. Oil rents, constituting more than 60 per cent of Syria's foreign exchange and supporting most public sector investments, are likely to dry up as the oil wells do between 2010 and 2015. See *al-Iqtisadiyyah*, 30 December 2001.

17. Interviews with former public sector workers who abandoned state employment for jobs in the private sector or abroad in the late 1970s and early 1980s. These former employees were radical Ba'this in their youth in the early 1960s and became disillusioned when the regime cast the party aside before, during and after the Corrective Movement that took place in 1970. They had access to mid-level regime inner circles that were in charge of financial operations intended to give the security apparatuses more leverage and more funds at the expense of the Ba'th Party, which, by then, was a 'mere mobilisationary tool for the countryside'. Though such accounts carry in them a deep injury of sorts, which contributes to some exaggeration, they are shared broadly by nearly all members of the older generation of Ba'this who either terminated their work with the state, were themselves terminated or are still working with the state for near subsistence living, refusing to move up in rank so as not be implicated with the kind of state operations to which they object. These individuals, including those from whom the quotes were derived, are to remain anonymous.

18. Interview with a former official at the Commercial Bank of Syria, Damascus,

8 March 1999. Syria was then desperately looking for economic exits and social stability. The regime knew, according to this former official and to other interviewees on the question of the 1970s coup, that it could not survive without a revived economy and a reduction in social polarisation, which would bring about the kind of social peace that 'a regime like that of 1970' could not afford to lose.

19. Interview with an economics professor working as editor of a Syria-based Palestinian publication sponsored by the public sector, Damascus, 20 April 1999.

20. See Raymond Hinnebusch, 'State and Civil Society in Syria', in Augustus Richard Norton, ed., *Civil Society in the Middle East*, vol. 1, Leiden 1995.

21. It is notable that, in the 1970s, it was not only the regime that had its gaze outwards, but also major segments of Syrian society, including the Muslim Brothers. Interview with economic professor cited above, Damascus, 20 April 1999. Also see Anoushirivan Ehteshami and Raymond A. Hinnebusch, *Syria and Iran: Middle Powers in a Penetrated Regional System*, London 1997.

22. See Perthes, *The Political Economy*, p. 50.

23. See articles on Syria's private sector and/or business community in Eberhard Kienle, ed., *Contemporary Syria: Liberalization between Cold War and Cold Peace*, London 1994.

24. Interviews with individual businessmen in the chambers of commerce who are beholden to regime officials through joint businesses started under Law Number 10 of 1991. It is not that these businessmen are all equally beholden to the regime or their partners therein: some sincerely dislike their partners, but appreciate prosperity far more – not to mention their reputations, which they must protect by paying lip service to private sector independence.

25. Ironically, or perhaps not, Tahsin al-Safadi (referred to by members of the old bourgeoisie as al-Hajj Tahsin al-Safadi, a sign of respect derived from his social position and from his pilgrimage to Mecca) was a true representative of the private sector on the authority of traders who did business at the time and whom I interviewed. Thus, the chambers had some claim to representation in the 1970s when they were virtually powerless, whereas today or since 1989 are virtually non-representative even though they play a more significant role in aggregating interests, albeit selectively. Interview with Nizar Qabbani, a notable textiles merchant in al-Hariqa, a business quarter adjacent to the traditional al-Hamidiyyah *suq*, Damascus, 28 April 1999.

26. Interview with Mahmud Salamah, a former government bureaucrat who co-ordinated relations between the public industrial sector, the private sector and labour. He was a driving force behind the public sector reform

project initiated in 1998, *al-Idarah bil-Ahdaf* (Goals Oriented Management) which gave public sector managers in the textiles industry (as a trial period) more decisional leverage and autonomy vis-à-vis government agencies in the Prime Ministry that traditionally scrutinise and interfere with public sector firms. See his 'Goals Oriented Management: Where To?' (*al-Idarah bil-Ahdaf: ila 'ayn?*), paper no. 3, 2000 Conference Series, Economic Sciences Association, Damascus 2000.

27. Interview with Riyad Saif, Damascus, 12 December 1998.

28. Interview with Ma'mun Tabba', Damascus, 30 May 1999.

29. This usually applies to merchants who act as intermediaries between large retailers and consumers in provinces outside Damascus or the countryside around that or other cities. Interview with Manar al-Jallad, Damascus, 24 April 1999. Similar situations occur in industry, across metropolitan cities or across the same city.

30. Interview with a businessman working in the newly established sector of the food and processing business, which the state monopolised until the early 1990s, 16 August 2001.

31. Interview with prominent public intellectual, Sadiq al-'Azm, with roots in the traditional bourgeoisie, Damascus, 10 December 1998.

32. Interview with Sadiq al-'Azm, 10 December 1998. Words in brackets are added by the author, but were translated from the interviewee's earlier statement that Saif represents businessmen who are '*mustaqillin wa musayyasin*' (independent and politicised).

33. Interview with Nizar Qabbani, 28 April 1999. Also see Hanna Batatu, 'Syria's Muslim Brethren', *MERIP Reports*, no. 110, 1982, pp. 12–20.

34. Interview with Manar al-Jallad, a textiles trader from the prominent al-Jallad family, with firm roots in the traditional bourgeoisie, Damascus, 7 April 1999.

35. Interview with Nabil al-Jajah, industrialist and board member in the Damascus Chamber of Industry, Damascus, 31 May 1999.

36. Interview with Riyad Saif, Damascus, 8 June 1999.

37. Interview with Rizqallah Hilan, Damascus, 15 March 1999.

38. Interview with Haitham Midani, Vice President of the Damascus Chamber of Industry, Damascus, 12 May 1999.

39. Interviews with Arif Dalila and a former official at the Commercial Bank of Syria, Damascus, 12 April 1999.

40. Interview with Riyad Saif, Damascus, 8 June 1999.

41. See Perthes, *The Political Economy*, p. 211.

42. Interviews with Ratib al-Shallah and 'Abd al-Rahman al-'Attar, both of whom have sat on Guidance Committee meetings (al-Shallah in his official capacity; al-'Attar as a delegate from the Damascus Chamber of Commerce). The president of the Syrian Union of Chambers of Commerce, al-Shallah, says

that the meetings are 'irregular' in terms of frequency, giving credence to its reactionary role, especially since the early 1990s. According to al-Shallah, the power of the Guidance Committee grew after 1986, and continued to grow in the 1990s, but the failure of the peace process slowed it down, as it did other reforms; Damascus, 9 May 1999. Al-'Attar, a businessman considered to be one of the symbols of regime–business partnerships in the 1970s, states that the Guidance Committee had a role in developing the private sector but that the private sector's role remains consultative. Al-'Attar's comments on the relationship between the regime and the private sector oscillate between criticism and praise. It is notable that, among other historic regime partners, al-'Attar businesses – diverse and multisectoral as they are – came under significant pressure from the offspring of the bourgeoisie in the late 1990s when they (that is, the children) began to enter into private business at higher rates as they matured. Al-'Attar finally affirms that 'he who would like to stay in business, must concede to their [the regime's] politics'. Interview in Damascus, 9 May 1999.

43.   In contrast to the account above, Perthes accords more weight to the general economic role of the Guidance Committee. Though this research reveals the more particularist dimensions of the Guidance Committee, it still recognises a residual general role, but not to the extent that Perthes observes:

> [The Guidance Committee] is a place for private-sector interests and demands to be officially injected into the process of governmental policy formation, as well as a corporatist body where private-sector and union representatives can bargain for their demands with government, party and each other.

It is notable that, since the early to mid-1990s when Perthes's statements were made, hopes were far higher for this institution, even among sceptics in the private sector. Nevertheless, it is unclear how labour unions bargained, what they bargained for and what benefits they ever received from the Guidance Committee after 1985 when the unions' powers were severely undermined by new laws. However, since the mid-1990s, the Guidance Committee has been viewed in a far more negative light because of the absence of any significant change in the economy by way of reforms. In fact, the role of the institution altogether has been reduced in favour of the earlier, more personalistic methods of distributing rents, as seen in 2000 and 2001 in the case of cellular telephone deals and free-trade zones expansion schemes that were won by relatives of the regime's top echelons. See *The Political Economy*, pp. 210–11.

44.   The expression 'corridor policies' refers to deals made in private between officials and businessmen.

45. Interview with Khalid 'Abd al-Nur, economist and academic adviser to the Aleppo Chamber of Industry, Aleppo, 2 April 1999.

46. Interview with one of the leading businessmen in Syria today, Haitham Jud, Damascus, 24 July 2007.

47. Interview with prominent economist Nabil Marzuq, Damascus, 22 July 2008.

48. Interview with seasoned economist and head of a leading business consulting agency in Syria, Syrian Consulting Bureau (SCB), Damascus, 23 July 2008.

49. See the 1995 report on private sector manufacturing firms, which shows a vast disproportion in the distribution of private sector firms across the country, with the provinces of Damascus and Aleppo getting the lion's share of 61 per cent; and see *Nata'ij Bahth al-Istiqsa' al-Sina'i fi-l Qita' al-Khass li-'Am 1995* (*Statistical Research Results of Private Sector Industry for the Year 1995*), Damascus 1998, pp. 4–5.

50. At the turn of the century, the Central Bureau of Statistics revealed a shrinkage of private sector firms. See *al-Hayat*, 23 March 2001. Compare with Khalid 'Abd al-Nur, 'Improving the Industrial Sector' (*Ta'hil al-Qita' al-Sina'i*), paper no. 6, 1999 Conference Series, Economic Sciences Association, Damascus 1999, p. 190.

51. See *al-Hayat*, 23 March 2001.

52. Ibid.

53. Interview with Riyad Saif, Damascus, 12 December 1998. Saif is among the independents who accumulated wealth in the textiles sector during the 1980s, but who had business roots in the 1970s. Said considers himself a social democrat.

54. See *al-Hayat*, 8 September 2001.

55. This view represents the bottom line for the regime's core officials, including the former and current president, their family and close relatives and those who have been most loyal to them in the government and army.

56. It is noteworthy that the two holding companies represent initiatives by individuals who are either close to the regime or are themselves within its networks.

57. Interview with 'Abdullah al-Dardari, 25 July 2007, Damascus, Syria.

58. Ibid.

59. See Bassam Haddad, 'The Formation and Development of Economic Networks in Syria' in Steven Heydemann, ed., *Networks of Privilege*, New York 2004.

THREE

Civil Law and the Omnipotence of the Syrian State

Zohair Ghazzal, Baudouin Dupret and Souhail Belhadj

It is a common assumption to place 1949 as a foundational date for modern Syrian law, since it was during the four and a half months of the Husni al-Za'im era (April–August 1949) that the core civil and penal codes were promulgated. If we accept 1949 as the key foundational date, other junctures in Syrian history, such as the various military coups from 1949 to 1953, the union with Egypt from 1958 to 1961 and the Ba'th Party's seizure of power in 1963 (all of which were politically decisive but had little impact on the legal system and the practices of the judiciary per se), look insignificant, as little changed in the structure, form and content of the laws that were implemented in 1949.

Only in the 1970s and 1980s, when President Hafiz al-Asad consolidated power under the so-called 'Corrective Movement' of the second Ba'th, did a few legal changes that affected the status of private property come into effect, imposing a de facto threat to the 'spirit' of the 1949 codes. Even such changes were more like piecemeal 'amendments' to civil law than ones that altered foundational structures. What is strange, then, is that the major political upheavals that had tremendous political repercussions, nonetheless left the legal system intact.

I

Let us begin with a brief survey of the main laws that have been passed since the 1970s.[1] These have mostly been 'economic laws' (*qawanin iqtisadiyyah*). Prior to 1966, there was only one 'economic law' that served to regulate the circulation of currencies between Syria and the external world, which was originally introduced in 1952 and which also laid out how the bureau for currency exchange should function. The rest was supposed to be regulated by the 1949 civil code itself. Between 1966 and 1986, four new crucial laws were promulgated: the Law of Economic Penalties (*qanun al-'uqubat al-iqtisadiyyah*) (1966), the Law of Contraband Repression (*qanun qam' al-tahrib*) (1974), the Law Organising the Tribunals of Economic Safety (*qanun ihdath mahakim al-'amn al-iqtisadi*) (1977) and the Law of Penalties against the Contraband of the Syrian Currency and Other Foreign Currencies and Precious Metals (*qanun 'uqubat tahrib al-'umlah al-suriyyah wal-'umulat al-ajnabiyyah wal-ma'adin al-thaminah*) (1986).

How can we explain the proliferation of such laws and what is their legal significance? Did such laws, which left the civil code for the most part unaltered since the 1958 abrogation of articles related to the freedom to associate, indirectly mitigate the 'civil' (or 'private') aspect of the law by subsuming private transactions to the authority of the state? As Alan Watson has noted in his pioneering studies on civil law systems, the institutional civil law tradition can be described as unnatural. In effect, natural law codes stress the importance of the state for human society, hence see the state regulating human affairs.[2] Modern Syrian law, therefore, even though it is rooted in the civil (unnatural) tradition, has nevertheless gradually shifted into guaranteeing the state a natural precedence in the management of human affairs, reducing the importance of free associations and private contracts, while giving priority to state projects that ultimately benefit the 'public good'. The state is therefore the primary agency that brings forth 'social cohesion' through control of the movement of privately triggered contractual settlements.

Reading the Syrian codes in conjunction with actual court settlements would soon turn into a macabre exercise of documenting individuals accused of favouring their own interests over those of the collectivity. Such case files would present traps for those same users, who simply thought that they were following procedures and doing the right thing. In sum, once the state positions itself as a natural agency for the protection of society, users are trapped into a judicial system that in principle favours private civil settlements, on one hand, and a vague political collectivism which remains poorly formulated, is more ideological than legal and is inconsistent with the private spirit of civil law, on the other.

Such collectivism is clearly visible in the texts of the economic laws promulgated in the two decades after 1966. These texts, which are quite short – ten pages on average – show how 'economic rules' were created in parallel to the civil code. But whereas the civil, commercial and penal codes follow long-standing French and Roman traditions, the collectivist 'economic rules' are nothing but an amalgam of political and ideological constructions without the concomitant legal procedures. Users are therefore incessantly trapped between the 'privacy' of their own transactions and the ideological collectivism of the Ba'thi state.

Since collectivism is a populist ideological construction with no clearly defined legal boundaries, the economic laws of the 1966–86 period tend to 'criminalise' private transactions which allegedly 'resist the socialist order'. Thus, instead of a tort law, to which civil transactions would be subjugated, the patchwork of economic laws either openly or de facto criminalises transactions whose intention is to resist the socialist 'economic' order. For example, the first article of the 1966 Law of Economic Penalties defines a new notion of 'public capitals' (*al-amwal al-'ammah*) which, besides moveable and immoveable state properties, includes ones belonging both to the venerable 'corporative associations' (*al-jam'iyyat al-ta'awuniyyah*) and to syndicates and 'popular organisations' (*al-munazzamat al-sha'biyyah*). The second article specifies that even the institutions of the Ba'th Party are part of the 'public capital', even though an authorisation from the general secretary is required to proceed with an investigation. The second chapter of the same code identifies 'major crimes' and their respective penalties, jail terms which vary from five to fifteen years prison with hard labour, with a particular focus on crimes of theft, illegal transactions involving state-owned properties or illegal contracts to promote individual interests. Article 9 goes even further by providing penalties for those who have 'voluntarily' contributed to 'lowering production' (*takhfid al-intaj*), for instance, by providing crucial information to a third party. Article 15 provides penalties of from one to three years of incarceration against all those who have 'resisted the socialist order' (*muqawamat al-nizam al-ishtiraki*).

From 1966 to 1977, criminal courts (*jinayah*s) in the provinces were responsible for adjudicating 'economic crimes', while the regular criminal courts proceeded with business as usual – thefts and burglaries, incest and rape, assaults on individuals and property, homicides and so on. However, in 1977 a new statute instituted 'tribunals of economic safety' (*mahakim al-amn al-iqtisadi*) in Damascus, Aleppo and Homs, which were presided over by their own judges, principally adjudicated on the basis of the 1966 law, and which were only abolished by presidential decree in 2004. Still, the 1966 law remains by and large valid, and continues under the jurisdiction of the regular penal and criminal courts.

II

This novel culture of 'economic crimes' reaches its full force once users are caught up in the labyrinth of the legal system between their civil rights (as formulated by the civil code) and collectivist, statist demands that come in rudimentary 'economic' formulas. An examination of concrete cases is helpful at this stage. The intention is not to 'illustrate' how the codes work – since code writing is a practice all its own, with its own autonomous rules and regulations – but rather to understand the language of users and how they document their own cases.

Consider the case of the merchant Muhammad Khair, a member of the Damascus Chamber of Commerce, whose commercial work required transferring capital between Syria and Egypt.[3] Since he was conducting business in Alexandria, the transfer of capital had to follow the regulations of both countries, which in essence implied following an 'equality' rule in terms of imports and exports. Moreover, every authorisation for import or export had to be conducted within a short, pre-approved time frame. In this case, his request to export food products to Egypt received approval from the Syrian central bank with the proviso that it be completed within six months, between 20 July 1972 and 20 January 1973. At the time, both Syria and Egypt were following strict regulations on the export and import of commodities and the flow of hard currency. Moreover, as the protection of the local currency came in conjunction with limitations on the products that could be exported or imported, merchants typically found themselves operating under regulations that severely limited their ability to compete freely, in particular with traders well connected to the political establishment. In some cases, such controlled transactions turned into a legal imbroglio.

In the case of Muhammad Khair, the inferno began when by martial order (*'amr 'urfi*) dated 2 October 1972, three months prior to the export deadline, all of his private and public banking capital was confiscated, which prevented him from completing his obligation to export within the original time framework set by the central bank. But it was only in March 1974, fourteen months after the export deadline had expired, that the Bureau of Hard Currencies (*maktab al-quta'*) issued a seizure (*dabt*) order, accusing him of carrying out illegal transactions in hard currencies, trafficking in foreign currencies and harming the national currency by receiving transmittances (*qabd hawwalat*) that originated in Egypt at prices equivalent to those of the central bank. In short, our merchant was accused of transferring money between two countries without having fulfilled his promise to export the commodities in the first place, as well as of failing to 'dump those commodities in the consumerist Egyptian market', while damaging the Syrian economy by an estimated 3,457,580 Syrian pounds ($70,000). Moreover, he was accused of sending the funds that he had received from Egypt to Lebanon, thereby using Lebanon as 'neutral territory' for 'money laundering'.

As the case proceeded, not much evidence was furnished that would have proved that our merchant did indeed abuse Syrian and Egyptian bureaucratic routines in order to exchange commodities (including currencies) at better prices than the officially imposed ones. The defence constructed its case around two main weaknesses in the public prosecution's argument: first, the accused was not even able to complete his transaction within the time frame set by the central bank, considering that the martial order came three months before the deadline and, second, the very legality of the martial order was questioned, on the grounds that the defendant did not represent a 'national danger' per se.

The seizure request from the currency bureau was expedited by the prosecutor general in Damascus, who in turn sent it on to the investigating judge. In the meantime, a second martial order came through in January

1980, transferring the dossier back to its point of departure, the investigative judge in Damascus. But even though the latter argued that there was lack of serious evidence against the defendant, the prosecutor general appealed the case to the tribunal of economic security in Damascus. The latter in November 1982 rejected the appeal regarding the charge of trafficking in public currencies. Since the tribunal's decision was irrevocable, the dossier was transmitted to the court of first instance in Damascus, which concluded in March 1988 that the defendant was not guilty on all counts. The tribunal even noted the illogical nature of the court martial order. The case then went through an array of further appeals, which we do not need to go through here. Suffice it to say that it was only in March 1991 that an upper administrative tribunal finally acknowledged that 'the martial order went beyond its initial legislative intention, considering that evidence was not furnished on the real dangers that the alleged illegal trafficking of hard currencies by the defendant would have caused to national security'. In December 1991, the same tribunal made the crucial point that the supervision of civil cases that touch upon 'the security of the state' should fall within its own jurisdiction, since only administrative law can determine whether the procedures are correctly followed by the various martial administrations. The case was permanently sealed in December 1992, twenty years after the court martial order was initially issued, in conjunction with a final ruling acknowledging that the martial judgment was null and void.

The issue here is not whether a country has the right to impose strict rules and regulations on the flow of currency and commodities across its borders, even though in the Syrian case the rules have been so tight and opaque that they bring commercial exchange to a crawl. What is significant is how a banal case of currency exchange, which at first involved the export of food commodities to Egypt, a country with which Damascus enjoyed friendly relations, on a comparative small scale, ended up as a state security matter and why it took two decades for a final verdict to unfold. Moreover, as various economic laws proliferated in the 1970s and 1980s, even more tribunals were created specifically to handle such laws, creating confusion among texts and jurisdictions. The outcome is that the spirit of the 1949 civil code, which protected individual freedoms of exchange and association, has been totally marginalised in favour of a blunt statism which is more ideological than legal.

From the security of the state to the wellbeing of the collective, the judiciary finds itself enmeshed in disputes whose legal aspects remain poorly defined. In other words, there is always a vague territory, situated at the margins of civil law, in which users find themselves suddenly entangled. Thus a small fraud can turn into an accusation of 'harming socialist production' or a minor currency exchange into a state security concern. More importantly, property confiscations are caught between the rules of civil law, which in principle protect private property, and those connected to the public good, based on statutes and regulations promulgated during the massive expansion of the state since the 1970s.

If the target of state intervention is all sorts of moveable and immoveable property, it is because the state presents itself as the natural guarantor of civil rights, placing political priorities over civil ones for the survival of collectivity. Although the 1949 civil code places strong emphasis on the personal side (*haqq shakhsi*) of transactions conducted by autonomous individuals, such rights have become marginalised as a result of ever-increasing statist natural rights, as if private transactions have become a threat to the very existence of the state.

The biggest obstacle to private property rights came in 1958, in the first year of the union with Egypt, when the authorities permitted municipalities to confiscate (*istimlak*) as much landed property as they needed, whether private or religiously endowed (*waqf*), in order to promote public housing. Since then, each city has adopted an 'organisational plan', which delineates a perimeter around the city, outside of which construction is forbidden. As rural zones are integrated into the plan, municipalities have confiscated newly incorporated properties for the purpose of transforming them into public projects.

This politics of confiscation was generalised in Law 60 of 1979 (which is often wrongly described as the Law of Confiscation), Decree Number 20 of 1983 and Law 26 of 2000 (which is a revision of Law 60 of 1979), all of which produce a complex mix of procedures for confiscations, appeals and refunds. In a nutshell, such laws and regulations induce in the property system a parallel set of constraints to the ones present in commodity transactions, with the state acting as the natural protector of eminent domain. Furthermore, as private property became the victim of the consolidation of state control over moveable and immoveable property, users had to find ways around normal channels of property transfer, whether within the family or with outsiders. Hence it has become common for people to be caught in judicial imbroglios whenever they transfer properties. Add to this the situation of millions of properties in poor neighbourhoods; for the most part these lack proper registration but are nevertheless routinely transferred through legally devised procedures formulated by the concerned users themselves.

In the 1970s, the heyday of Hafiz al-Asad's Corrective Movement, all kinds of limitations were imposed on the transfer of property, in particular Law 3 of 1976 which formally prohibits the so-called 'double sale' of non-built urban properties from one proprietor to another. In other words, one buyer cannot in principle sell to another buyer, unless there is a commitment to use the property for some sort of residential or manufacturing project. The purpose of the law was, in a period when the price of urban properties was skyrocketing and there was a lack of genuine investment possibilities in both the financial and manufacturing sectors, to reduce speculative investment that would have pushed prices even higher. Moreover, the law appeared in parallel with other restrictive statutes and decrees, such as various zoning regulations, confiscation procedures and restrictions imposed on dividing large family properties (including *shuyu'* landholdings) among individual users.

Let us consider the case of a certain Nadhir, who in February 1982 filed a lawsuit against the mayor of Damascus. The mayor had allegedly authorised Nadhir to proceed with construction on his own land, with the proviso that Nadhir would cede (*tanazala*) a portion of his property for the sake of safeguarding the 'collective properties' (*al-amlak al-'ammah*). The plaintiff claimed that the transfer (*faragh*) of a portion of his property did in effect take place, but did so against his will; he therefore proceeded with a contract with the mayor only after appending his reservations on the contract sheet itself. In the suit, Nadhir recapitulated such reservations and requested a refund for the lost part of the property.

The mayor claimed that Article 773 of the civil code warns proprietors that, notwithstanding their right to privacy and the safety of their properties, they should nevertheless take into consideration the laws and decrees that would protect the common good (*al-maslahah al-'ammah*). And the mayor referred in his own defence to Article 12 of Decision 350 of

1978 regarding the regulation of the Damascus habitat, which states that 'whenever the ongoing plan, at the moment of the construction application, demands that part of the property be annexed to other private or public properties, then the permit will only be granted once the part to be annexed has been properly assessed and received full payment'. In sum, a gratuitous concession (*tanazul majjani*) over a portion of a property, made in order to receive a construction permit over the non-conceded part, does not authorise the owner to recoup later the price of the property which had already been conceded for the public good.

In February 1983, the tribunal of first instance rebuked (*radd*) the suit: 'The Cassation Court had already reasoned [upon the examination of another file] that once the plaintiff had conceded part of his property for the public good in order to obtain a construction permit, such a practice is acceptable and legal, and would not be looked upon as acting under duress (*ikrah*), considering that the plaintiff would have received in exchange his construction permit. In other words, as long as there is a shared "common interest", it would make no difference whether the plaintiff stated any reservations or not [when drafting the contract], since the concession took place legally.'

In a decade-long succession of replies and counter-replies, what stands out most is indeed the notion of constraint or duress (*ikrah*), for the simple reason that the court differentiated between a violation against a personal right, on one hand, and the wilful act of exchange within an administrative procedure for the sake of receiving a construction permit, on the other. Thus, even the reservations that were appended to the original contract were an indication that the plaintiff was aware of the concessions that had been proposed to him. In the final analysis, it was the notion of constraint that predominated and the plaintiff received a positive verdict in February 1991 from an appellate tribunal in Damascus, which compensated him 1,215,000 Syrian pounds ($24,000) for the illegally exchanged property.

One thing seems clear: the original spirit of the 1949 legal code has been irreversibly betrayed, even though the text itself stands intact. Syrian citizens have lost a great deal of their civil liberties, not simply in the political arena but also with regard to the right to exchange and associate freely, as originally devised by the civil code. An understanding of Syrian law would, however, be incomplete without looking at parliamentary legislation.

III

According to the terms of the 1973 constitution, legislative responsibility belongs to the People's Assembly. In practice, however, the president's legislative powers largely counterbalance those of the assembly. This is because the president is authorised to legislate whenever the assembly is not in session, and parliamentary recesses are very long, and also because the constitution gives the president wide latitude to issue decrees. Indeed, the laws that have had the greatest impact in Syrian life in recent years have originated with the president.

Nevertheless, the provisions of the constitution make the People's Assembly the only institution that limits – formally and virtually but also actually – the extent of presidential power. In the following paragraphs, we analyse the passing of a law to demonstrate how the assembly is embedded within the institutional network and the political game. The draft law originated in the cabinet, more precisely with the minister of justice, Nizar al-'Asasi, himself a former member of parliament. It also involved the minister of labour and social affairs, Ghada al-Jabi, because the prime minister considered that she enjoyed, as a former president of the General Union of Syrian Women, particular influence with regard to the issue at hand.

The draft discussed by the assembly proposed to modify the age of child custody when parents divorce. It is therefore a component of personal status law, that is, the law dealing with marriage, divorce and inheritance. Syria promulgated a personal status code on 7 September 1953 (Law 59 of 1953). This text, which applies to all Syrians – Muslims and non-Muslims alike – forms part of the so-called 'legislative revolution' that took place during the short presidency of Husni al-Za'im, although it was actually enacted during the presidency of Adib al-Shishakli (1951–3). In 1975, the Code of Personal Status was amended and important changes were introduced with regard to polygamy, dowry, alimony, consensual divorce (*khul'*) and children's age of custody. Concerning the latter issue, Article 19 of Law 34 of 1975 provides that 'the duration of custody [by the mother] ends when the boy reaches the age of nine and the girl [the age] of eleven'. The same provision was once again amended by Law 18 of 2003, approved by the People's Assembly on 19 October and issued by the president of the republic a week later. Article 146 of the Code of Personal Status now stipulates that 'the duration of custody [by the mother] ends when the boy reaches the age of thirteen and the girl [the age] of fifteen'. It is this amendment that sparked the debate to which we now turn.

A close look at the way in which the debate unfolded constitutes a good introduction into Syrian parliamentary life. The debate started with the president of the assembly reminding members of the procedure to be followed: submission of a draft law by the government; a session of the assembly's Commission of Constitutional and Legislative Affairs and the submission of the bill as amended by the Commission to the People's Assembly. The secretary of the assembly would read the texts of the government's project and the commission's project, after which the floor would be open to representatives who would express their desire to speak. In the initial step, the debate unfolded smoothly, with some interventions in favour of the commission's amended project and others asking for amendments. Then, one member requested that the debate be closed (*qifl bab al-niqash*), and voting be commenced on the bill. The closure motion was put to the vote and was adopted by a majority of members. Once closure was adopted, the president of the assembly summoned the secretary to proceed with the reading of Article 1. It was only at this stage that closure was contested, a move that launched a second round of debate during which a further series of statements was made. The renewed debate, which proved to be a bit chaotic, divided supporters of the government's original proposal from supporters of the commission's and supporters of the amendment suggested by an independent member, Muhammad al-Habash. A second closure motion was introduced, which was in turn adopted by the majority. The commission's project was then put to a vote and was rejected. The situation became even more confusing, and the president of the assembly suspended the session.

When the session resumed, a third step of the debate began, which was characterised by procedural adjustments and a series of votes on several propositions made by members. While two of these adjustments were rejected, al-Habash's was adopted. However, procedural motions were raised concerning the voting procedure, which led the president to ask for a 'standing–sitting' vote, which confirmed al-Habash's amendment by a twelve-vote majority. Then, the president opened debate on the entire law, which initiated new discussions on the competence of the courts and various procedural rules related to whether or not a quorum was present. The debate ended with one member stressing the idle character of the discussions and the president putting the whole draft law to a vote, as amended by the al-Habash proposal. Once the draft was approved, the president of the assembly declared that 'the project is adopted and ... becomes a law' and moved on to the next item on the assembly's agenda.

This example shows that the president of the assembly plays a key role in determining the process of legislative activity. Drawing on the by-laws, the president shapes discussion. Through many operations, which may look like mere parliamentary intrigue, the president orients and channels debate in very specific directions. He systematically allocates turns to speak, he interrupts, he contradicts, he cuts short, he synthesises, he is ironic, he proceeds to the voting. In short, he orchestrates the whole process.

At the same time, the assembly's by-laws and procedural provisions constitute a powerful instrument in the hands of the members and a means that offers them some room for manoeuvre and contestation. As Jon Elster puts it,[4] such procedures are a resource that is provided by the political system itself. More precisely, they make it possible to use procedural devices to disrupt the system or, at least, to make rulers 'pay the price' for the marginal role to which they confine the parliament. In Albert Hirschman's typology, these procedures allow members to exercise voice; that is, to express criticism from within the system itself. In our case, this voicing does not take the shape of open contestation but instead constitutes an exasperating strategy whereby the procedural rules, which are provided by the system and which it cannot elude, are used to extreme effect.

IV

Studying the way that laws are passed is one way to observe how political institutions function. In contemporary Syria, there is a deliberative process within the People's Assembly. This process proves to be largely uncertain, since it involves the collaboration of representatives who act in personal ways, on the basis of personal motives. Even in an authoritarian regime, the operation of representative institutions multiplies infra-decisional means through which members can undertake initiatives corresponding to what they believe to be suitable for the collectivity and in accordance with their own personal interests. Representatives draw practical maps that delineate the borders between what is permitted and what is forbidden within the institutional framework. Such maps leave open a broad margin of uncertainty, all the more because the popular legitimacy of the regime must be (at least formally) rehearsed inside the assembly.

Needless to say, Syria's People's Assembly presents some peculiarities. The election of representatives is not the outcome of free and transparent polling. Nevertheless, the assembly functions in accordance with, and in turn produces, a body of legal texts that constrains and is equally constrained by the institutional environment in which politics occurs. There is a circle, either virtuous or vicious, in which legislative activities are embedded in rules and procedures that they themselves create. Far from being simply constraints on the members' work, these rules and procedures also offer resources that members can and do use to assert themselves, to voice preferences, to express disagreement or simply to address a broader audience. To sum up, despite the authoritarian nature of the Ba'thi regime, the legal system is one site where complex political dynamics operate, which transcend the ruler's autocratic power and reflect complicated relations of dependence and autonomy between the People's Assembly, the Ba'th Party and the president of the republic.

Notes

1. *Majmu'at al-qawanin al-iqtisadiyyah*, Damascus 2003.
2. Alan Watson, *The Making of the Civil Law*, Cambridge, Mass. 1981, p. 115:

> The basic structure of the Code civil is that of the institutional tradition; and it can even be described as unnatural. Thus, unlike the Code civil, natural law codes stress the importance of the state for human society and emphasize the legal relationship between the individual and the state. Other omissions from the Code are inexplicable on any notion of a law of reason. The most striking of these omissions is commercial law, which became the object of its own code, the Code de commerce, which came into effect on January 1, 1808. On any normal understanding, commercial law is a part of private law, the law between citizens. And the incorporation of commercial law into the Code civil would have been particularly easy, given the existence of what was in effect a code of commercial law in Colbert's ordinance for mercantile

law. Moreover, the hostility of the revolutionaries to the commercial class ought logically to have brought about the disappearance of any separate commercial law and the incorporation of rules appropriate to all transactions and classes of the people in the Code civil. The explanation for the omission of commercial law from the Code is simply that commercial law was not thought of as 'civil law', and the explanation for that is that commercial law formed its own distinct legal tradition, had no obvious forerunners to which it could be attached in Roman law and above all was not to be found in Justinian's Institutes and hence not in the institutes of French law. The same explanation applies to the same omission from the Austrian ABGB and the German BGB.

3. The two cases in this section are summarised in Muhammad Fahr Shaqfah, *Qadaya wa-abhath qanuniyyah*, Damascus 1997.

4. Jon Elster, 'L'usage strategique de l'argumentation', *Negociation*, vol. 1, no. 2, 2005, p. 60.

FOUR

Sunni Clergy Politics in the Cities of Ba'thi Syria

Thomas Pierret

Given the ruthless repression of lay Islamic activists, Sunni clerics have come to occupy a hegemonic position on Syria's religious scene. By actively supporting the regime, some of these clerics (*'ulama*) have been able to monopolise access to official institutions and media, following the example of the late Grand Mufti Ahmad Kaftaru and the Kurdish-born scholar Sa'id Ramadan al-Buti. In its quest for legitimacy, however, the Ba'thi regime of President Bashar al-Asad has been forced to widen its support base by giving freer rein to previously hostile but popular religious trends. Relying on two years of fieldwork among Syrian Islamic circles,[1] this article aims to scratch the surface of 'official Islam' and shed light on lesser-known players whose role is likely to increase in the future.

The scope of this article is limited to people commonly considered to be *'ulama*. In contemporary Syria, the category is loosely defined, since it supposes neither official appointment nor graduation from an Islamic university. Rather, the social construction of this status is a complex process that involves formal and informal religious criteria, career orientation, self-presentation and family background. It consequently sometimes overlaps with the group of lay Islamic activists and intellectuals, who are not included in the present study.

In the absence of a unified public sphere, Syria's *'ulama* are fragmented into a number of local scenes that are marginally interconnected. Regional identities remain very strong, as illustrated by the proverbial antagonism between Damascus and Aleppo, which is still deeply felt in relations between the two cities' religious elites. The choice made here to focus on the country's two largest urban centres results not only from practical considerations but also from the fact that tight control by the security apparatus in smaller cities and towns, including Homs and Hama, restrains both the clergy's dynamism and the possibilities for field research.

Informal Networks

Most Syrian *'ulama* adhere to a text-oriented version of Sufi Islam,[2] because state repression helped this trend to marginalise its more radical Salafi rival. The main gatekeeper of this orthodoxy is Sa'id Ramadan al-Buti,[3] who is also the chief mediator between the regime and the Sunni clergy. As a result, he has come to occupy a kind of 'papal' position. The latter implies that he is not clearly identified with any particular network, making him different from the vast majority of the country's Sunni clerics, who generally belong to Sufi brotherhoods and more influential groups known as *jam'iyyat*.

Sufi Brotherhoods and Jam'iyyat

In the second half of the twentieth century, Syria's Sunni scholars were mainly affiliated with the Shadhili and Naqshbandi orders.[4] The former is frequently dubbed al-Hashimiyyah after Muhammad al-Hashimi (d. 1961), an Algerian shaikh who spread the order throughout the country.[5] Thanks to the latter's charisma, as well as to the Shadhiliyyah's distinctly elitist orientation, this Sufi way became a favourite one among local *'ulama* and the urban middle class. In the capital, al-Hashimi's main contemporary successors are Hisham al-Burhani, a renowned Hanafi jurist who lived in exile in the United Arab Emirates until 1995, as well as 'Abd al-Rahman al-Shaghuri (d. 2004).

Al-Shaghuri was the most prestigious Shadhili shaikh of his time and many Damascene *'ulama* recognised him as a spiritual master. His deputies are even found in Aleppo, most notably Mahmud al-Husaini, a rising star of the local religious scene; that is, on the other side of the generally rigid north–south divide. In central and northern Syria, al-Hashimi's deputy was 'Abd al-Qadir 'Isa (d. 1991), who went into exile during the uprising of the late 1970s. His successor Ahmad Fathallah Jami still lives in Turkey but several of his disciples are prominent Sunni scholars in Aleppo (Nadim al-Shihabi, Bakri al-Hayyani) and Homs (Sa'id al-Kahil, the shaikh of the city's Grand Mosque, and 'Adnan al-Saqqa, who became the leading figure of the city's clergy after his return from exile in 2000).

Syrian branches of the Shadhili order have always retained 'traditional' structures, that is, non-centralised networks that almost inevitably fragment among the leading disciples of the shaikh after he dies. In contrast, by adding a sense of social mission to the transmission of religious knowledge, several – mostly Naqshbandi-affiliated – scholars have managed to create more cohesive movements known as *jam'iyyat*. The latter emerged in the middle of the twentieth century in the context of what was retrospectively called the 'awakening of the shaikhs', a traditionalist reaction to the spread of secular ideas. In a bid to 'bring society back onto the path of Islam', some of these shaikhs concentrated on setting up formal schools to teach the future religious elite; these shaikhs included Hasan Habannaka (d. 1978) and Salih al-Farfur (d. 1986) in Damascus, as well as 'Abdullah Siraj al-Din (d. 2004) in Aleppo. All of these *'ulama* had Sufi affiliations and their authority relied more on vertical spiritual ties than on the functional structures they set up. Two of their peers, Ahmad Kaftaru (d. 2004) in Damascus and Muhammad al-Nabhan (d. 1974) in Aleppo, were famous both as founders of successful educational institutions and as heads of large Naqshbandi brotherhoods, which spread to Beirut (under the direction of Kaftaru's disciple Rajab Dib)[6] and to the Iraqi province of al-'Anbar.

Leaders of other *jam'iyyat* more exclusively relied on a Sufi-inspired organisational model and developed no formal structures. Instead they based their action entirely on spiritual bonds, informal circles (*halaqat*) and daily lessons in the mosque. Their goal was not to train religious specialists but rather to educate lay people in order to turn them into models of piety. The largest of these *jam'iyyat* were led by two Naqshbandi-affiliated shaikhs, 'Abd al-Karim al-Rifa'i (d. 1973) in Damascus (Jam'iyyah Zayd) and Ahmad al-Bayanuni (d. 1975) in Aleppo (Jam'iyyah Abi Dharr),[7] both of which attracted hundreds of young people from the educated middle class.

The political positions of the *jam'iyyat* evolved in very different ways. The groups established by Kaftaru, al-Farfur, Siraj al-Din and al-Nabhan maintained good – or at least satisfactory – relations with the authorities, with the result that they have remained to date the main private provider of formal Islamic teaching in the country. However, whereas Kaftaru was appointed grand mufti in 1964, his rival Habannaka (whose group was named Jam'iyyah al-Midan after the neighbourhood that constituted its stronghold) became the spearhead of the religious opposition to the Ba'th Party. He was briefly jailed in 1967 and his al-Tawjih al-Islami Institute was shut down. As for Zayd and Abi Dharr *jam'iyyat*, they were dragged into the 1979–82 Islamist uprising after some of their young adepts succumbed to the calls of militant groups. Abi Dharr was annihilated and one of its rare remnants is led by Ahmad al-Bayanuni's son Abu al-Fath. A prominent academic in Saudi Arabia, he was allowed to settle in Aleppo in 2006 and was quickly reinstated as a distinguished member of the local religious elite.

As for Zayd, it suffered badly from state repression during the 1980s and its leaders were forced to take refuge in Jiddah. It survives thanks to older and second-rank shaikhs who were allowed to remain in Syria. In order to lessen the resentment of Zayd's wide popular base, which includes a significant part of Damascus's merchant middle class, al-Rifa'i's sons 'Usama and Sariya were allowed to come back in the mid-1990s and progressively rebuilt the movement. After the 2000 presidential succession, the 'new' regime turned to them to improve its shaky legitimacy and Zayd was allowed to expand its charitable activities. With twenty to thirty mosques and very popular shaikhs who attract thousands of people to its weekly gatherings, most notably the al-Rifa'i brothers and Na'im al-'Arqsusi, Zayd is by far the most popular religious trend in Damascus today.

Mosque Politics

Given the state's lack of economic and symbolic resources, the process of bureaucratisation of the Syrian clergy has remained embryonic. Of course, the economic and political power of the Ministry of Religious Endowments (*awqaf*) is considerable, as it possesses gigantic properties and is responsible for the appointment – and dismissal – of mosque personnel.[8] At the same time, its relative isolation from the actual religious elite severely curtails its ability to set up a credible state-sponsored clergy. In fact, the Ba'thi regime has never even tried to produce its own brand of religious scholars: Syria has no institution like al-Azhar in Cairo, and the only state-owned school for higher Islamic studies is the Shari'ah Faculty of the University of Damascus which was never, as will be shown below, a proper incubator for an Islamic bureaucracy. Most Syrian *ulama* still emerge as the result of complex, informal processes of social recognition that take place inside the 'infrastructure' of the religious scene, rather than from administrative appointments.

As a consequence, the regime's preferred strategy for managing the Sunni elite has been the co-optation of personalities who have a genuine social base, rather than merely manufacturing 'Ba'thi shaikhs' out of the void. The best illustration of this policy is the decade-old alliance between the authorities and the late Ahmad Kaftaru, whose popularity preceded – and survived – his 1964 regime-imposed appointment as grand mufti. Informal partnership with Sa'id Ramadan al-Buti is another good example, since the latter managed to balance his vocal support for the two al-Asads and the preservation of his credibility among local religious circles. Even presently isolated pro-regime clerics such as the Islamic member of parliament Muhammad Habash stem from larger *jam'iyyat* and have achieved significant popularity before 'burning their wings' by moving too close to the state.

Such a strategy has brought only limited results, since even the powerful Kaftaru network never managed to establish itself solidly outside its historic stronghold in northern Damascus. Consequently, the regime had to rely on religious actors who could be called quietist rather than enthusiastic supporters, like al-Farfur's group in Damascus and al-Nabhan's in Aleppo, whose shaikhs filled part of the void created by the repression of the 1980s uprising. The former trend is probably the most widespread in the capital's suburbs, while the second has trained today's most famous preachers in Aleppo, namely Mahmud al-Hut, 'Abd al-Hadi Badla and Nabih Salim. In Damascus, even rebellious *jam'iyyat* like Zayd and al-Midan have never been rooted out of their traditional fiefdoms.

In order to understand the regime's inability to 'format' the religious scene according to its own interests, it is necessary to stress the fact that the central administration's power to appoint mosque staff is limited. The government has no candidates of its own to fill the posts and only offers nominal salaries, whereas existing religious networks can provide trained clerics and substantial economic resources. In addition, thanks to its social capital and financial incentives, the *ulama*–merchants nexus exerts significant pressure on the administration and security apparatuses alike.

Formal Institutions

In the wake of the limited liberalisation of the regime's religious policy that started in the early 2000s, educational institutions, charities and mass media have increasingly represented the different trends that can be found in Syria's Islamic scene. This process now also involves administrative and political structures.

Formal Schools

Formal Islamic teaching is mainly represented by secondary *shari'ah* institutes. In the larger cities, most of these schools were established before 1963 and are controlled by the *jam'iyyat* and the families that established a hold on the religious scene in the middle of the last century: in Damascus, al-Ansar (Kaftaru), al-Fath (al-Farfur), al-Furqan (Zayd), al-Gharra (al-Daqr) and al-Tahdhib wal-Ta'lim (al-Khatib);[9] in Aleppo, besides the government-affiliated Khusrawiyyah, the two main ones are al-Nabhan's al-Kiltawiyyah (now headed by the popular preacher Mahmud al-Hut) and Siraj al-Din's al-Sha'baniyyah (directed by Nur al-Din 'Itr, Siraj al-Din's son-in-law and Syria's leading scholar in the study of the traditions of the Prophet [*hadith*]).

In the last few years, détente between the regime and the religious elite has resulted in the opening of new *shari'ah* institutes in Damascus at a rate unseen since the March 1963 revolution. In order to accommodate the popular but distrustful students of Hasan Habannaka, the authorities have begun to hold out the prospect of allowing the reopening of his al-Tawjih al-Islami Institute, which was closed in the late 1960s. Certain local observers see a co-ordinated move in the 2007 appointment of Hasan, the son of Mustafa al-Bugha, as the head of the Shari'ah Faculty of Damascus University. Mustafa al-Bugha, the most prominent student of Habannaka still living, was privately visited twice by President Bashar al-Asad, an extremely rare honour for a Sunni scholar. Al-Bugha now routinely occupies top-level positions at official religious ceremonies.

Traditional *jam'iyyat* also run the only two private Syrian institutes for higher Islamic studies – the Shaikh Ahmad Kaftaru Academy (formerly known as Abu al-Nur and now headed by Kaftaru's son Salah al-Din) and the al-Fath Institute (directed by Salih al-Farfur's son Husam) – that were allowed to open an academic section in 1991.

As for Damascus University's Shari'ah Faculty, it has never constituted a reliable means to train a religious elite loyal to the state. It is thus a marginal producer of mosque personnel, since derisory salaries do not render this career very attractive for university graduates. Beside academic functions in Syria and abroad, many alumni choose to work as religious teachers in secondary schools or engage in business activities. For the same economic reasons, those who end up as mosque preachers or teachers also engage in business; graduation from the faculty is no more than a means to improve academic credentials. It is neither necessary nor sufficient to have such qualifications to obtain a position in a mosque. The backing of established *'ulama* is usually essential too.

The problem posed by the faculty is also political. Despite failed attempts at Ba'thisation in the 1980s,[10] this institution, founded in 1954 by the Muslim Brothers, has continuously included professors known either for their political independence (such as the present mufti of Aleppo, Ibrahim al-Salqini) or for their sympathy for the Muslim Brothers (Wahba al-Zuhaili). It has also attracted scholars who belong to previously repressed traditionalist currents like Habannaka's student Mustafa al-Bugha and the Shadhili shaikh Hisham al-Burhani, who joined the teaching staff immediately after his return from exile in the mid-1990s. Some of these scholars owe their rather unexpected appointment to the support of the influential al-Buti, who has taught there for almost half a century. Moreover, the faculty appears to be a nursery for reformist, politically minded Islamic intellectuals like 'Imad al-Din al-Rashid, the young vice dean of the faculty, whose 'Muslim democratic' views are avowedly influenced by the experience of the Turkish AKP.

Charitable Associations

The 1963 revolution made the foundation of Islamic charities extremely difficult and several of them were banned in the wake of the 1979–82 uprising. As a result, most of Syria's Islamic charities go back to the pre-Ba'th era and are often controlled by the *jam'iyyat* that emerged during that period. Since the 1990s, however, charitable activities have grown in number and scale as a result of worsening economic and social conditions.[11]

Given its underlying legitimacy problem, the regime is in no position to extract spontaneous donations from society. Moreover, traditionally regime-friendly Islamic networks such as Kaftaru's have relied on too narrow a social base to bear the burden of welfare privatisation by themselves. As a result, the regime has allowed the takeover of Damascus's charitable sector by the Zayd movement, because of the latter's popularity among the merchant middle class and its ability to attract funds from the private sector. Relying on a network of neighbourhood associations set up in the 1950s, Zayd has launched the Hifdh al-Ni'ma (Preservation of Grace) project, which collects surpluses of food, medicine, clothes, furniture and books to aid more than 6,000 families. In 2006, Zayd-linked businesspeople were allowed to take control of the Union of Charitable Associations in Damascus, which co-ordinates and represents the city's charities. Since 1997, the union has also set up large-scale projects such as Sunduq al-'Afiya (The Health Fund), which covers surgical expenses, and Sunduq al-Mawadda wal-Rahmah (The Love and Mercy Fund) that subsidises marriages.

Media

Syria is one of the less hospitable Arab countries for Islamic mass media. In the mainly state-owned daily press, the only religious column is that of Muhammad Habash, which comes out every Friday in the official *al-Thawrah*. In the 2000s, Habash emerged as a prominent personality in Syrian and global media as well as in local parliamentary politics. The son-in-law of Kaftaru, he was expelled from the latter's circle because of his liberal positions regarding women's status and inter-faith relations.[12] Since then, his estrangement from the conservative religious elite has been matched by his rapprochement with the regime and he increasingly appears as the government's unofficial public information officer.

As for monthly journals, the Ministry of Religious Endowments' *Nahj al-Islam* ('The Way of Islam') is the only one to have been authorised since the early 1980s. Conceived at first as an ideological weapon against the Muslim Brothers, *Nahj al-Islam* subsequently watered down its tone and now increasingly welcomes authors from outside the narrow circle of notoriously pro-regime clerics, such as Zayd's Sariya al-Rifa'i. In the private realm, disciples of Ahmad Kaftaru have actively sought to bypass restrictions on Islamic press. Between 1996 and 2002, they printed the monthly *Sada al-Iman* ('The Echo of the Faith') in Beirut and, in 2006, they obtained authorisation to release the 'generalist' *al-Ijtima'iyyah* ('The Social Review'), which dealt extensively with religious issues. However, it was forbidden the following year, after one of its editorials called on readers to 'urinate' on the radical secularist intellectual Nabil Fayyad.[13]

Until the 2000s, appearances by Sunni scholars on official audio-visual radio and television programmes were limited to a select few pro-regime clerics like al-Buti and Kaftaru's right-hand man, Marwan Shaikhu (d. 2001). During the present decade, the state monopoly in this realm has been formally broken, thanks to the extensive religious programmes broadcast by Radio al-Quds of Ahmad Jibril's Popular Front for the Liberation of Palestine – General Command, which include the extraordinarily popular lessons of Ratib al-Nabulsi. The latter is a peculiar phenomenon on the local religious scene, since he is an independent shaikh and does not belong to any *jam'iyyah*; his fame comes exclusively from his media performances.

As for television, Muhammad Habash was responsible for the religious transmissions made by the first, but short-lived (2006–7), private Syrian channel *al-Sham* of the Idlib businessman and deputy Akram al-Jundi. Since 2007, the Kuwait-based *al-Risalah* satellite channel has aired mosque lessons by a dozen Syrian Sunni scholars who were chosen according to their popularity, like Zayd's 'Usama al-Rifa'i and Na'im al-'Arqsusi.

Heads of the Religious Administration

The purely religious authority of top religious civil servants is at best marginal. The grand mufti and his subordinates rarely issue the kind of widely publicised edicts (*fatwas*) that are common in Egypt. Instead, most of the activities of the head of Syrian Sunni Islam consist of 'faith-based diplomacy' through incessant journeys abroad and welcoming foreign delegations. In the absence of any real autonomy that would allow official religious figures to express themselves on social and political issues, the only rationale for issuing *fatwa*s would be to answer the regime's wishes. Except when in dire need – for instance during the 1979–82 uprising – the authorities have avoided inscribing their decisions in an Islamic normative framework that might prove constraining in the long term.

The current policy of appointment to official religious positions reflects both the authorities' continued reliance on their most loyal partners and a slow, calculated opening towards more distant ones. Kaftaru's succession clearly followed the first trend: when he died in September 2004, rumours evoked the possibility of his replacement by a prominent 'non-Kaftari' Damascene religious figure like al-Buti or Wahba al-Zuhaili. However, the regime was just entering a period of deep internal and foreign crisis, with the result that it was unwilling to reinforce the already too powerful religious establishment of the capital. The government found the issue so delicate that it waited almost a year and eventually bypassed the legal procedure of election by the Higher Council for Ifta, instead appointing the new mufti by presidential decree. The beneficiary was the young mufti of Aleppo, Ahmad Hassun, the son of Adib Hassun (d. 2008), Muhammad al-Nabhan's leading deputy as a Sufi master. The first non-Damascene occupant of the post since its creation in 1947, Ahmad Hassun was more famous for his career as a member of parliament than for his scholarly credentials.[14] Appointments to the post of minister of religious endowments illustrate the same cautiousness, since Ziad al-Ayyubi, a disciple of Ahmad Kaftaru, was replaced in 2007 by his assistant Muhammad al-Sayyid,[15] the former mufti of Tartus and son of 'Abd al-Sattar al-Sayyid, a long-time supporter of the regime who headed the same ministry between 1971 and 1980.

At the local level, however, the picture is more nuanced. In Damascus, the Shafi'i and Hanafi *ifta* have been handed over to representatives of, respectively, the Kaftaru trend (Bashir al-Bari, since 1986) and the al-Fath Institute ('Abd al-Fattah al-Bazam, since 1993). Since early 2008, the latter current also headed the directorship of the city's religious endowments (Ahmad Qabbani), but a new player made an appearance through the appointment of a shaikh of the Zayd movement (Ziad al-Musalli) to be director of the Damascus countryside's religious endowments. As for

Aleppo's Islamic scene, it has been dominated until recently by the sons of two prominent disciples of al-Nabhan, Muhammad al-Shami (d. 1980) and Adib Hassun. When the former was assassinated by Islamic militants, he was succeeded at the head of religious endowments by his son Suhaib. The latter was dismissed in 2005 after his arch-rival, Hassun's son Ahmad, left his position as mufti of Aleppo to become grand mufti of the Republic. Al-Shami was replaced by a Ba'th Party member but in an opening move, the city's muftiship was entrusted to the politically independent Ibrahim al-Salqini. Unsurprisingly, therefore, the latter was flanked with a more 'reliable' second mufti in the person of Mahmud 'Akkam, another leading cleric of the post-1980 local religious scene. A former member of Abi Dharr, 'Akkam received a doctorate in Paris under the supervision of Muhammad 'Arkun. Once very popular among the educated youth, he has been increasingly reproached for his close ties with the authorities and interest in Shi'i Islam. In 2006, he was entrusted with the supervision of the newly founded University of Aleppo's Faculty of Shari'ah.

Preaching at the Grand 'Umayyad mosque in Damascus has traditionally been the responsibility of Kaftaru's disciples, as well as members of the al-Khatib family, whose most outspoken representatives, Mu'adh and his brother 'Abd al-Qadir, were dismissed in 1995 and 2003 respectively. In early 2008, al-Buti was appointed as the mosque's chief preacher and director of teaching. This decision constituted an important shift in relations between the regime and the Kurdish scholar, since it was the first time that the latter had accepted a prominent position in the religious administration. Al-Buti quickly left his mark on the institution by completely reorganising the lesson schedule and appointing eminent *'ulama* from groups that were previously barred from teaching at the capital's most prestigious place of worship, like Krayyim Rajih and Mustafa al-Bugha (al-Midan) as well as 'Usama al-Rifa'i and Na'im al-'Arqsusi (Zayd). Correspondingly, al-Buti's promotion occurred at the expense of the regime's historically privileged Islamic partner, as none of the Kaftari shaikhs included in the previous schedule had his mandate renewed.[16]

Political Representation

In an authoritarian system like Syria's, the main access for religious actors to the authorities remains the *nasiha,* that is, private advice to the ruler. This role has been mainly played by al-Buti since he declared his open support for the regime during the 1979–82 uprising. Al-Buti's aid was of crucial importance because of his personal prestige, which resulted from the fact that he was among the very rare Arab writers to combine impeccable, Azhari scholarly credentials with a 'modern' literary style characteristic of contemporary Islamic literature. After 1980, because most of this literature was forbidden in Syria, al-Buti was the only major writer of the contemporary Islamic awakening *(sahwah)* whose books were easily available in the country's bookshops.

After coming out publicly for the regime, al-Buti has repeatedly praised the Syrian leadership in exchange for a progressive softening of restrictions on non-political Islamic activities and amnesty for some exiled Sunni scholars. At the same time, he has managed to retain credibility by refusing any material reward and formal position, at least until his 2008 appointment as the head of the 'Umayyad mosque.

As far as formal politics is concerned, Sunni *'ulama* have sat in the People's Assembly as 'independent' deputies since the early years of the al-Asad era. From 1980 onwards, all of them have been carefully chosen from among pro-regime clerics, following the example of Kaftaru's disciple Marwan Shaikhu, present Grand Mufti Ahmad Hassun, the late brother of Suhaib al-Shami 'Abd al-'Aziz (d. 2007) and Zakariya Salwaya of Latakia.

The coalitions of businessmen that overwhelmingly dominate the campaigns for independent seats frequently include Muslim scholars, as illustrated by the two winning lists in Damascus in April 2007. Whereas Muhammad Hamshu, a crony of the ruling family, enrolled 'Abd al-Salam Rajih, the dean of the Shari'ah Faculty of the Ahmad Kaftaru Academy, his rival Hashim al-'Aqqad allied with Muhammad Habash. Hamshu's list managed to get the backing of the city's religious establishment but, in most cases, this was simply compensation for widely publicised pious donations rather than a mark of genuine political involvement.

In 2004–5, Muhammad Habash and Ahmad Kaftaru's son Salah took advantage of the regime's weakening to issue calls for democratic reform which, according to a common pattern of liberalising authoritarianism, would have favoured the clients of the regime. However, because of its cautiousness and distrust of parliamentary politics under Ba'thi rule, the majority of the clergy viewed the establishment of a syndicate of *'ulama* as a more suitable way to increase political influence. There already existed an Association of 'Ulama headed by Habash, but this charitable and cultural organisation composed of second-rank clerics could not play such a role.

In 2006, two factors pushed the regime to envisage the creation of a more convincing representation of the clergy: the religious elite had to be rewarded for its loyalty during the 2004–5 crisis, and a need was felt to answer the establishment of the League of the 'Ulama of Syria by Majid Makki, an exiled cleric from Aleppo with strong ties to the Muslim Brothers, but whose moderate discourse was obviously aimed at attracting Syrian-based religious scholars. As a result, the League of the 'Ulama of Bilad al-Sham was founded in April 2006, whose headquarters and leadership were rather unsurprising (the Kaftaru Academy, with Wahba al-Zuhaili as president, and al-Buti as 'mastermind'). Nevertheless, the organisation was genuinely representative of all of Damascus's major Islamic networks.[17] The league could thus have been a very influential player, if political restrictions and internal rivalry had not led to its final paralysis a few weeks later.

Conclusion

The Syrian regime never possessed sufficient economic means and religious legitimacy to set up the institutional tools that would have enabled it to produce a Sunni clergy that was sympathetic to the Ba'th Party's ideological orientation. Consequently, the *'ulama* remained outside the state apparatus, and nothing like an official 'Islamic bureaucracy' ever emerged. Rather, the authorities have dealt with existing religious networks whose social capital is produced by mechanisms that are mostly beyond the reach of the state. Therefore, official religious policy can only be conceived in terms of selection: compliant actors have been rewarded, neutral ones tolerated and hostile trends suppressed. Such a course of action, however, is difficult to maintain in the long term, since the very partners whose loyalty was of crucial importance during the Islamic uprising of the late 1970s increasingly used their connections with the regime to intercede on behalf of formerly repressed religious players. As a result, exclusive support for a handful of compliant figures has progressively given way to a more pluralist policy of inclusion.

Bashar al-Asad's leadership is going through a delicate transition in its relations with the Sunni clergy, as it slowly leaves the repressive context that followed the uprising and returns to the more permissive posture that prevailed in the 1970s. In the meantime, radical social and cultural transformation has turned the *ʻulama* into a much more influential force than it had previously been. Formerly marginalised actors are no longer satisfied with mere tolerance but instead demand full normalisation on the basis of a true partnership. This means not only more freedom of action in the field of education, charitable activities and the mass media, but also wider access to administrative positions and political representation. Such a process has improved the regime's short-term stability by widening its social base. In the future, however, balancing the Sunni clergy's demands against the reservations of the ʻAlawi-dominated, secular-minded security apparatus and state intelligentsia may turn out to be an increasingly complicated game.

Notes

1. This article mostly relies on interviews with anonymous Syrian sources, which explains the limited number of references.
2. See Itzchak Weismann, 'Sufi Fundamentalism between India and the Middle East' in Martin Van Bruinessen and Julia Howell, eds. *Sufism and the 'Modern'*, London 2007, pp. 115–28.
3. Andreas Christmann, 'Islamic Scholar and Religious Leader: A Portrait of Muhammad Saʻid Ramadan Al-Buti', *Islam and Christian–Muslim Relations*, vol. 9, no. 2, 1998, pp. 149–69.
4. For a theoretically informed overview of Sufi brotherhoods in Syria, see Paulo Pinto, 'Sufism and the Political Economy of Morality in Syria', *Interdisciplinary Journal of Middle Eastern Studies*, vol. 15, 2006, pp. 103–36.
5. Itzchak Weismann, 'The Shadhiliyya-Darqawiyya in the Arab East' in Eric Geoffroy, ed. *La Shadhiliyya – une voie soufie dans le monde*, Paris 2004.
6. Annabelle Böttcher, 'Official Islam, Transnational Islamic Networks, and Regional Politics: The Case of Syria' in Dietrich Jung, ed. *The Middle East and Palestine: Global Politics and Regional Conflict*, New York 2004, pp. 125–50; Leif Stenberg, 'Young, Male, and Sufi Muslim in the City of

Damascus' in Jorgen Baeck Simonsen, ed. *Youth and Youth Culture in the Contemporary Middle East,* Aarhus 2005, pp. 68–91.

7. Al-Bayanuni is the father of present Muslim Brothers' leader 'Ali Sadr al-Din al-Bayanuni. He was succeeded at the head of Abi Dharr by another of his sons, Abu al-Nasr (d. 1987).

8. Annabelle Böttcher, 'Le Ministère des Waqfs', *Maghreb – Machrek*, no. 158, 1997, pp. 18–30.

9. An important exception is the Badr al-Din al-Hasani Institute, which is more bureaucratically organised and open to various doctrinal trends.

10. Bernard Botiveau, 'La Formation des Oulémas en Syrie. La Faculté de Shari'a de l'université de Damas' in Gilbert Delanoue, ed. *Les Intellectuels et le pouvoir: Syrie, Égypte, Tunisie, Algérie,* Cairo 1986, pp. 67–91.

11. Soukaina Boukhaima, 'Le Mouvement associatif en Syrie' in Sarah Ben Nefissa, ed. *Pouvoirs et associations dans le monde Arabe*, Paris 2002, pp. 77–94.

12. Paul Heck, 'Religious Renewal in Syria: The Case of Muhammad Al-Habash', *Islam and Christian–Muslim Relations*, vol. 15, no. 2, 2004, pp. 185–207.

13. *al-Rayat* (Doha), 17 October 2004.

14. *al-Mar'at al-Yawm* (Abu Dhabi), 16 April 2005 and *Akhbar al-Sharq* (London), 17 July 2005.

15. *Cham Press* (Damascus), 8 December 2007.

16. *al-Thawrah*, 15 February 2008.

17. *al-Ray al-'Amm* (Amman), 28 April 2006.

FIVE

The Shi'i Mausoleums of Raqqa: Iranian proselytism and local significations

Myriam Ababsa

Raqqa, former capital of the 'Abbasid empire and today the administrative centre of the pioneering agricultural front of eastern Syria, is located 200 kilometres east of Aleppo on the Euphrates River. In 1988, the city acquired the largest Shi'i mausoleums in the country, built by the Islamic Republic of Iran. They consist of two symmetrical buildings dedicated to 'Ammar bin Yasir and 'Uwais al-Qarani, companions of the Prophet Muhammad who died at the battle of Siffin in 657 (37 AH). The new buildings put Raqqa among a group of pilgrimage sites that replaced the Iraqi holy places of Najaf and Karbala, which were closed to Iranian pilgrims for two decades after 1980. The substitute sites in Syria also include the mausoleum of al-Sayyidah Zainab, south of Damascus, and that of al-Sayyidah Ruqiyya, near the 'Umayyad mosque in the capital.

Although the mausoleums at Raqqa stood unfinished for seven years (from 1994 to 2001), they are now attracting Iranian pilgrims who visit them on half-day trips from Aleppo. Since the summer of 2002, the blue dome of the mausoleum of 'Ammar dominates the city's skyline. However, the signification of these buildings is problematic for Raqqa. The structures stand at the place of tombs that have been instrumental in the construction of identity for several generations of local inhabitants. Moreover, some of the city's intellectuals are concerned about Shi'i proselytising, which is developing around these buildings in the form of teaching sessions (*majalis husainiyyah*) and specialised bookshops. At the same time, the region's population, particularly members of formerly semi-nomadic tribes, has undertaken to reappropriate this key aspect of Raqqa's historical heritage through renewing the practice of visiting the tombs.

This article examines the complexity of the symbolic structuring of the city of Raqqa by looking at these emblematic sites, whose meaning has evolved over the twentieth century. In places that once expressed the identity of the local population, the mausoleums have become sites of memory and, after their reconstruction by Iran, sites of power.

Reinterpreting the Battle of Siffin

Eight hundred metres from the Euphrates, on a high terrace dominating the valley's plantations, east of the 'Abbasid remains in Rafiqah,[1] stand two square mosques, fifty metres wide, with domes shaped like flower buds and minarets to the side. They are joined by two storeys of arcades, which surround a sixty-metre-long courtyard parallel to the east–west axis of the river. Each dome houses the catafalque of a 'saint', which, for fifteen years, was a simple concrete base covered with carpets; today the catafalques are surrounded by silver railings. They are adjoined by a third, smaller mausoleum, dedicated to 'Ubai bin Ka'b, the Prophet's secretary.[2] Started in 1988, work was interrupted between 1994 and 2001, due to a financial dispute between Syria and Iran. The work was completed in 2005, at the time of the beginning of the construction of an entire hotel complex east of the site, on former agricultural land adjoining Siffin cemetery.

The mausoleums of Raqqa have been built over the tombs of two of the Prophet's companions and heirs (*tabi'un*) who died at the battle of Siffin. This clash took place forty or so kilometres west of Raqqa, on the road to Aleppo near the village of Abu Huraira. During the Middle Ages, the many tombs scattered between the village and Raqqa were Shi'i pilgrimage destinations and formed a geographic link between Siffin and Raqqa.[3] For centuries, the Prophet's companions have been worshipped by Shi'i pilgrims and by the region's Sunni nomads and semi-nomads alike.

'Ammar bin Yasir was named governor of the town of Kufa in 21 AH. His mother, Sumayya, was the first female martyr of Islam.[4] 'Uwais al-Qarani was a shepherd from Yemen, who is said to have been appointed by the Prophet as the best of his followers, despite the fact that the two never met. Many pious tales (*hadiths*) have turned him into the 'prototype of Islamic asceticism' and the first 'religious extremist' of Islam.[5] He is renowned for the invisibility and immateriality that characterised his spiritual training, which is said to have been conceptualised by the Prophet himself.[6] Since the Second World War, several hagiographies published in Baghdad and Beirut have made these two into Shi'i 'martyrs'. This is especially true of 'Ammar,[7] whose death at Siffin led to the creation of a Shi'i anti-'Umayyad tradition based on unauthentic *hadiths* and Quranic allusions to his skill, which aim to prove that he chose to support 'Ali. The production of this martyrdom story is the intellectual expression of Iranian Shi'i proselytism, which has become manifest through the 'restoration' of the tombs of 'Ammar and 'Uwais.

1. Raqqa mausoleums
   Source: Ababsa, 2007

Syria and the Topology of Shi'i Pilgrimage Sites

Raqqa's Shi'i mausoleums are amongst a number of substitute pilgrimage sites that replaced Iraq's holy sites between 1980 and 2003 and Saudi Arabian sites where pilgrims are subject to a strict quota system.[8] In Iraq, the main examples are Najaf and Karbala, where the martyrdom of 'Ali and Husain took place. In 1998, these two sites were opened to coach trips of aged pilgrims, following the reopening of the Syrian–Iraqi border near Albu Kamal. In 2003, since the fall of the Ba'thi regime in Iraq, Iranian pilgrims have returned to Najaf and Karbala and the festivals of 'Ashurah have been widely celebrated. In 1991, 140,000 Iranian pilgrims visited Syria. This figure dropped in the mid-1990s due to the Iranian recession but has once again been on the rise since 1997, reaching nearly 233,000 in 2002, and more than 270,000 in 2006:[9]

Table 5.1: Iranian Entries into Syria (1991–2007)

1991	1992	1993	1994	1995	1996	1997	1998
139,092	145,358	103,797	54,836	47,297	63,124	78,669	77,423
1999	2000	2001	2002	2003	2004	2005	2006
64,897	61,515	97,255	232,985	213,931	196,699	247,662	270,915

Sources: *Syrian Statistical Abstracts* for 1996, 2000, 2003 and 2007

Most Iranian pilgrims arrive by road, passing through Turkey. Their main destination is the town of Sayyidah Zainab, located seven kilometres south of Damascus, which houses the mausoleum of 'Ali's daughter, the Prophet's granddaughter.[10] Sayyidah Zainab, which had a population of only 800 in 1960, became a veritable Shi'i holy city of almost 200,000 inhabitants in the 1970s, following the arrival of displaced people from the Golan in 1967 and Iraqi Shi'i refugees during the Iran–Iraq war of 1980–8. Dedicated to pilgrimage and religious teaching, Sayyidah Zainab has two hotel complexes of over 600 rooms each,[11] dozens of bookshops specialising in the diffusion of Twelver Shi'i teaching and the sale of religious souvenirs, half a dozen *husayniyyah*s and nine religious schools (*hawza*s), attended by over a thousand students. The existence of these schools, along with the saint's mausoleum, makes Sayyidah Zainab a religious centre comparable to Qom in Iran, and an alternative to Najaf as a centre of Arab Shi'ism.[12]

During the twentieth century, the al-Sayyidah Zainab mausoleum became 'Shi'itised': its first major renovation dates back to the 1950s at the initiative of a committee of Syrian Shi'i notables, with the help of a wealthy Iraqi citizen, al-Hajj Bahbahani, who raised funds from Iranian believers.[13] Thus the saint's tomb is a 'gift from the Iranian people' and not the result of government intervention, as was the case with al-Sayyidah Ruqiyya or the new structures in Raqqa.[14] Visiting al-Sayyidah Zainab is considered to be 'the pauper's pilgrimage' (*hajj al-fuqara*) for those who cannot make it to Mecca, Najaf or Karbala.

It is a political act to construct a Shi'i mausoleum in the middle Euphrates district, where fierce struggles took place at the very birth of the 'party of 'Ali'. Doing so allows the Syrian state, at little expense, to establish strong symbolic ties to Iran by providing the Islamic Republic, which aims to dominate the Twelver Shi'i world, with the possibility of extending its religious territory across Syria, a country that is dotted with mausoleums (*dharih*) and memorials (*maqam*). Raqqa, lying at the heart of an emerging geography of Shi'ism, was chosen in a context of geopolitical collaboration between Syria and Iran. Indeed, the Syrian regime, whose leaders belong to the 'Alawi minority, is concerned about *taqrib*, the act of creating ties with 'orthodox' Shi'is.[15]

The topology of the pilgrimage sites that have been appropriated by Shi'is in Syria can be traced through an analysis of a religious souvenir that was sold in Sayyidah Zainab in 1999: it consists of a montage of forty-five photographs, reproduced in Figure 5.1 and classified in Table 5.2. On it, the Raqqa mausoleums appear beside the holy sites of Damascus, Aleppo, Hama and Sayyidah Zainab in Syria, but also Mashhad, Najaf, Samarra, Karbala, Cairo, al-Madinah and Mecca.

2. Main Shi'i Sites shown on al-Sayyida Zaynab souvenir card
   Source: Ababsa, 1999

Table 5.2: Topology of Shi'i Pilgrimage Sites According to a Poster Sold in Sayyidah Zainab in 1999

City	Name of Holy Place
Raqqa	*Maqam* 'Ammar bin Yasir and 'Uwais al-Qarani
Najaf	*Maqam* and *dharih* al-Imam 'Ali bin Abi Talib
Aleppo	*Dharih* Muhassin bin al-Imam al-Husain *Mashad* Ras al-Husain
Karbala	*Maqam* and *dharih* al-Imam al-Husain *Maqam* al-Imam Musa al-Kadhim *Maqam* al-Imam Muhammad al-Jawwad
Mecca	Ka'ba
Samarra	*Maqam* al-Imam 'Ali al-Hadi and al-Imam Hasan al-Askari *Sirdab* al-Imam al-Mahdi *Dharih* al-Imam al-Qassam wal-Jawwad *Dharih* al-Imam Hasan al-'Askari *Dharih* Abu al-Fadl al-'Abbas
Hama	*Maqam* and *musala* al-Imam Zain al-'Abidin

al-Madinah	*Dharih* and mosque al-Nabawi al-Imam Hasan, Zain al-ʻAbidin, al-Baqir and al-Sadiq Sayyidah Haba bint ʻAmas, Hamida bint Muslim ibn ʻUqail and Maymuna bint Hasan Umm Salim and Umm Habiba
Mashhad	*Maqam* and *dharih* of al-Imam ʻAli Rida
Damascus	*Maqam* al-Sayyidah Ruqiyya Abu al-Dirda *Mashad* Ras al-Husain *Maqam* of the martyrs' heads *Maqam* Fatima al-Sughra *Maqam* ʻAbdullah *Maqam* Bilal al-Habashi *Maqam* Saint John the Baptist *Maqam* al-Nabi Ezekial *Maqam* al-ʻArbain, Qubay and Hubay *Maqam* Sayyidah Sukaina bint al-Husain
Sayyidah Zainab	*Maqam* al-Sayyidah Zainab
ʻAdra	*Maqam* Hijr bin ʻUdai al-Kindi
Cairo	*Maqam* al-Sayyidah Zainab and Sayyidah Sukaina bint al-Husain

The major Shiʻi holy sites are mixed with Sunni ones, such as the Kaʻba in Mecca and the tombs of the Prophet's wives, as well as with more general sacred sites, such as the tombs of Saint John the Baptist, of Cain and Abel and of the prophet Ezekiel. The montage sold in Sayyidah Zainab gives priority to Damascus, since most of the city's holy sites are depicted.

Early 2004 saw the official announcement of a new construction project concerning Shiʻi sites in Syria, that of the 'Convoy of Prisoners' (*mawqib al-sabaya*). It consists of all the sites through which Husain's severed head is said to have passed during its journey from Karbala to Damascus in 680, under the orders of the caliph Yazid. Mosques and *maqams* have existed for centuries at the sites of the main 'stations' where the head is said to have been set down or lost blood. The most renowned is the *Mashad* Ras al-Husain (Mosque of the Drop of Blood from Husain's head) in Aleppo, where a block of green stone marked with a red stain is revered. However, Iran would like to mark out the entire route from Karbala to Damascus with commemorative monuments of this major event of Shi'i martyrology, thereby giving pilgrims further opportunity to commune in Syria following the steps of 'Ali's son. In this context, Raqqa's Shi'i mausoleums form one stage of the funeral route.

Even though some sources claim that Husain's head rested in Raqqa[16] and others remind us that the city's 'martyrs' cemetery' once included a column marked with 'Ali's autograph, which was transferred to Aleppo in the twelfth century,[17] Raqqa has never been a centre of Shi'i culture. Unlike Dair al-Zur, which had a Shi'i minority of some 200 people out of a population of 20,000 at the end of the nineteenth century, Raqqa has never been home to a Shi'i community.[18] The reconstruction of tombs into Shi'i mausoleums signifies the power of the state to permeate the boundaries of national territory, all the more so since the sites were previously used by the local inhabitants for specific practices.

Conversion of a Place of Local Memory

The mausoleums of Raqqa stand out from the city's other public buildings by their architecture, exogenous cultural practices and the lack of discourse about them in official publications. Analyses of their shape and symbolism reveal the conflicts at play between state and locality in this marginal region of the country. The mausoleums take on multiple symbolic dimensions, in terms of both identity and religion, for they replace tombs which had been the focus of a local cult and which local legends had made essential places of memory.

The two mausoleums are rarely mentioned, either by the authorities or by the local population. Texts published by the Ministry of Culture are discreet about the identity of the saints who are buried at Raqqa, devoting only one page out of 440 to the battle of Siffin in the governorate's official history. No book published by the Raqqa municipality or the governorate mentions them. At most, passing visitors are taken there to admire the panorama of the city and the surrounding valley from their terraces. They live up to the medieval legend according to which the tombs of the martyrs of the battle of Siffin become invisible as soon as one approaches them. Thus the famous historian and geographer Ibn Hawqal twice describes in his work *The Configuration of the Earth (Kitab Surat al-Ard)*, an 'extraordinary thing' that he witnessed first hand:

> Siffin is situated on the plain, near the Euphrates, between Raqqa and Balis; it was the site of the battle between 'Ali – peace be upon him! – and Mu'awiyya. While visiting the site, I saw something extraordinary: we were passing below the area on the Euphrates; there is a large hill where we counted eight or nine tombs. Above it lies a higher hill, on which we counted over ten tombs, clearly visible to anyone looking carefully; we all agreed on the number of tombs at the two sites. We then climbed to the points where we had seen these tombs, and yet we saw no trace of a single one.[19]

At the time of my first investigations, in 1997, local contacts, who were members of established families in the city, denied the presence of Shi'is within the population, thereby refusing to vindicate the construction of the mausoleums. It would appear that during the 1960s, Shi'i foundations often attempted to renovate the mausoleum of 'Ammar. However, the worksites were sabotaged during the night. It was said to be a miracle worked by 'Ammar himself, 'who was so great that his foot emerged from his *qubba* and he thus destroyed it'. This joke expresses the resistance of the townspeople, as well as a gentle mocking of 'Ammar, who is considered to be far less important than 'Uwais.

'Uwais al-Qarani, Patron Saint of Raqqa

'Uwais al-Qarani is considered particularly important in Raqqa. Since the origins of the city, he has been the focus of a local cult encouraged by Raqqawi notables who were originally semi-nomadic families from the outskirts of Musil in Iraq, the desert area south of the Euphrates and 'Urfa in Anatolia. His name was given to the martyrs' cemetery, which became the cemetery of 'Uwais. He intervened in the daily life of the town's inhabitants: semi-nomads and sedentary groups, notables and new arrivals alike, dedicated a huge mulberry tree to him east of the town, between the Baghdad Gate and the cemetery. The 'Uwais mulberry tree is a holy site, a *haram* placed under the protection of the saint. Semi-nomadic families left their belongings at the foot of the tree when they departed on the summer migration of livestock along the banks of the Balikh River, certain to find them safe four months later. This custom was followed until as late as the 1940s, and elderly Raqqawis have assured me that no one dared to touch the belongings out of fear of the saint's revenge.

'Uwais al-Qarani also played the role of mediator among the townsfolk of Raqqa, particularly following thefts or the disappearance of valuable objects. A very precise ritual helped to explain cases of theft that were unsolved by notables or which existed between the two factions that made up the city's population.[20] This consisted of a procession through all of the roads and back streets of Raqqa involving a large copper cup that was covered by a green sheet, the 'Uwais Cup. It was carried by a public crier (*dallal*), who was appointed by the wronged family from among several *dallals* reputed for their personality and their voice. One Raqqawi quoted from memory the ritual imprecation that was called out by the *dallal*: 'Hark ye here, O people! Whosoever knows anything about the theft or the missing object is called upon, by the 'Uwais Cup, to inform me of it or to return it.'[21]

During these processions, the entire city was regarded as sacred. For a while, it became 'a place of condensation', a term defined as the setting of a collective experience through which a society establishes and demonstrates its values.[22] The codification of these religious practices made Raqqa an intermediary place between a city, structured by mosques and *madrasahs*, and a tribal environment dedicated to the cult of saints, to the devotion of *sayyids* (deceased saints) and populated with spirits (*jinns*).[23] The 'Uwais cult was normalised and used by notables in order to keep social peace and tribal order, whereas his tomb outside the town remained an 'arena of free religious expression and the conservation of ancestral rites', like other rural tombs in the Arab world.[24] The 'Uwais tomb was the linchpin of a religious territory organised around the *haram* mulberry tree, which expanded to fill the whole town during the ritual processions. The territory spread across the valleys of the Euphrates and Balikh through visits to the tombs (*ziyaras*). The principle of territoriality that links these holy sites is based on an assertion of the Raqqawis' community identity.

This attachment to 'Uwais al-Qarani, apparent in specific cultural practices, is not the result of any particular piety on the part of the local inhabitants but of their political will to appear as fully capable residents, able to organise their own religious and social practices within a defined area. The prestige of the tombs of the Prophet's companions fuelled local pride and demonstrated the autonomy of the town's families in relation to those of Aleppo, whose merchants dominated investments in Raqqa. Nevertheless, the mausoleums were not destroyed but have instead been 'restored'. Therefore, Raqqawis may continue to pray at the 'Uwais tomb, and are in fact in the process of reappropriating the site.

The Synecdoche Mausoleums of Opposing Territories

Different types of pilgrim mix in the mausoleums of Raqqa. Apart from a few Iranian pilgrims, the mausoleums are visited by many Shawaya, members of semi-nomadic tribes in the district, as well as by the inhabitants of Raqqa themselves, albeit with diverse rhythms and meanings. After the al-Aqsa uprising (*intifadah*) in Palestine, which broke out in September 2000, these holy sites have been given a new geopolitical meaning.

Iranian pilgrims can be recognised by their dress and practices. The women wear black, remain in groups, are often seated and cry together

3. 'Uwais al-Qarani shrine in Raqqa
   Source: Ababsa, 2007

when listening to accounts of the martyrs 'Ali and 'Ammar bin Yasir. They pray using small spots of earth from Karbala, which are placed on their foreheads. They mostly gather in the mausoleum of 'Ammar. They attach pieces of green material to the silver railings of the catafalque.

Since the opening of the Iraqi border at Albu Kamal in 1998, road traffic has resumed along the Euphrates route. After April 2003, Iranian pilgrims can combine visits to Syrian sites with trips to Najaf and Karbala. According to a municipal official in Raqqa, the Iranian government predicts that every month some 18,000 pilgrims will visit Raqqa's mausoleums; that is, 216,000 per year. This seems like a plausible figure, considering that 232,985 pilgrims entered Syria in 2002 (see Table 5.1). However, since hotel accommodation is practically nonexistent in Raqqa and the hotel projects associated with the new mausoleums are still being drafted, one wonders how the city will cope with such a boon. It is highly likely that the pilgrims' visits will in fact benefit Aleppo more than they do Raqqa.

Unlike the intellectual minority, the majority of the population of Raqqa has welcomed the intervention of Iran in making 'improvements' to the 'Uwais

4. Pilgrims at the 'Uwais al-Qarani shrine in Raqqa
   Source: Ababsa, 2001

and 'Ammar tombs. Moreover, this population, made up of bedouins and semi-nomads who settled in the region during the 1930s, partly considers itself to be like the Husainis, the descendants of Husain. This is the case with the Hlaissat and the Bu Assaf, but also with the Baggara further downstream.

A Syrian anthropologist from the Baggara tribe analysed this pursuit of prestigious *nasab*: 'Driven by what Jean Weuleresse calls the "cult of noble blood", all Arab tribes seek to claim a distinguished ascendance. The Beggara claim to be Husaini, tracing their genealogy back to al-Husain the martyr, son of Fatima and 'Ali; they therefore consider themselves to originate from Hijaz.'[25] This Husaini genealogy does not contradict Sunnism. The Shawaya who claim to be Husainis call themselves Sunnis. Certainly most of them come from villages that in the past had no mosque, and the religious custom of gathering for Friday prayers is more characteristic of the towns. At best, the village shaikh gathered men for prayer in his *madafa*.[26]

The renovation of Raqqa's mausoleums was welcomed by the region's semi-nomads because they subscribe to the Sufi brotherhood for which 'Ali, Husain and more generally the House of the Prophet (*ahl al-bayt*) are essential figures.[27] The semi-nomads are members of the local Sufi brotherhood Marindiyyah, a branch of the Qadiriyyah, which is widespread across the outskirts of Raqqa.[28] Paulo Pinto describes the presence of portraits of 'Ali and Husain, printed in Iran, in most of the Sufi brotherhoods of Aleppo, whether they are connected to the Qadiriyyah or the Rifa'iyyah. According to a Sufi shaikh of the Rifa'i order in Aleppo, these portraits help worshippers to feel the spiritual presence of the Imam 'Ali.[29]

According to a construction worker, who is considered to be like a shaikh due to his knowledge and who claims to be Sunni, 'Seventy per cent of the [Euphrates] valley's Sunnis [come] from the Prophet's family.' In the municipality of Raqqa, he considers the most important *maqam* to be the tomb of 'Ammar and the mosque of Sayyidah Fatima al-Zahra in Tabqa, which was built in 1998. He considers 'Ammar to be far more important than 'Uwais, since the former is a companion of the Prophet (*sahib*) and the latter is simply one of his followers (*tabi'un*). Some Raqqawis claim that conversion to Shi'ism has been encouraged by Jamil al-Asad, the late president's brother, through a foundation that supports 'Alawi religious practices, the Jam'iyyah 'Ali Murtada. The foundation finances the construction of mosques and sponsors the pilgrimage to Mecca for members of the 'Alawi community.[30]

Shawaya pilgrims are mostly women, in Bedouin dress, with two fine and brightly coloured headscarves tied around their heads. They wear plastic shoes, indicating relative poverty, and the older women have tattoos. They do not cry, but instead kiss and stroke the carpets and Qur'ans, and leave behind carpets to attract the blessing (*baraka*) of the saints. The inhabitants of Raqqa tend to mock the faith and credulity of the inhabitants of the valley. Thus they scorn the Hlaissat tribe, which is pledged to the 'Afadla tribe and which settled around the 'Uwais tomb in the nineteenth century. The Hlaissat, whose name means 'those who possesses nothing', looked after the saint's tomb and received the offerings made to him. In reality, the inhabitants of Raqqa affirm that 'the Hlaissat consider 'Uwais as their grandfather; when they have no money, they steal from him'. In the same vein, an intellectual from Raqqa told me of the latest 'miracle' that had been witnessed in the governorate in the early 1990s. A young soldier had recently been buried in his village of Dair 'Affar on the road to Aleppo, when the rumour of a miracle spread through the countryside. A light emanated from his tomb, day and night. Hundreds of people began to converge on the new holy place. The spontaneous pilgrimage lasted for three months, during which the Shawaya of both sexes made offerings and remained beside the tomb in the hope of being cured through contact with the saint. This lasted until the day when the parents of the soldier quarrelled over their respective shares of the pilgrims' offerings. The hoax was then brought to light: the families had lit the tomb from the inside. By recounting this story, the Sunni intellectual distances himself from the beliefs of the majority of the population, half of which remains illiterate.

The Faithful Women Pilgrims

'Uwais remains so important in Raqqa that several local expressions carry his name. One swears on the 'Uwais Cup, *'Bi tass 'Uwais'*, and one gives thanks by citing him. Visiting his tomb remains a major religious practice for the women of Raqqa on the occasion of religious celebrations, deaths in the family or at the time of school examinations. In 2001, while waiting for the results of their high-school diploma, many young women gathered at the 'Uwais mausoleum.

The people of Raqqa readily recount that during their childhood, Friday was 'Uwais day. Women went to the tomb to pray, to get together or to ask for a husband or children. They spent the day there with their families and neighbours and cooked chicken. People made wishes for the saint to fulfil. Along the wall of the tomb they laid out silver coins, or if they had none, they would use marrow seeds; if the coin or seed remained stuck, the wish was granted. Rites and women's songs were dedicated to 'Uwais. For example, one of the women's games involved climbing to the top of the minaret and dropping their cloaks (*'abayas*) from the summit. If the *'abaya* unfurled, the young woman would soon marry. If it fell in a bundle, she would stay single. This is one of the songs dedicated to 'Uwais:

> O 'Uwais, I came to see you,
> And my *'abaya* flies like a bird.
> My aunt criticised me for the flight.
> All the girls are wed
> And I am still alone.

The pilgrimage practices in Raqqa, like the body language analysed by Henri Lefebvre, allow us to 'link the representations of space and the spaces of representations'. For Iranian pilgrims, the prayers and the tears that are left at the holy places along the Euphrates River, on sites comparable to Karbala, make Raqqa a Shi'i site. For the bedouin and the Shawaya, the renovation of the buildings gives a renewed attraction to 'Ammar and 'Uwais. For the townspeople, the persistent attachment to 'Uwais results in continuing visits and intercession.

Manipulation of the Mausoleums in the Struggle against Zionism

In order to understand the territorial significance of the renovated mausoleums of Raqqa, we must emphasise that they are the subject of political manipulation by Iran and Syria. This manipulation initially took the form of conferences organised by the Iranian cultural centre and held in the Arab cultural centres of Raqqa and al-Thawrah in 1997 and 2000. The organisers invited Shi'i dignitaries, like the Iranian ambassador in Syria and the great Shi'i scholar Muhammad Husain Fadlallah, the spiritual leader of the Lebanese Islamist organisation Hizbullah. The conferences focused on the personality of the Prophet's companions buried in Raqqa and on their struggle to promote Islam. The holding of these conferences shows an attitude of openness towards Shi'i doctrine in Syria, which has been accepted all the better by the population because Shi'ism is presented as being linked to Hizbullah's struggle against the Israel Defense Forces.

In the spring of 2000, an Iranian cultural week was organised in the al-Asad Cultural Centre in Raqqa. It included a book fair and the showing of Iranian films. Thereafter, weekly teaching sessions were held in Raqqa's mausoleums, during which the martyrdoms of 'Ali, Husain and 'Ammar were recalled. In Raqqa, the *husainiyyah*s brought together forty or so people around an Iraqi or Iranian shaikh. The mausoleums contain a small bookshop that distributes Shi'i religious encyclopaedias, as well as films and cassettes. The liberation of South Lebanon in May 2000 considerably strengthened the aura of the Hizbullah in Syria. In Raqqa, portraits of Fadlallah are sold in the markets and displayed in the apartments of several officials.

With the beginning of the al-Aqsa uprising, cultural events organised in the mausoleums became bigger and far more politicised. Thus, following the 'crimes' perpetrated at the Jenin camp in April 2002, a large gathering was organised on Friday the 26th by the Iranian embassy and the local Ba'th Party at the mausoleums of 'Ammar and 'Uwais, under the title 'Celebration of Solidarity with the *Intifadah*'. According to *Akhbar al-Sharq*, no fewer than 5,000 people gathered in the mosque of 'Ammar. The crowd was made up not only of the inhabitants of Raqqa, but also of people from other governorates, demonstrating the new-found centrality of this highly politicised site. The demonstration, which lasted for five hours, is sometimes described as a celebration and sometimes as a festival, the latter term referring to the diversity of participants and the variety of events. The Hizbullah orchestra was invited to represent its party and Palestinian university students 'reminded the public of the principle of the martyr since the time of the companion 'Ammar bin Yasir up until today'.[31]

Conclusion

The transformation of the shape, use and signification of Raqqa's mausoleums sheds new light on the territorial issues that have affected the city since its nomination as the administrative centre of the Euphrates Project. What is at stake is the continued control of earlier borders of the Syrian state, the Iranian-sponsored expansion of Shi'i religious territory into Syria and the assertion of a formerly autonomous Raqqawi identity over territory administered by tribal factions. Such issues relate to reference territories at different scales, which express specific value systems. Thus, Raqqa's mausoleums are considered by the Syrian state to be among a number of new buildings in a city that stands on the pioneering front of national agriculture; by the Iranian authorities to be Shi'i centres in the struggle for hegemony over the Twelver Shi'i world; and by the Raqqawi notables as vital sites in a Sunni community.

Notes

1. Rafiqa, 'Raqqa's companion', was buit by the caliph al-Mansur between 770 and 775, following the same circular design as the *madinah al-salam* in Baghdad. A five-kilometre-long brick surrounding wall and the first mosque with arcades in Islamic architecture still remain there. The caliph Harun al-Rashid set up his capital on the site from 796 to 808. M. Meinecke, 'al-Rakka', *Encyclopedie de l'Islam*, nouvelle edition, vol. 8, 1995, pp. 424–8.

2. The presence in Raqqa of a tomb dedicated to 'Ubai bin Ka'b is questionable since nothing links him to the town, or to northeastern Syria. His tomb is mentioned in Damascus and in Raqqa, but is more likely to be in Medina. Even the inhabitants of Raqqa acknowledge that he should not be in their town, although his tomb has been proclaimed there by their ancestors since the nineteenth century. J. Sourdel-Thomine, *Le Guide des lieux de pèlerinage d'al-Harawi*, Damascus 1957, p. 35.

3. In the thirteenth century, Ibn Shaddad reported the existence of Shi'i pilgrimage sites in Raqqa, 'several in relation to Siffin'.

4. I. Calzoni, *Sayyida Zaynab*, Venice 1988, p. 145.

5. Eric Geoffroy, *Le soufisme en Egypte et en Syrie sons les derniers mamelouks et les premiers ottomans.Orientations spirituelles et enjeux culturels*, Damascus, 1995, p. 595.

6. This initiation by the *ruhaniyyah*, or 'spiritual entity' of deceased prophets or saints, is peculiar to the 'Uwaisi, mystics whose eponymous guide is

al-Qarani. 'Uwaisism opposes Qadirism in Muslim mysticism. 'Uwais is so notorious that he has dozens of tombs and memorials (*maqam*) in the world: in Zabid in the Yemen, in Damascus, in Alexandria, in Diyarbakir, at the summit of an Uzbek mountain in Karakalpakistan where he is known as Veys Baba but also in Beirut, in Mardin, in Bursa, in Erzurum and, of course, in Raqqa. In his guide to pilgrimage sites, which dates from the beginning of the eighth century, al-Harawi wrote: 'Only God knows the truth, but it is most probable that the correct site is in Raqqa', (Sourdel-Thomine, *Le guide*, p. 34). According to the Shi'i guide (*marja*), Muhsin al-Amin, author of an encyclopaedia of influential Shi'i figures, the tomb of 'Uwais is in Siffin, and 'is still celebrated there today'. Muhsin al-Amin, 'Uwais al-Qarani', *A'yan al-Shi'ah*, Beirut 1963, pp. 512–16.

7. G. al-Faqid, *'Ammar bin Yasir*, Beirut 1992; A. al-Subaiti, *'Ammar bin Yasir*, Baghdad 1946. I thank Sabrina Mervin for informing me of these two sources.

8. Yann Richard, *L'Islam chiite*, Paris 1991, p. 258.

9. These figures are minute compared with pilgrimage movements within Iran, especially in Mashhad, where the mausoleum of 'Ali Ridha, the eighth Imam, attracted eight million pilgrims *per year* in 1988. See N. Hakami, *Pèlerinage de l'Imam Reza*, Tokyo 1989.

10. S. Mervin, 'Sayida Zaynab', *Cahiers d'Etudes sur la Méditerranée orientale et le monde turco-iranien*, no. 22, 1996, p. 149.

11. The hotel complexes in Sayyidah Zainab were largely developed thanks to the initiative of a rich Syrian Shi'i property developer, Sa'ib Nahhas, honorary consul of Senegal and vice president of the Franco-Arab Chamber of Commerce, who developed a free zone there for tax-free luxury products, the 'Nahhas Free Shop'. See Joseph Bahout, *Les entrepreneurs syriens*, Beirut 1994.

12. M. Bazin, 'Qom: ville de pèlerinage et centre régional', *Revue Géographique de l'Est*, vol. 13, pp. 77–136.

13. Mervin, 'Sayyida Zaynab', p. 153.

14. 'The case is completely different concerning the mausoleum of Sayyidah Ruqiyya, whose renovation and extension were entirely and directly financed by the Iranian government, in co-operation with the Syrian Ministry of Religious Endowments. In order to do so, part of an old quarter was demolished, causing discontent among the inhabitants of the old city. An accord had been drawn up between the two states, over and above Syria's Shi'i community, which in a way has been dispossessed of the mausoleum', Mervin, 'Sayyida Zaynab', p. 154.

15. A. Böttcher, *Syrische Religionspolitik unter Assad*, Freiburg 1998.

16. 'According to other sources, the head is said to have been buried in Madina,

Kufa, Najaf, Karbala, Raqqa on the Euphrates and even in a *ribat* [religious fortress] of faraway Merv', H. Halm, *Le Chi'isme*, Paris 1995, p. 21.

17. Meinecke, 'al-Rakka', p. 424.

18. However, neighbouring Aleppo has significant Shi'i communities, estimated in 1959 at 6,000 Shi'is in the 'Azaz district and 4,778 in the Idlib district. A. R. Hamide, *La Région d'Alep*, Paris 1959, p. 146.

19. Ibn Hawqal, *Configuration de la Terre (Kitab Surat al-Ard)*, Paris 1965, p. 34.

20. The two factions were those of the Akrad and of 'Asharin. L. Deheuvels, *Les Recherches de Sonia Farra sur la croissance d'une ville moyenne dans la Syrie d'aujourd'hui: Raqqa et ses dimensions sociales*, Paris 1979; M. Ababsa, *Idéologies et territoires dans un front prionnier du monde arabe: Raqqa et le Projet de l'Euphrate en Jazira syrienne*, Tours 2004.

21. The 'Uwais Cup contains holy oil. This inclusive borrowing from Christianity can be explained, according to the writer Ibrahim Khalil, by the close proximity of the 'Uwais tomb to Tell Bi'a, well known for its Byzantine monastery, Dair Mar Zaqqar.

22. B. Debarbieux, 'Le Lieu, le territoire et trois figures de rhétorique', *l'Espace Geographique*, no. 2, 1995, p. 97.

23. In reality it is more complex, since the towns were also the setting of popular cults. In Hama, for example, the name 'Uwais, among others, was given to children to protect them.

24. H. Chambert-Loir, *Le Culte des saints dans le monde musulman*, Paris 1995.

25. Rabah Naffakh, 'La Conception du monde chez les Beggara', *Revue d'Etudes Islamiques*, vol. 39, no. 1, 1971, pp. 119–43.

26. The *madafa*, or house of hospitality, is the attribute of a tribal clan chief and the institution of hospitality which allows him to practise his functions of protection and generosity. M. Ababsa, 'La Madafa a Raqqa', *Geographies and Cultures*, no. 37, 2001.

27. P. Pinto, 'Pilgrimage, Commodities, and Religious Objectification', *Comparative Studies of South Asia, Africa and the Middle East*, vol. 27, no. 1, 2007.

28. Its name is the distortion of that of an Iranian town, Marand. The shaikhs of the Marindiyyah order introduce themselves as Ashraf. The brotherhood is based in Taiba-Jahja, in the north of Raqqa governorate. However, its members have centres in Raqqa Samra (southeast of Raqqa), Aleppo, the village of Afras and the countryside of Damascus. It is said that the brotherhood owns bread ovens and land, such as in al-Khanawi in al-Hasakah governorate. Its role is to treat the mentally ill. It recruits members from the Bu Assaf tribe, affiliated members of Jaiss, whose lands are near Sluk. The brotherhood meets during major Islamic celebrations.

During these sessions, 200 to 300 disciples pierce their bodies with iron spikes (*shish*), 'without any blood dripping and without pain'. Interview with a member of the brotherhood in Raqqa, December 2003.

29. Pinto, 'Pilgrimage, Commodities and Religious Objectification'.

30. See Nikolaos Van Dam, *The Struggle for Power in Syria*, London 1996.

31. *Akhbar al-Sharq*, 28 April 2002.

SIX

The 2004 Events in al-Qamishli: Has the Kurdish question erupted in Syria?

Julie Gauthier

Translated by Diana V. Galbraith

Events in al-Qamishli in the spring of 2004 ended the obscurity of a community that, despite an increasing sense of identity since the 1970s, has not been able to transform its demographic weight (two million citizens, or 10 per cent of Syria's total population) into a substantial political force. Syria's 'Kurdish question' has been a tangible presence on the national scene for many years. But a relaxation of tensions, however relative and ephemeral, brought about by the change of president in Damascus and especially by the hopes raised by the American–Kurdish 'alliance' in Iraq, has been perceived by Kurdish political activists as an opportunity to bring their community's issues to the fore and adopt a more assertive opposition strategy.

Kurdish Nationalists in Syria

During the 1980s and 1990s, the Kurdish national movement in Syria was polarised into two very different wings. On one side stood the Kurdistan Workers' Party (PKK), a mass party with a tightly hierarchical guerrilla organisation, whose leader Abdullah Ocalan was the protected guest of the Syrian authorities. The ultimate objective of the PKK – complete liberation of Kurdistan through martial valour and a cult of leadership – was endorsed with great enthusiasm by Syrian Kurds. It was in the name of this absolute, almost sacred, nationalism that the supporters of the PKK renounced their specific identity as Syrian Kurds.

At the other end of the nationalist chessboard stood an assortment of small partisan groups, a number of which had evolved as splinters (almost twenty), from the Kurdish Democratic Party of Syria, a group much older than the PKK, but one concerned with similar issues. It was founded in 1958 after the model pioneered by Mustafa Barzani. Faithful to the moderate line adopted at its inception, it advocated complete integration of the Kurds into the Syrian state, an end to discrimination and democratic reform of the regime. At the same time, these groups strongly supported Kurdish nationalists in Iraq. The 'Kurdistani'[1] orientation of the Kurdish parties in Syria favoured cultivating neutrality in their relations with the regime in Damascus.

But the new international order that took shape in the early 1990s with the Second Gulf War would change the Syrian regime's approach to the Kurdish question. In the first place, the weakening of the Ba'thi regime in Baghdad after the American intervention reduced Damascus's interest in an alliance with the Iraqi Kurdish parties. On the contrary, the creation of a Kurdish security zone in northern Iraq now appeared to be a new threat. This novel Kurdish danger and various other issues, like the question of water and the isolation of Syria after its failed negotiations with Israel, pointed Syria towards a rapprochement with its traditional enemy, Turkey, a reconciliation that was solidified in 1998 with the expulsion of Ocalan from Syrian territory. Bashar al-Asad's visit to Ankara in February 2004 and the routine extradition of PKK prisoners from Syria (seventy since 2003) have contributed to solidifying the alliance between the two nations.

Since the 1990s, a unifying tendency has led to the formation of two Kurdish coalitions, al-Jabhah (the Front) and al-Tahaluf (the Alliance). At the same time the Yakiti Party was born, mobilising a new generation of militants around figures such as Fuad Aliku, Marwan 'Usman, 'Abd al-Baki Yusif and Isma'il 'Amr. The founding act of these emerging organisations would be the practice of *mulsaqah*, whereby a handful of militants – to commemorate the thirtieth anniversary of the 'extraordinary census'[2] – glued posters denouncing government policies towards the 'undocumented' Kurds on walls and public buildings in the larger Syrian and Kurdish towns. The novelty of this act lay not so much in the content of the posters as in the heightened visibility of the demands. The authorities did not fail to respond, however, and a wave of arrests commenced against the new party.

Debates and Declarations at the Demonstrations

On 10 December 2002, to mark International Human Rights Day, the Yakiti Party organised a demonstration in front of the parliament building in the heart of Damascus. At 11 o'clock in the morning, 120 people marched, brandishing signs that read 'Syria is the country of all, be they Arab or Kurd', 'We demand that the Syrian constitution recognise Kurds as the second official ethnicity of the country' and 'We demand a definitive solution to the Kurdish question in the framework of national unity'.[3] This gathering, though modest, represented a marked contrast to the usual gatherings and memorial ceremonies undertaken by the Kurdish parties. Because of the messages on the placards, the ideology of the regime was displaced from the street, a space that had long been confiscated and manipulated by the state for its own glorification. This was also a way to revive the 'peaceful and democratic struggle', long advocated by the Kurdish movement, but which over time had become a symbol of, or justification for, its own impotence. Finally, this gathering was a message addressed to the politically powerful, signifying that the Kurds planned to increase pressure with the support of the new post-September 2001 international order.

But this change, far from creating cohesion with the other Kurdish groupings, caused Yakiti to break with the rest of the nationalist movement. The party's isolation became evident at a demonstration that occurred in December 2002. Despite fifteen days of intense discussion, the other Kurdish parties refused to participate, citing regional issues (especially American threats to the Middle East), the general climate of official détente towards the Kurds (President Bashar al-Asad had just returned from al-Qamishli and a historic visit to 'Afrin) and the argument that a confrontation with the government could be damaging. Yakiti would be penalised by the arrests of Marwan 'Usman and Hasan Salah, but this proved to be no obstacle to their meeting with the president of the Chamber of Deputies in the wake of the demonstrations.

It was another six months before another demonstration of this kind took place. On 25 June 2003, Yakiti organised a 'parade of children' in front of the UNESCO building in Damascus on the occasion of the International Day of Children's Rights. This time, Yakiti did not find itself alone, because other Kurdish parties, Yassari, Ittihad and Wahdah, chose to participate. But al-Tahaluf, under the influence of Hamid Hajj Darwish, declined to join because it opposed the use of placards during the demonstration, which it felt would provide the authorities with 'a pretext for repression'. This shows to what extent public visibility, indicated here by banners and posters, is a determining factor in the subversive nature of this political discourse. There would be no signs at the next demonstration, on 6 October 2003, in front of the Council of Ministers, to commemorate the 'extraordinary census'. This time, Yakiti bowed to the wishes of the assembled Kurdish parties: the gathering would be silent, limited to the demands of the 'undocumented' and with no overtly politicised messages. For Yakiti, this was a retreat from its offensive strategy and showed the incapacity of the Kurdish movement to mobilise jointly and break with the authorities. However, it was also the first demonstration where indications of collaboration between Kurds and the Arab opposition were apparent, with the participation (however discreet) of certain human rights organisations.

This co-operation was solidified on 10 December 2003, International Human Rights Day. The demonstration was preceded by a meeting between Kurdish and Arab parties where the slogans and the location were determined. One year after the December 2002 demonstration, things had changed dramatically. Yakiti broke its isolation and obtained the support of a number of groups, even if it had not always contributed to achieving a united Kurdish front for common action. This tactic of regrouping achieved positive results: the number of participants in the demonstration more than tripled.

Co-ordinated demonstrations in front of the courts that were holding trials of Arab Kurdish political militants happened during this period with regularity and on a new scale. On 20 December 2003, the Tajammu', several humanitarian organisations and the Kurdish parties organised a gathering in front of the military tribunal in Aleppo where a trial of fourteen Arab and Kurdish intellectuals was under way. The defendants had been arrested in Aleppo on 24 September 2003, as they were getting ready to attend a meeting of the al-Kawakibi club. This demonstration drew a thousand participants. 'Abdu 'Abd al-Hamid, a Kurd, was placed under arrest. Less than two months later, on 22 February 2004, 500 people gathered in Damascus in front of the Military Security court where the trial of seven Kurdish activists who had been arrested at the children's march was under way. One week later, the release of Marwan 'Usman and Hasan Salah, the two militants from Yakiti who were arrested in 2002 at the demonstration for human rights, provoked a mobilisation that easily overwhelmed the military forces' ability to contain it. The procession that accompanied the two former prisoners to al-Qamishli extended four kilometres and 15,000 people gave them a triumphant welcome to the city. The celebrations lasted for three days.

Finally, this increase in political activity manifested itself in a space that had experienced lengthy repression and had not experienced greater freedom during the Damascus Spring of 2000–1: the domain of students, particularly at the University of Aleppo, where Kurdish students are numerous. The fall of the Ba'thi regime in Baghdad in April 2003 provoked a certain degree of agitation among Kurdish students. The threat of Turkish intervention in Iraq, plus the anniversary of the Halabja massacre, became occasions for rallies and assemblies to which Arab students were invited. This new groundswell of student interest, at first uniquely Kurd, did not escape the notice of the authorities, who proceeded to carry out targeted arrests. The detentions did not, however, prevent two more demonstrations, one month apart, on 27 January 2004 and 26 February 2004. The first, in front of the College of Medicine, brought 200 students together to demand the autonomy of student unions from the Ba'th Party. The second started with a more precise and less political protest against the decree that abolished the state's obligation to employ engineers and architects after they obtained their diplomas. It drew 500 people, of whom 100 were not affiliated to the university.

Despite the modest size of the gatherings (300 people on average), their brevity (generally two hours before they were dispersed by the authorities) and their negligible impact (rarely going beyond a small group of militants), the regularity of the demonstrations, the novelty of the places used and the diversity of actors involved – students, civil associations, Kurdish and Arab political parties – combine to make these protests an undeniably new phenomenon. They represent an organised and enduring union of democratic forces. The predominance of the Kurdish element in the opposition movement solidified and intensified during the month of March. For this reason, 8 March 2004 – three days before the al-Qamishli events – is significant because three kinds of movements occurred.

In the majority of Kurdish towns, crowds appeared spontaneously in the streets celebrating the re-emergence of federalism in Iraq. Almost simultaneously, in Damascus, another demonstration was unfolding, organised by Kurdish and Arab parties in front of parliament, on the anniversary of the 1963 revolution in which the Ba'th Party came to power. This counter-demonstration corresponded to the collective actions that had taken place for two years. The novelty resided in the numerous interviews (of some thirty to a hundred people) carried out by Aktham Naissah, the spokesman for the Committee of Human Rights, along with Lebanese and American journalists. More importantly, the security forces remained content just to watch the demonstration on 10 December. The same day, residents of al-Qamishli gathered in massive numbers, in the suburbs, to celebrate International Women's Day. In spite of the inclusive title, the participants were exclusively Kurds and the gathering exhibited a festive mood, with folklore groups and poetry readings in Kurdish. That this kind of celebration, normally tolerated under surveillance, ended with numerous arrests foreshadowed the response of the authorities to the events in al-Qamishli three days later. The events were immediately followed by an offensive move on the part of the state and a popular struggle that radicalised community spirit and politicised ethnic divides.

Events in al-Qamishli

The events in question unfolded over some ten days, from 12 to 25 March 2004. They began in the al-Qamishli stadium with an altercation between supporters of the Dair al-Zur football team and those of the Kurdish city's team. Circulating in buses through the streets of the city, supporters of Dair al-Zur chanted insults against the Kurdish nationalist leaders, Mas'ud Barzani and Jalal Talabani, and brandished pictures of Saddam Hussein. The unrest spread into the stadium, to the disadvantage of the Kurds. Young supporters of the Dair al-Zur team were not searched when they entered the stadium, unlike the Kurds, and therefore were able to carry in weapons. It was in these circumstances that police fired on the crowd, under orders from the governor of al-Hasakah, Salim Kabul. The shooting caused ten deaths; all were Kurds, several were children. Rumours of a massacre started to spread. That evening, Kurdish students from Damascus University made their way to the front of the United Nations building carrying signs of protest. The following day, thousands of people marched peacefully in al-Qamishli at the funerals of the victims, whose caskets were draped with the Kurdish flag. The authorities responded by once again firing into the crowd. Kurdish young people then became violent, going as far as to destroy a statue of the former president, Hafiz al-Asad.

Protests spread rapidly to the other, largely Kurdish, towns of northeastern Syria. At Ras al-'Ain, stores closed and armed young people threw stones at the commissariat. In Darik, a solidarity demonstration that attracted at least 25,000 people (practically the entire town) quickly degenerated: a Ba'th Party building was burned, as was a government vehicle, the agricultural club, the customs office, the district headquarters, as well as other administrative buildings. The revolt resulted in five deaths and twenty injuries. Similarly, the towns of Darbasiyyah and 'Amudah seemed for a moment to be surrounded by angry crowds. In the latter, another statue of Hafiz al-Asad was destroyed.

The regime wasted no time responding: units of the Republican Guards travelled by train to Darik. Soldiers were deployed along the borders with Turkey and Iraq, surrounding the border towns. At Ras al-'Ain, and especially in the mixed town of al-Hassakah, street fights exploded between demonstrators and Arab Ba'thi militias, which were armed by the government and composed mostly of *'amar*, poor farmers who had received land that was confiscated from the Kurds during the operation 'Arab Encirclement'.[4] The militias pillaged Kurdish stores and properties. Tribal rivalries, particularly ones that involved the family of Ibrahim Pasha, killed three Bedouin. The unrest extended to other major Kurdish regions, including Kawbanah, 'Afrin and Aleppo.

The anniversary of Halabja on 16 March brought a resumption of uprisings. The list of 'martyrs' extended to ten dead. In Zawrafa, a town of 5,000 and a Kurdish enclave in the suburbs of Damascus, situated just below the presidential palace, repression was particularly cruel, causing one death and just under 1,000 arrests, twenty-five of which involved children. Kurdish students were also very active. In Damascus, as in Aleppo, they organised a number of gatherings on the university campus, avoiding the town proper. On 14 March 2000, Ba'thi students encircled Kurdish students in front of their university dormitories, facilitating their arrest and blocking them from entering the streets of the capital. Some students, nonetheless, carried out a demonstration in front of parliament. Calm returned for the month of April, but the oppression continued apace. Police raids resulted in summary arrests, and Kurdish parties claimed that four deaths occurred as a result of torture. The intervention of President al-Asad on the television channel al-Jazirah on 1 May accompanied the release of one hundred prisoners, marking a new step and serving as a temporary conclusion to the series of events.

By overtly siding with the Arabs of Dair al-Zur in what was at first a small scuffle, the Syrian state seemed to have almost deliberately precipitated the violence. The initial repression was not, however, on a scale comparable to the government's reaction to the subsequent demonstrations. The regime tried to justify its disproportionate response by spreading rumours that foreign infiltrators, both Kurdistani and American, had instigated the movement. This allowed the authorities to accuse the demonstrators of divisiveness (*fitnah*) and treason and raised the prospect of a Kurdish fifth column that would pose a constant threat to national sovereignty. However, these security-related arguments could not mask a veritable offensive against the Kurds. There was a jump in repression – fifty dead, many injured, two thousand arrests, forty raids on student offices, and widespread destruction of private property; – which was long lasting. Numerous young people were arrested, with a number killed, several as a result of torture. Moreover, the persecution was systematic. Every Kurdish region was affected, even Hama. All these aspects testify to the role of the authorities in a concerted campaign against the Kurds.

These offences contrast with the relatively benign policies that the government of Hafiz al-Asad had implemented with regard to the Kurds and more closely resemble the Ba'th Party's early offences against the Kurdish community at the time of the party's seizure of power in 1963. Recalling the memory of those dark years, one thinks of General Mansurah and the *'amar* tribunals that contributed to the implementation of the 'Arab Encirclement' as part of the repression.

However, the reason for a renewed assault on the Kurds by those in power is difficult to explain, especially given the international context. According to the Kurdish-language media, an American aeroplane was about to land at al-Qamishli on the second day of the confrontation, with an American and Kurdistani delegation on board that intended to plead for calm with Mahir al-Asad and Mansurah. Is this false rumour a Kurdish fantasy of protection and support by the Americans or is it a reflection of the reality of a reordering of the international order in which Syria finds itself in a position of weakness? Must we then concur with the opinions of certain Kurdish observers, according to whom the violence of the reprisals are a fantasised transposition of the situation in Iraq?

Sawdi Hadidi, a Syrian journalist and opposition figure, was also astonished by the unusual permissiveness of the authorities when faced with the young people of Dair al-Zur, considering that the image of Saddam Hussein had up to then been banned in Syria. Though he does not support the idea of direct manipulation, Hadidi suggests that the regime might have profited from the events by reorienting the Sunni opposition towards Islamic/pan-Arab solidarity.[5] Nevertheless, the reactivation of tribal rivalries and the use of Ba'thi students during the course of the repression reinforce the views of those who see in the al-Qamishli events a deliberate attempt to create a schism between Arabs and Kurds in order to tighten Arab ranks in defence of the regime. In addition to reflecting the nervousness of the authorities in the face of a growing American presence in the region, the al-Qamishli events could therefore constitute a response to the growing reconciliation of Kurds and Arabs opposed to the regime.

The intervention of Bashar al-Asad indicates an awkward relationship with the security services. Contradicting the official media and the forces of order, President al-Asad asserts that the al-Qamishli events represent an internal problem for Syria rather than a foreign threat. He declares that the Kurdish people are an integral part of the national fabric (*nasij*) and history of Syria. He finally admits the existence of the 'undocumented' Kurds and the importance of this question. His declaration appears to be historic in the sense that it marks the recognition of a high point in relations with the Kurds of Syria, breaking a taboo that has persisted for decades. However, if the intervention of the president marked the end of mass arrests, it was not followed by any concrete measures. Rather than responding to the Kurdish question, it seemed like the habitual boundaries of the authoritarian regime were in crisis. Other, more discrete, signs, like the arrest of seventeen medical students, all Kurds from Hama, reduced the impact of his gesture, but they did not expose it as a mockery. They restored the presidential intervention to one of balance between détente and repression, false political announcements and real security action.

This testifies perhaps to the irresolution of the regime regarding the question of Kurdish politics. The passive discourse of President al-Asad, leading at the extreme to the restoration of a place for the Kurds in the Syrian nation, could not attenuate the strong feeling of exclusion and alienation harboured by the Kurdish community, a sentiment that was exacerbated by the al-Qamishli events. Whatever allegiances it may restore, this gesture testifies to the extraordinary impact on Kurds in Syria of developments in Iraq, which pose a new milestone in the relationship between the Syrian Kurdish community and the state, setting a course towards overt confrontation in the future.

Direct confrontation between the police and 'the street' signals an extremely rare configuration on the Syrian political scene. On the Kurdish side, we must go back to the confrontations of 1986 that set the stage for the partial legalisation of the Nawruz celebration to find a mobilisation of the same magnitude. It is therefore not surprising that certain Kurdish actors and observers applied the term 'uprising' (*intifadah*) to the events, a term that has the double merit of rejecting the pejorative nature of words such as 'disorders' and 'acts of sabotage' and which includes the positive connotations of the Palestinian struggle. At the same time, the term underscores the popular and spontaneous nature of the uprising. Without yet possessing the necessary elements that would give us a more precise understanding of the relationship and its political implication, we can already say that the 'martyrs' of the stadium and the demonstrations that followed were not necessarily activists. The 2,000 arrests that were carried out by the authorities involved no more than ten political cadres.

Otherwise, through acts of violence and vandalism, the systematic destruction of public buildings, and the rejection and subversion of symbols of the state, one does not see 'peaceful combat' as set forth by the nationalist organisations, guided by legality and respect for institutions. In contrast to the reprisals that habitually reinforce the relationship of Kurds to the (Syrian) nation, the '*intifadah*' of March 2004 brought to the fore elements that are exclusively (Kurdish) nationalist and transnationalist. The slogans 'Long Live Kurdistan, Martyrs Never Die' that were brandished by the students show that popular mobilisation stretches outside the realm of existing territorial boundaries and their religious phraseology reaches far beyond the mundane arena of political bargaining.

The tenor of the slogans – and the violence of some of the actions – instead evokes the style of the PKK. The immolation of a young man at a central location in Aleppo, in honour of the victims of al-Qamishli, recalls the highly visible character of the forms of action used by PKK militants. This fact had not been conveyed by the Kurdish media until it appeared on the front page of the PKK newspaper *Ozgur Politika*. Other signs confirm the participation of elements close to the party, like the immense banners bearing the image of Apo that were displayed at the burials of the 'martyrs' of the stadium incident. Similarly, the unexpected mobilisation in the 'Afrin region, in particular around Kawbanah, where Kurdish parties are only weakly established, seems difficult to explain without bringing in the PKK. Since the fall of Ocalan and the end of the armed struggle, we have been expecting the resurrection of the party that in 2002 adopted a new name, Ittihad Dimukrati. Also awaited was the revision of the political programme that has since been axed and the installation of other Kurdish parties that raise demands that are predominantly local rather than Kurdistani, including the cultural and political rights of Kurdish Syrians and the installation of democratic principles.

The programmes on Roj TV, the PKK's television channel, reflect this change of direction by giving an increasingly important role to Kurdish Syrians and their political representatives. The events in al-Qamishli gave the party the chance to reappear on the Syrian Kurdish political scene through a militant action that distinguished it from other parties: while other parties cancelled Nawruz as a sign of mourning, the Ittihad Dimukrati urged Syrian Kurds to carry on with the celebration. The success of this invitation (3,000 people in al-Qamishli) demonstrated once again the PKK's ability to capture public sentiment. However, the action was so innovative that the Kurdish media did not pick up the story and the fact that the demonstrators carried images of Barzani along with the inevitable portraits of Ocalan seemed to indicate that the '*intifadah*' had introduced a new flexibility of beliefs. This represented a sharp break with the 1980s and 1990s, which were marked by great hostility between the PKK and Barzani's party.

The March uprising consecrates in particular the mobilisation of youth and students. We must examine the link between the students and the political arena. The eruption of these new actors raises additional questions: is their participation in the action simply a flash in the pan, followed by their retreat from the political scene, or could this be the birth of a new and autonomous movement? In the latter case, what would be the relations that would keep the connection between this 'March generation' and the Kurdish political movement intact?

We must revisit more precisely the role of the Kurdish parties that were caught off guard by these events. In the first place, they refused to meet with the security services, stipulating that before any negotiations could take place, an investigative commission must be formed to establish responsibility for the acts of violence. They also demanded an end to arbitrary arrests and attacks on private property, as well as reparations for the families of victims. But this posture of refusal crumbled rapidly. Hamid Darwish did not hesitate to meet on two occasions with one of the principal responsible parties, General Mansurah.

After 13 March, the al-Jabhah and al-Tahaluf parties reunited with leaders of the Ba'th Party, including the governor of al-Hassakah, Salim Kabul, and representatives of the Arab democratic forces. Rather than formulate a politics of popular protest, the parties agreed to pacify the street (in which their influence had already been reduced), worrying more about being seen by the regime as mediators than about legitimising their base. According to other groups, like Yakiti, the best way to cultivate broader popularity is not necessarily to compromise with the regime, but they did not know how to undertake the initiatives that were promised by the movement's leaders and retained a wait-and-see attitude.

Nor did the Kurdish parties know how to seize the occasion to strengthen their ranks and create true unity, a fruitless wish that had always been delayed. The desire to come together, which was indicated by the signature of joint declarations during the crisis, was quickly abandoned in the power game that the authorities set in motion among various parties. Parties that had otherwise been discredited emerged as interlocutors to the detriment of others. This is also how the delegation charged with meeting Mustafa Tlas at the end of April, composed uniquely of representatives from four parties stemming from al-Tahaluf, ended up shackling the Kurdish movement. Yakiti and Ittihad al-Sha'b were soon brushed aside. During the brief meeting, which lasted barely half an hour, the delegation was satisfied with accepting the promises of the former minister of defence regarding the future of 30,000 'undocumented' Kurds.

Emergence of a Community

For the first time, mass mobilisation of Kurds around their ethnic identity took the form of direct confrontation with power. Also for the first time, the popular resistance movement touched the network of Kurdish territories, including even the most isolated enclaves such as Kawbanah, and thereby reinforced the symbolic unity of a Kurdish Syrian space. The statement that 'the *intifadah* of March delineated the map of Syrian Kurdistan', by 'Abd al-Basit Hamu', a Kurdish militant based in Germany, clarifies the importance of *intifadah* for a community that discovers an affirmation of its existence inside the lines of demarcation that are drawn by revolt. By providing a geographic symbol, the events in al-Qamishli mark a decisive step for Kurdish nationalism in Syria.

At the same time, the confrontation creates a space of confidence regarding Kurdistan, which becomes a symbolic sanctuary: Shivan, the Kurdish nationalist singer, even composed a song to honour the 'martyred' city of al-Qamishli and the solidarity demonstrations that took place in Sulaimaniyyah and Diyarbakir, and in Europe. Barzani abandoned his typical reserve on the subject of Kurds in Syria, and demanded that a solution be found for the problems affecting 'Kurdistan in Syria'. This indiscreet terminology enraged Syrian officials, and not even a visit by Hushyar Zibari, the Iraqi minister of foreign affairs, could calm them down. The new-found interaction between the Syrian Kurdish and Iraqi Kurdish arenas, as illustrated by Zibari's attempt at mediation, could not but arouse an awareness of the unprecedented strategic position of the Kurds in Syria and the shift in power between them and the Syrian state.

Conclusion

The March 2004 episode demonstrates the ability of the Kurds to mobilise popular action even at the centre of Syrian society, as we saw in Aleppo and Damascus, with the help of the student movement. The combined force of the two movements testifies at once to the cultural integration of the Kurds in Syria and their long-standing political frustration. In spite of the gains in visibility that were achieved by the Kurdish community as a result of the al-Qamishli events and the concomitant change in the community's relations with the state, the disjunction between the social and economic integration of the Kurds and the persistent denial of their national rights looms ever greater. In effect, the basic terms of the Kurdish question have remained constant since the coming of the Ba'thi regime. Nevertheless, the events of al-Qamishli show that the status quo between the government and the Kurdish community has now been transformed: the nature of the conflict will continue to be revolutionised and the awakening of a Kurdish national identity in Syria will no longer be a marginal political question.

Notes

1. An Arabic neologism, it designates either 'Kurds of Kurdistan', that is, the 'Kurdish Land' in its entirety, transcending state boundaries, or the inhabitants of the Kurdish region in Iraq. Here it designates non-Syrian Kurds.

2. The 'extraordinary census', carried out by the Ba'th Party in the early 1960s, enabled hundreds of thousands of Kurds to be stripped of their Syrian citizenship. It is estimated that more than 300,000 Kurds never regained their legal status in Syria. The reinstatement of these Kurds' citizenship is one of the principal demands made by Kurdish parties today.

3. All the information about these demonstrations comes from various independent Kurdish websites such as <www.efrin.net>, <www.qamislo.com> and also from the site of the Committee for the Defence of Human Rights.

4. Operation 'Arab Encirclement' was envisaged in the 1960s by Muhammad Talib Hilal in his famous 'Study of the Jazirah Region', in which he proposed to empty the frontier zones of the region of their Kurdish inhabitants. Partially implemented, it led to the confiscation of a number of farms and the creation of Arab colonies, especially between the towns of Darik and 'Amudah. Here state officials relocated the *'amar*, that is,

poor farmers from the Raqqa province whose lands were flooded during the construction of the high dam across the Euphrates River.

5.   Interview in Paris, August 2004.

SEVEN

The Syrian Opposition:
The struggle for unity and relevance, 2003–2008

Joe Pace and Joshua Landis

On 10 June 2000, Hafiz al-Asad died. He had ruled Syria for three decades, bringing stability to a country that had been rocked by military coups and revolving governments. Stability came with a price, however. Al-Asad tightened emergency laws, eliminated political liberties and ruled with an iron fist. One Syrian dissident expressed the mood upon al-Asad's death by remarking, 'The strong man is dead. Now we have a chance.'[1] His son's ascent to power kindled hope that the leadership would embark on much-needed political reform, bringing about what came to be known as the Damascus Spring.

Indeed, the first few months under the new leader were auspicious. In his inaugural speech to parliament, Bashar al-Asad appealed for 'creative thinking' and recognised the 'dire need' for constructive criticism, reform and modernisation.[2] In a move to patch up relations with Islamist groups and end the bitter war between the regime and fundamentalists, Bashar closed down the notorious Mazzah political prison, which had become a symbol of the regime's brutality. Human Rights Watch estimated that Syria held some 4,000 political prisoners in 1993.[3] The new president whittled the number of known political detainees down to between 300 and 1,000 within the first years of his rule.

Almost immediately, Syria's once catatonic intellectuals began to show signs of life and human rights organisations and discussion forums began proliferating across the country. Encouraged by what seemed to be a real social base for dissent, a number of prominent establishment figures – parliamentarians, businessmen, academics and former opposition leaders – also stepped into the reformist limelight. The Damascus Spring activists produced a manifesto to give direction and a semblance of unity to the flood of reform demands emanating from Syria's long-suppressed public. More than 1,000 civil society activists signed the Statement of One Thousand in January 2001, calling for comprehensive political reforms.[4] The following week, parliamentarian and vocal regime critic Riyad Saif announced the formation of the Movement for Social Peace. These developments, however, proved too much for the regime to bear.

Hardliners, anxious that the criticism was escalating beyond control, inaugurated a crackdown that would become known as the Damascus Winter. The regime unleashed its attack dogs, publicly impugning the opposition's nationalist credentials and even physically assaulting its critics. Vice President 'Abd al-Halim Khaddam warned that the calls for change had gone too far and claimed that the regime would not tolerate threats that could drive Syria into civil war. By the end of the summer, eight of the most prominent civil society leaders had been imprisoned and all but one of the civil society forums were shut down.

Despite its brevity, the Damascus Spring achieved several lasting, if modest, aims. For the first time since the late 1970s, individuals could vocalise critical views of the regime in public settings. The new-found freedom drew scattered and secretive activists out of the shadows. Even if ideological disputes persisted, dissidents at least became aware of each other's existence and the language of reform was injected into political discourse.

Notwithstanding these successes, the Damascus Spring failed to produce anything resembling a unified opposition. Almost all of the opposition groupings agreed on a basic set of demands, but even such shared commitments proved tenuous. Trifling ideological disagreements, personality conflicts and interference from state security forces compounded substantive disputes over everything from the question of Kurdish rights to the role of foreign assistance. These troubles produced a fragmented and ineffectual opposition composed of often competing human rights associations, political parties, civil society forums and committees, independent activists and intellectuals and underground Islamist groups.

Human Rights Groups

Approximately ten human rights organisations and two centres for human rights studies, as well as a series of smaller, single-issue associations, such as the Free Political Prisoners Committee, have been operating in Syria since 2003. Because no agency within the state is receptive to the concerns of these organisations, their main function has been to collect information on human rights violations and issue press releases with condemnations or calls for a detainee's release. These groups are arguably the most effective parts of the Syrian opposition. The increasing frequency with which families file reports with these organisations is indicative of the trust they have built with vulnerable segments of the population.[5] They have also become more communications savvy, feeding a constant flow of information to international non-governmental organisations, thereby deterring the most egregious abuses.

Unfortunately, these groups are not without their problems. Membership is trifling and of those who formally belong, only a fraction actively participates. For example, all of the Human Rights Association of Syria's research, reports, correspondence and press releases in 2004 were the products of one woman. The Syrian Organisation for Human Rights splintered: the core group has only ten members and the split-off has one who is widely suspected of being a state security agent. Even organisations that are better staffed run on shoestring budgets, relying on membership dues that rarely surpass a total of a few hundred dollars per month or on the personal wealth of their founders.

The constant financial strain has undermined democratic practices within these organisations. Often, the only organisational real estate is an activist's personal office, which gives him or her undue influence over internal operations. One activist who severed his relationship with a human rights association lamented that its founder and office owner 'ran the association like a personal fiefdom'.[6] There is no neutral meeting space;

if a personal conflict flares up between the proprietor and another activist, the latter is forced to capitulate or disaffiliate.

Then there are the personal conflicts between organisations, illustrated by the decision of multiple human rights organisations to boycott a demonstration in front of the High National Security Court during activist Aktham Naissah's trial, no small slight for a community that shows its utmost solidarity when its members are facing sham political trials.[7] These squabbles limit co-operation and information sharing and lead to redundant and inefficient uses of organisational resources.

Civil Society Forums and Committees

Civil society in Syria is a wasteland. Even at the height of Bashar's reformist fervour, the regime refused to license dissident groups, choosing instead to tolerate their illegal operation until political convenience dictated otherwise. The few civil associations that have been licensed are either pet projects of regime figures, such as the president's wife's development associations, or professional syndicates, whose leadership is by law drawn from Ba'th Party loyalists.[8]

Aside from human rights associations, the only civic associations to survive the Damascus Winter were the Committee for the Revival of Civil Society and the Jamal al-'Atasi Forum for Democratic Dialogue; the latter was shut down in the spring of 2005. The stated goals of these associations were multifaceted. They were supposed to provide a forum to voice critical viewpoints, be a staging ground for cobbling together a united platform and act as a counterweight to sectarianism by facilitating dialogue between different ethnic and religious groups.[9]

Report cards were mixed. The Jamal al-'Atasi Forum's monthly meetings regularly attracted hundreds of participants, consistently more than demonstrations, but the meetings never produced tangible results. In the words of one activist, 'People voice their views, others disagree; and when the forum ends, people go home without ever resolving the argument. Three hours of talk once a month is not going to produce a unified opposition.'[10] All the same, the al-'Atasi Forum provided an important venue for opposition figures to be seen and heard in public. It was a signal to the secular left that the public conscience had not been erased. Its existence was also a useful talking point for a president who tried to project a façade of greater tolerance for free speech.

Political Parties

Political parties have always been the weakest link in the opposition. With the exception of the Kurdish parties, whose members are resoundingly nationalist, none has managed to plant roots in society. The most popular non-sectarian party's membership is less than 1,000, leaving active members vastly outnumbered by security agents.

Contrary to the popular presumption, Syria does not suffer from a shortage of opposition parties. In fact, the problem is that there is a glut of these parties, despite the fact that all of them are technically illegal. Straw-man parties, consisting of two or three political entrepreneurs, are being formed with such frequency that people have stopped keeping track.[11] The combination of security pressures and lack of internal democracy has rendered the parties brittle and prone to splintering. State agents easily infiltrate the organisations, foment internal discord and form breakaway parties with disaffected members.[12] There is no better example of Syria's fissure-prone opposition than the prodigious number of Kurdish parties, whose total changes so frequently that rarely will two opposition watchers report the same number.[13]

Although other indicators – popular protests, civil society gatherings, dissident presence in the media – indicate that opposition activity increased from 2002 to 2005, party membership actually decreased. Parties have proven particularly inept at recruiting youth. Riad al-Turk, the opposition's most highly esteemed party leader, tried to rejuvenate his party with this dilemma in mind: 'We don't have a platform suitable to the present conditions this society is facing ... University students, the youth, those from the countryside – none of them are finding anything within [the opposition] that suits them.'[14]

The Nasirists, who still adhere to former Egyptian President Gamal 'Abd al-Nasir's platform of pan-Arab nationalism and socialist economics, and leftists, who dominate Syria's largest opposition party alliance, the Democratic National Gathering (DNG), are widely viewed as relics of the past, clinging to an ideology that collapsed along with the Soviet Union.

Turk's party, the second largest in the DNG, has been one of the few success stories. Formerly the Syrian Communist Party, it was refashioned into a liberal party with a renovated platform and newer, younger leadership.[15] By most accounts, before the latest crackdown it was the only party with a steadily rising membership base.

Due to the fragmentation of Syrian political society, the spine of the opposition in the post-Damascus Spring period had become intellectuals and independent activists, who at best had a readership and no following. As activist 'Ammar Qurabi noted, 'Really, there is no such thing as "the opposition". There are [only] individual activists and writers.'[16]

An Islamist Resurgence?

Despite Bashar al-Asad's pardoning of hundreds of Muslim Brothers during his first three years in office, and repeated, albeit abortive, efforts at reconciliation, there is no indication that the regime is growing more tolerant of Islamist political activity. The memory of the Hama massacre, which crushed the Muslim Brothers' uprising in February 1982, and Law Number 49, which punishes membership in the Muslim Brothers organisation by death, have inhibited the re-emergence of an organised presence inside Syria.

Although it is impossible to ascertain the extent to which the public sympathises with the Muslim Brothers, growing religiosity and a dearth of credible liberal trends would make the organisation a formidable political force if it were allowed to mobilise. Nonetheless, despite alarmist predictions, it is unlikely that it would monopolise Syrian politics. The roughly 30 per cent of Syrians who are Kurds, Christians or 'Alawis generally oppose the Muslim Brothers by default, as do many upper-middle-class urbanites who are weary of Islamist puritanism.

The only Islamist party inside Syria is the Liberation Party (Hizb al-Tahrir), which has fewer than 1,000 members, according to its own activists.[17] It has become a cliché for journalists to note the increase in veiled women and bearded men, archetypal signs of a religious awakening. In general, however, the type of Islam that is resurging in Syria is neither fundamentalist nor militant. Rather than fall victim to it, the regime has managed to harness its energy by monopolising the religious establishment and burnishing its Islamic credentials. The puritanical Salafi and Wahhabi trends are divided

– some advocating political silence or even co-operation with the state, others counselling political agitation – and their activities are largely limited to tiny, scattered discussion groups. There is no established network.

After Syria's withdrawal from Lebanon, there have been scattered clashes between security forces and what the government claims were Islamist militants. Plausible theories have been proffered that the regime staged at least some of these attacks in order to evoke sympathy from the West and justify its internal crackdown.[18] Even if the attacks were the work of hostile Islamists, their occurrence testifies only to the spread of isolated militant cells. They command very little popular support in a Syrian street that is still wary of the kind of violent clashes between Islamists and the regime that erupted in the early 1980s. Given the regime's stranglehold on political Islamic trends, it is highly unlikely that Islamists will emerge as a major opposition force inside Syria, regardless of how well the Muslim Brothers fare in exile.

The Iraq War: Energising or enervating?

For proponents of the so-called reverse domino theory – that Saddam Hussein's collapse would send a tidal wave of democratic fervour through the region – the US-led war turned out to be a double-edged sword. Activists amplified their calls for reform in the name of protecting Syria from Iraq's fate, but the war also shocked the general population into rallying behind the Ba'thi regime, whose chief boast was that it could maintain stability. The Bush administration's new-found democratisation fervour forced Damascus to adopt the language of reform, but it also facilitated government efforts to label dissidents as lackeys of the West. Saddam's collapse kindled an awakening among the Kurdish opposition, but in so doing exacerbated tensions between the Kurdish and Arab oppositions.

Even though the vast majority of Syrian dissidents harshly condemned the Iraq war, they coupled their scathing rebukes with calls for domestic reform. In May 2003, a mere month after the fall of Baghdad, civil society activists submitted a petition to the president warning against the 'aggressive, racist, egotistical and evil policies and ideology' of the United States and Israel and appealing for reform to strengthen Syria against external threats.[19] On 8 May 2004, opposition activists staged an unprecedented sit-in in front of the People's Assembly.[20] At the same time, however, they found themselves increasingly vulnerable to accusations of treachery. For example, the one exception to the media blackout concerning the sit-in was an article by the editor in chief of *al-Ba'th* newspaper that accused the protesters of trying to 'reinforce pressures being exercised from outside'.[21]

Arab activists were ambivalent about the Iraq war but the Kurds greeted it with nearly unanimous glee. The fall of Saddam, the figurehead of Kurdish repression, ignited a revival of Kurdish nationalism inside Syria. Kurdish opposition groups began agitating for Kurdish rights, including the return of confiscated lands in the northeast, the right to teach and study the Kurdish language, the redressing of systematic discrimination against the Kurds in the official bureaucracy and the nationalisation of Kurds who had been stripped of Syrian citizenship in 1962. A smaller number of parties began demanding greater political autonomy and a federal government.

Masha'al Temu, spokesman for the recently founded Kurdish Future Trend, observed, 'The Iraq war liberated us from the culture of fear ... [People] saw a Kurd become president of Iraq and began demanding their culture and political rights in Syria'.[22] In March 2004, a soccer match erupted into clashes between Kurds and Arabs in the northeastern city of al-Qamishli, spawning Kurdish protests throughout Syria's major cities.[23] The Syrian regime did not hesitate to crush the so-called *intifadah*, rounding up thousands of activists and flooding the Kurdish-dominated northeast with security forces.[24]

The effect of the rise of the Kurds on the opposition as a whole was again mixed. In some ways, the sudden outburst of Kurdish nationalism in the midst of increasing US and Israeli pressure on Syria – months earlier, Israel had launched an air strike on Syrian soil – played directly into the regime's hands. While the state-run press accused foreign agents of initiating the riots, the security agencies stoked suspicions that the Kurds constituted a fifth column – secessionist and in favour of US military intervention – thus containing the agitation within Kurdish circles.[25] Even nervous Arab activists, who had once been sympathetic to the Kurdish plight, hesitated to support a movement whose leaders affectionately referred to President George W. Bush as Abu Azaadi (Father of Freedom).

Nevertheless, the size of the uprising forced Arab activists to recognise that the Kurds were a force that could no longer be ignored. The Arab opposition struggles to move 300 supporters onto the street while the Kurdish opposition brings out hundreds of thousands. Prior to this uprising, the Arab opposition had largely ignored the Kurdish issue, being suspicious that Kurdish activism was a cover to pursue an independent Kurdistan. Kurds stood accused of exaggerating their hardship and revising history to establish the Kurdish claim to Syrian lands.

Soon after the uprising, Arab and Kurdish leaders began making contact and engaging in low-level co-ordination. The Arabs hoped to piggyback on the Kurds' manpower while the Kurds hoped to insert Kurdish rights into the Arab opposition's agenda. The goals were to surmount the mutual suspicion that had been so carefully cultivated by the regime and create a united front for reform. The increasing importance of Kurdish forces in the opposition was recognised by the Muslim Brothers, which issued a statement of solidarity with the Kurds exactly one year after the uprising. It was the first time the Muslim Brothers had publicly acknowledged the legitimacy of Kurdish grievances.[26]

Hariri's Assassination Gives New Life to the Opposition

On 14 February 2005, a massive bomb ripped through former Lebanese Prime Minister Rafiq Hariri's convoy, killing him and twenty-two others. Washington blamed Damascus and worked closely with both France and Saudi Arabia to ratchet up diplomatic and economic pressure on the Syrian regime in order to hold it responsible before an international investigation and court of law. A popular uprising in Lebanon, quickly dubbed the Cedar Revolution, brought more than a million citizens of the fractured state together to protest the killing of their leader and demand that justice be done.

Bashar al-Asad insisted on Syria's innocence and warned fellow Syrians against foreign conspiracies and an international witch-hunt. Nevertheless, bowing to overwhelming pressure, he withdrew Syria's armed forces from Lebanon, ending a thirty-year presence that most Lebanese had come to view as an occupation. Syria's humiliating expulsion from Lebanon and growing international isolation had a profound psychological effect on the opposition. For the first time, many opposition leaders believed that the regime might face a truly concerted international effort to bring it down or force it to accept real reforms. The opposition had to step up to the plate and prove to the Syrian people that it could provide an effective substitute for Ba'thi rule. According to Kamal al-Labwani, 'For the first time, the possibility of regime collapse, even if improbable, was in view, and people began to think more seriously about providing an alternative.'[27]

The opposition spent the spring of 2005 engaged in its first serious effort to unite since the collapse of the Damascus Spring. First, low-level contacts between Arabs and Kurds gave birth to the National Co-ordination Committee for the Defence of Basic Freedoms and Human Rights, the most inclusive opposition alliance to date.[28] In April, the Committee for the Revival of Civil Society, Syria's largest civil society formation, issued a statement calling for the 'opening of channels of dialogue' with all segments of Syrian society, including the Muslim Brothers.

For the first time since the infamous 1982 Hama massacre, an opposition group inside Syria had called for dialogue with the Muslim Brothers.[29] One month later, activist and writer 'Ali 'Abdullah, standing up at the al-'Atasi Forum in central Damascus, read aloud a letter from Muslim Brothers Secretary General 'Ali Sadr al-Din al-Bayanuni that encouraged the co-operation of all of Syria's political movements; even the ruling Ba'th Party. It was the first time the Muslim Brothers had been publicly represented inside Syria since 1982.[30] Soon thereafter, ex-communist leader Riyad al-Turk sat next to al-Bayanuni and announced his intention to form an alliance with the Muslim Brothers. The groundwork was being laid for a broad opposition coalition that would unite the many strains of Syria's opposition, whether ethnic or religious.

The Damascus Declaration

On 18 October 2005, five days before the scheduled release of the United Nations' first report on the Hariri assassination, the newly invigorated Syrian opposition unveiled the Damascus Declaration, a document establishing a unified platform for democratic change. The declaration grew out of a clandestine trip to Morocco a few months earlier by two leading members of the Damascus-based secular opposition, where they met with the leader of the Muslim Brothers. The Christian journalist and leftist Michel Kilu was one of the two delegates to meet with al-Bayanuni. They hammered out the rudiments of a compromise unity document. The two sides agreed on four guiding principles: pluralism, non-violence, oppositional unity and democratic change. Al-Bayanuni delegated authority to his secular counterparts to shop the draft copy of their agreement around Damascus to be amended and approved by as many other opposition groups as possible. The result was a broad-based alliance that seemed to bury the hatchet between secular and Islamist factions.[31] The publication of the declaration only days before the first UN findings were released gave a boost to the accomplishments of the opposition, as it was able to ride a wave of press reports on Syria, a country that is seldom discussed in the international news.

Five political parties and civil society organisations, along with nine prominent intellectuals, signed their names to the declaration. Within hours, dozens of additional parties, inside and outside Syria, began to declare their support. For the first time in decades, it seemed that Syria's bickering political parties, outspoken intellectuals and civil society groupings were finding common ground. Kurdish, Arab and Assyrian nationalists put aside their ethnic squabbling. Socialists, communists, liberals and Islamists were willing to unite over a single platform of democratic change and respect for one another. Civil society activists who had previously turned their noses up at political parties joined forces with them and a deliberate effort was made to ensure that signatories of the declaration hailed from a majority of Syria's provinces.[32] According to one activist, '[Only] with the Damascus Declaration could we speak about a "Syrian opposition".'[33]

The document sidestepped many of the niggling issues that had dogged opposition groups to that point. It refrained from declaring a state religion. It avoided clear statements about the economy or saying whether Syria should remain socialist or turn to free markets. It proposed no clear solution to the Kurdish problem, other than to insist that it should be dealt with within a democratic and inclusive framework. Another significant feature of the Damascus Declaration was that, unlike previous declarations, it was followed up by the creation of a committee to oversee continued co-ordination among its signatories.

In many ways, the criticisms of the Damascus Declaration were evidence of the pettiness of the divisions that plague the opposition. A clause that stresses Syria's affiliation to the 'Arab Order' drew fire from both Arab and Kurdish nationalists. Some Arab nationalists disparaged this as a despicable compromise of Syria's Arab heritage, and some equally extreme Kurds decried the mere reference to Arab identity as evidence of unceasing Arab chauvinism.[34] As these criticisms revealed, many dissident efforts failed to gain widespread support because of phraseology, not content.

The more substantive criticisms of the declaration revolved around the special reference to Islam, which it referred to as the 'religion and ideology of the majority' and 'the more prominent cultural component in the life of the nation and the people' and the treatment of Kurdish rights. Some commentators warned that such efforts to court the Muslim Brothers would exacerbate sectarian tensions.[35] One argued that the drafters had 'surrendered, without so much as fluttering an eyelid, [Syria's] long history of secularism and the separation of church and state'.[36] As for the Kurdish issue, three Kurdish groups praised the declaration's demands for democratic change but ultimately rejected the document on the grounds that it was deficient on the issue of Kurdish rights since it did not explicitly recognise the Kurds as an independent national group with historic ties to the land.

The pact between secular groups and the Muslim Brothers was a tremendous boon for both sides. The Muslim Brothers could project its voice through the conduits of Syrian civil society, while secular elements gained the endorsement of the country's most prominent Islamist movement. After a disappointing Ba'th Party conference, secular activists hoped that this connection would mitigate popular suspicions that the secular opposition was anti-Muslim, elitist and pro-Western.[37]

The coalition set off alarm bells for a regime that had struggled for two decades to deny the Muslim Brothers a foothold in Syrian society. The regime counter-attacked through its proxies within intellectual and dissident circles. Rihab al-Bitar, of the quasi-opposition Free Democratic Gathering, impugned the motives of the declaration's signatories, parroting the regime's logic that amidst the onslaught of international pressures, any challenge to the state endangered the security of the Syrian people.[38] The regime cast itself as the guarantor of stability and accused the opposition of disregarding US and Israeli treachery or, worse, facilitating it by seeking to undermine the state.[39] Unfortunately, indictments of the opposition's loyalty still resonated with an anxiety-ridden public.

The Opposition Goes Global

A debate has long raged within the Syrian opposition about the role of foreign forces. At one extreme stands a sizeable group of nationalists that rejects any form of outside assistance, especially from the United States. Their ideology is encapsulated in the slogan, 'We will not ride to heaven on the back of Satan.' At the other extreme is a smattering of marginalised liberals who welcome any and all pressure that could weaken the regime. The moderate contingent recognises the need for foreign assistance but rejects anything that influences the opposition's agenda or takes power out of its own hands.

Two developments empowered advocates of internationalising the reform movement. First, opposition groups in exile began proliferating in 2004, beginning a concerted effort to forge ties between foreign and domestic forces. Second, and more important, the regime commenced a new clampdown on activists within Syria in March 2005 and has steadily escalated repression since that time, prompting activists to travel abroad and encourage their counterparts in exile to lobby their respective governments.

The regime intensified its repression of activists during the 2005 with-drawal from Lebanon to levels unseen since the Damascus Winter. It began to arrest and harass civil society activists and scrambled to deny them a voice in the media. In mid-March 2005, the Ministry of Information yanked the licences from the US-sponsored channels al-Hurrah and Radio Sawa, because they covered a 10 March protest in front of the Palace of Justice.[40] A website featuring frequent articles on the opposition, called Elaph, was blocked along with the critical newsletter *All4Syria*. This sent a clear message to remaining journalists not to engage with or cover the opposition.

In May 2005, security forces arrested the entire administrative committee of the Jamal al-'Atasi Forum for reading aloud a message from the Muslim Brothers. All of its members were subsequently released except one, and the forum – the last association to survive the Damascus Winter crackdown – was closed indefinitely. The number of arbitrary arrests and security summons skyrocketed. By mid-summer, all oppositional gatherings had been banned, and those trying to skirt the ban found their houses and offices besieged by security forces. One activist explained the impact on the opposition: 'It [was] becoming almost impossible for us to do anything inside of Syria. So people [had] two choices: they [could] regress and revert to secretive work like what they did in the 1980s and 1990s or they [could] travel and organise abroad.'[41]

Meanwhile, Farid Ghadri, a Syrian businessman and founder of the Washington-based Reform Party of Syria, began touting himself as the leader of the opposition in exile. Although Ghadri had no discernible following inside Syria, he managed to ingratiate himself with neo-conservative officials like Richard Perle and Paul Wolfowitz. Describing himself as 'the Syrian Ahmad Chalabi', he called for the overthrow of the Ba'thi regime.[42] Associations with the United States destroyed his credibility within Syria's domestic opposition, but they may have stoked the regime's anxiety.

After several abortive conferences, the internal and external opposition – minus Ghadri – successfully linked up in Washington in January 2006. The conference did not create a new coalition but its attendees from inside Syria all attested to its singular accomplishment: it marked an important first step in breaking down the walls of mistrust between activists inside Syria and expatriates residing in the United States.[43]

Khaddam's Bombshell Reinvigorates the Opposition

On 30 December 2005, former Vice President Khaddam, once a staunch critic of the opposition, stunned regime and opposition alike by lashing out at the authorities on the al-'Arabiyyah news network. It had been an open secret that he opposed Bashar al-Asad's inheritance of the presidency, and was posturing to assume the position himself. After Bashar came to power, Khaddam found himself increasingly marginalised until he resigned from – or was forced out of – the vice presidency.

After the interview, he relocated to Paris, where he announced an alliance with the Muslim Brothers. In March 2006, a conference in Brussels ended with the announcement of a new opposition coalition known as the National Salvation Front (NSF). It stressed liberal values: religious, ethnic, political and intellectual pluralism, rotation of power and an end to discrimination against the Kurds, whom it described as 'partners in the homeland'.[44]

Khaddam's defection and the formation of the NSF were bigger blows to the regime's confidence than the Damascus Declaration. At best, the declaration heralded greater unity within the opposition. By itself, it did not enhance the opposition's standing within Syrian society. Whereas dissidents struggled to network internationally and were consistently starved for funds, Khaddam possessed a personal fortune, a wealth of important connections and an intimate knowledge of the inner workings of a notoriously opaque regime.

The alliance bolstered the positions of Khaddam and the Muslim Brothers alike. By linking up with the secular Khaddam, the Muslim Brothers showcased an eagerness to prioritise political pragmatism over narrow ideology. It may have alleviated the anxieties of 'Alawis and military leaders who believed that the Muslim Brothers' first move in power would be to purge regime loyalists. Khaddam could appeal to Ba'this in a way that al-Bayanuni never could. The former vice president issued an open letter to regime Ba'this, appealing to them to reject the small family clique ruling Syria and give their loyalty instead to the fatherland, represented by the NSF. The Muslim Brothers also benefit from Khaddam's international and internal connections. Meanwhile, the Muslim Brothers gave Khaddam an Islamic imprimatur, so he could now piggyback on whatever support it enjoyed inside Syria.

The NSF reopened some fissures within the domestic opposition, however, that the Damascus Declaration had hoped to seal. No activists within Syria openly declared their support for the NSF – doing so would have assuredly carried a stiff prison sentence – but most dissidents divided into two camps. One camp strenuously objected in principle to dealing with Khaddam, an icon of the oppressive Ba'thi regime and an architect of the Damascus Winter. Some in this first camp condemned the shift in the opposition's centre of gravity from Damascus to Europe, given that Khaddam had fled to Paris. Some criticised the gall of the participants in the NSF conference for not including any activists from inside Syria. Other critics bemoaned the Muslim Brothers' failure to consult their new Damascus Declaration allies. Some on the declaration's temporary committee in fact flirted with the idea of officially expelling the Muslim Brothers from the declaration's ranks.[45]

The second camp, while cautiously optimistic about the NSF as a political formation, and elated about the emergence of a new opposition alliance, remained wary of Khaddam's character. This contingent was dominated by liberals, dissidents receptive to foreign assistance, along with those who had been most severe and uncompromising in their opposition to the regime. Riyad al-Turk, who in October 2005 boldly called for Bashar's resignation, said on the record, 'While we do not have to support Khaddam, we will not fight him on behalf of the regime', adding that the opposition was open to everyone, including defectors from the Ba'th Party.[46] A sizeable number of foreign opposition movements endorsed the NSF, even while holding their noses. The fact that the formation of the NSF did not fracture the opposition was one of the few concrete testaments to the cohesive force of the Damascus Declaration. The declaration provided the wrangling camps with an agreed-upon set of ideals and no committed activist wanted to see the fledgling opposition's single greatest achievement unravel only months after its birth.

The NSF quickly embarked on a diplomatic campaign to partner with regional forces hostile to Bashar, setting up meetings and offices in Turkey.[47] It also consolidated ties with anti-Syrian elements in Lebanon, raising fears in Damascus that Lebanon might be turned into a beachhead for opposition forces. The Syrian regime also had to fear that anti-Syrian leaders in Lebanon would use their lobbying skills in the US to convince Washington to abandon its hostility to the Muslim Brothers and consider support for a Sunni Islamist party as an alternative to Syria's secular, 'Alawi-dominated regime. The Muslim Brothers discussed the mechanisms for opposing al-Asad with Lebanese Druze leader Walid Jumblatt.[48] Jumblatt stopped in Paris twice to confer with Khaddam on trips to Washington. The opposition's success in building a broad, even if fragile, coalition and its ability to gain tentative support from foreign governments prompted the regime to go on the offensive.

The End of the Opposition

The repression that began in 2005 and grew in intensity following Khaddam's defection became draconian following the Beirut–Damascus Declaration of May 2006. Several developments emboldened the regime to intensify the crackdown. First, the Ba'thi regime felt that it had dodged a bullet when the UN investigation into the Hariri murder began to run into serious difficulties following the first and most dramatic report issued during the fall of 2005, which squarely accused Syria of masterminding the assassination. A number of key witnesses either recanted, claiming they had been paid by Hariri's allies to give false testimony, or turned out to be unreliable. Secondly, Israel signalled during the last months of 2005 that it would not support regime change in Damascus. The third, and perhaps the most reassuring, development for Syria was the weakness of the anti-Syrian coalition in Lebanon. The parliamentary elections of 2005 revealed deep divisions among Lebanon's Christian community, half of which allied itself with Lebanon's Shi'ah rather than the country's pro-American Sunni leadership.

The Israeli invasion of Lebanon in the summer of 2006 further emboldened Syria. Israel failed to destroy Hizbullah, which quickly rearmed with Syrian help and proved that it could protect Syrian interests in Lebanon. Another factor that convinced Bashar al-Asad that he could move against the opposition without provoking serious opposition inside or outside Syria was the failure of President Bush's Middle East plans. Iraq had turned into a disaster and democratic elections in the Middle East brought to power Islamists hostile to the US wherever they were held. The January 2006 elections in Palestine that brought HAMAS to power with a sweeping victory gave Bashar al-Asad an important political boost. After all, HAMAS's leader Khalid Mash'al lived in Damascus. President Bush's freedom agenda had clearly backfired.

In March 2006, no doubt anxious about the build-up of opposition forces abroad, the regime amplified its persecution of dissidents by outlawing contact with foreign elements. Al-Labwani was immediately arrested following his return after meetings with European and US officials in Washington; he was initially charged with belonging to a banned organisation, inciting sectarian strife, and 'damaging the nation's image', the worst-case scenario being a ten-year prison term.[49] The regime later levelled a new charge against al-Labwani: 'communicating with a foreign country and prompting it to direct confrontation', which carries a sentence of life imprisonment or death.[50] Since the summer of 2006, virtually no Syrian dissident has been allowed to leave the country.

The Beirut–Damascus Declaration

On 12 May 2006, 300 Syrian and Lebanese intellectuals signed the Beirut–Damascus Declaration, calling for a normalisation of relations between Lebanon and Syria. At first glance innocuous, the regime interpreted this document as evidence that the Syrian opposition was teaming up with the anti-Syrian government in Lebanon.[51] The fact that a delegation that included Khaddam and several Muslim Brothers met with Walid Jumblatt – Lebanon's most vociferous anti-Syrian politician, who had called for both US military intervention in Syria and the assassination of Bashar al-Asad – lent credence to this interpretation. Many Syrians were piqued at what they perceived to be Lebanese ingratitude for Syria's sacrifices to maintain Lebanese security. The regime played on this upsurge in anti-Lebanese sentiment to paint opposition figures as treacherous agents of pro-Western intervention in Lebanon.

The regime went for the opposition's jugular vein and has had its teeth implanted therein ever since. An editorial in the state newspaper *Tishrin* accused the signatories of '[forgetting] all Syria's victims and sacrifices for the sake of Lebanon and [joining] the evil and open attack led by the Bush administration against Syria'.[52] Two days after its release, secret police called Kilu, the declaration's main author, to come in for questioning. He was held for a year, and then sentenced to three more years for 'weakening national sentiment, spreading false news and inciting sectarian strife'.[53] Kilu's arrest sent shockwaves through the opposition and prefigured a broader campaign to target every element of the dissident community – human rights advocates, Arab nationalists, Kurds, leftists and liberals alike. The state was intent on warning the opposition that no one would be exempt from retribution if they forged alliances with outside governments. Activists began to speak of the 'final liquidation' of the opposition.[54]

Throughout 2007, the regime dispensed with almost every significant opposition figure, starting with the signatories of the Beirut–Damascus Declaration. Michel Kilu, Mahmud 'Isa, Sulaiman Shummar and Khalil Husain were each sentenced to three years.[55] Prominent human rights attorney Anwar al-Bunni was sentenced to five. The wave of repression prompted statements of condemnation from the presidency of the European Union and the US State Department, but nothing more.[56] Throughout this period, state security forces prevented Damascus Declaration members from meeting. In early December, the regime signalled a new zero-tolerance policy for such gatherings. After breaking up a National Council of the Damascus Declaration meeting, security forces fanned out across the country and arrested more than a dozen people who had been in attendance, including Akram al-Bunni, Fida al-Hurani and 'Ali 'Abdullah.[57] Shortly thereafter, secret police stormed the house of former Member of Parliament and Damascus Spring luminary Riyad Saif, and hauled him away.[58]

Not only has Syrian security jailed the opposition's leaders, but it has also taken steps to ensure that a new leadership does not emerge. Arrests of part-time activists and those who criticise the regime are not unusual. The virtual world, once the refuge for expressions of dissent, is monitored and restricted. The crackdown on the Internet includes the blocking of such domain names as 'Blogspot', 'YouTube' and 'Facebook'. Some 160 websites have been blocked, including many news outlets and social networking sites.[59] In 2007 a new regulation requiring website operators to list the name and email address of anyone who posted on the site was issued.[60] Internet cafes have been ordered to register the identification numbers and names of users.

The End of Containment

Syria broke out of its diplomatic and political isolation during the last half of 2008. The reasons for this are several. First, Bashar al-Asad turned out to be a more astute adversary and capable ruler than most analysts gave him credit for. Second, the Syrian opposition was never able to rally more than a few hundred followers for public protests. This failure was due to the pervasive fear of Syria's security forces that has created a generation of apathetic and depoliticised Syrians, but it is also due to the opposition parties' ineffectiveness at recruiting adherents. Even in exile, few Syrians would turn out when summoned. Third, the Bush administration failed to convince Middle Easterners that democracy could solve their problems. The importance of sectarianism, tribalism and ethnic divisions undermined efforts at national unity and reform. As a consequence, authoritarianism was bolstered rather than weakened by America's experiment in Iraq. Syria, which has opened its doors to an influx of some 1.5 million Iraqi refugees, has been traumatised by the civil war that ripped apart its neighbour. Far from being a spur to Syrians to rise up and demand freedom, the Iraq example taught a new generation of Syrians to appreciate the stability and security of rule by a strong man. Authoritarianism throughout the Middle East is being refurbished and modernised.

Recognition of Syria's status as a major regional player and the resulting engagement have not redounded to the benefit of the opposition. The West's diplomatic blockade of Syria concluded with a visit by EU foreign policy chief, Javier Solana, to Damascus. Despite public pleas for Solana to broach Syria's abysmal human rights record, Solana was explicit that the three areas of concern were noninterference in Lebanese affairs, shutting down Palestinian terrorist organisations in Damascus and securing the border with Iraq.[61] Shortly thereafter, a delegation of Republican Congressmen broke ranks with the Bush White House and visited President al-Asad in Damascus. This was a prelude to the much-publicised visit by US Speaker of the House, Nancy Pelosi. Once again, discussions revolved around Lebanon, Iraq and the Israeli–Palestinian conflict. Conspicuously absent was discussion about the dozens of activists imprisoned and awaiting trial. Three months later, in reward for Syria's constructive role in resolving Lebanon's political crisis, French President Nicolas Sarkozy resumed ties with Syria by announcing his plans to send two senior envoys to Damascus. This preceded Sarkozy's visit to Damascus in September 2008.[62] Syrian–French relations had officially recovered from the Hariri assassination fall-out.

Even Syria's enemies are reaching out to it. In May 2008, Israel and Syria announced that they were pursuing comprehensive negotiations.[63] As for the United States, its policy of refusing to deal with Syria will most likely expire with the Bush administration.[64]

Conclusion

The combination of international engagement and regime crackdowns has ended all significant opposition activity inside Syria. Aiman 'Abd al-Nur, who produces the web-based newsletter *All4Syria* and who now lives in exile, explains that Syria's improved relations with the West provided the regime with 'shelter to use force against its militant enemies, and even against civil society, without generating a global outcry'.[65] Yasin Hajj Salih, perhaps the government's most articulate leftist critic who has not been jailed, wrote in *al-Hayat* in October 2008 lamenting the complete fragmentation and debasement of the opposition by the government. He argued that 'the opposition must change itself first in order to be an example of change to society'. He continued, 'Neither communism nor Arab nationalism can solve the problem. The democratic opposition ... needs new ideas about Syrian patriotism and about the current economic and social transformation taking place in Syria ... It must be independent from the outside.' Salih concludes, 'The only way to exit this crisis of failure is to focus on rebuilding the self and developing knowledge of Syrian society which the opposition in all its different branches lacks completely.'[66] Such scathing self-criticism is prevalent within the ranks of Syria's opposition. The opposition is busy trying to explain why the ordinary Syrian citizen did not rally to its call while devising a plan for rebuilding itself.

Notes

1. Alan George, *Syria: Neither Bread nor Freedom*, London 2003.
2. 'President Bashar al-Asad's Address to the People's Council', Damascus Online, 17 July 2000.
3. Human Rights Watch, *World Report 1994: Syria.*
4. 'The One Thousand Statement Calls for Democracy and the Revival of Civil Society in Syria', *Arabic News*, 12 January 2001.
5. Joe Pace, 'Razan Zeitouneh, "The State of the Syrian Opposition"', *Syria Comment*, 4 October 2005.
6. Syrian activist, interview with author, Damascus, 5 June 2005.
7. 'Syrian Activists Boycott Demonstration because of Disagreement of Naisse's Accusation that Some Sit at the Table with Security Agencies', *al-Rai al-'Am*, 25 April 2005.
8. Jihad Matsui, interview with author, Washington DC, 29 January 2006.
9. George, *Syria.*
10. Syrian activist, interview with author, Damascus, 30 August 2005.
11. Syrian activist, interview with author, Damascus, 5 September 2005.
12. 'Ammar Qurabi, interview with author, Aleppo, 25 August 2005.
13. Kurdish and Arab activists, interview with author, al-Qamashli and Damascus, 10–25 June 2005.
14. Joe Pace, 'Riyad al-Turk interviewed by Joe Pace on Mehlis, the Opposition, Ghadry', *Syria Comment*, 8 September 2005.

15. 'Syrian Democratic People's Party New Name for the Syrian Communist Party – Political Office', *Akhbar al-Sharq*, 8 May 2005.
16. Qurabi interview.
17. Zaitunah, unpublished manuscript.
18. Joshua Landis and Joe Pace, 'The Syrian Opposition', *The Washington Quarterly*, vol. 30, no. 1, Winter 2006–7, pp. 45–68.
19. Carsten Wieland, *Syria: Ballots or Bullets? Democracy, Islamism, and Secularism in the Levant*, Seattle 2006.
20. 'Damascus: Demonstrators Detained before the Syrian Parliament', *Arabic News*, 9 March 2004.
21. Mahdi Dakhallah, 'Pressure through Intimidation', *al-Ba'th*, 10 March 2004.
22. Masha'al Temu, interview with author, al-Qamashli, 14 June 2005.
23. 'Gains by Kin in Iraq Inflame Kurds' Anger at Syria', *New York Times*, 22 March 2004.
24. Amnesty International, 'Syria: Amnesty International Calls on Syria to End Repressive Measures against Kurds and to Set Up an Independent Judicial Inquiry into the Recent Clashes', Public Statement, 6 April 2004.
25. 'Usamah Shihadah, Syrian Arab TV1, 15 March 2004.
26. 'Statement from the Muslim Brotherhood in Syria on the Occasion of the First Year Anniversary of the Intifada of 12 March 2004', *Akhbar al-Sharq*, 12 March 2005.
27. Kamal al-Labwani, interview with the author, Zebadani, 2 July 2005.
28. Razuq al-Ghawi, 'Twelve Unlicensed Organisations of Syria from Committee for the Defence of Freedoms', *Asharq al-Awsat*, 20 January 2005.
29. 'The Syrian Opposition on the Inside and Outside Begin Steps to Unify their Ranks', *Quds Press International*, 4 April 2005.
30. 'Letter in the Name of the Muslim Brothers in a Conference which Representatives of the Ba'th Party Attended in Damascus', *Akhbar al-Sharq*, 9 May 2005.
31. Interview with activist and Andrew J. Tabler, 'Democracy to the Rescue', *ICWA Letters*, March 2006.
32. Hazem Nahar, 'Story of the Damascus Declaration', *al-Mawqif al-Dimuqrati*, November 2005.
33. Syrian activist, interview with author, Beirut, 1 July 2006.
34. Syrian activists, interviews with author, Beirut, 1 July 2006 and Syrian activist, email message to author, 7 July 2006.
35. Muhammad Jidid, 'I'alan Damashq al-Mawlud al-Muntathar ... Walakin', *al-Mawqif al-Dimuqrati*, (special report obtained by the author).
36. Wa'il al-Sawah, 'Syrian Competition between the Authorities and the Opposition for the Islamic Street', *al-Hayat al-Lunduniyyah*, 5 July 2005.
37. Syrian activisits, interviews with author, Damascus, 5 July 2005.

38. 'Syrian Party Doubts the Nationalism of Opposition Parties that Signed the Damascus Declaration', *Agence France-Presse Arabic*, 18 October 2005.

39. 'Syrian Security Prevents Press Conference', *Elaph*, 1 February 2006.

40. 'Syria Bans Correspondent from U.S.-funded Broadcasters', *BBC Monitoring International Reports*, 21 March 2005.

41. Syrian activist, email message to author, 5 February 2006.

42. Salim Abraham, 'A Power Struggle from Washington to Damascus: Syria's Ahmad Chalabi', *Syria Comment*, 25 March 2007.

43. Syrian activists, interviews with the author, Washington DC, 31 January 2006.

44. 'Meeting of Syrian Opposition Elements, Khaddam and Bayanuni Announce the National Salvation Front', *Akhbar al-Sharq*, 17 May 2006.

45. 'Abd al-Athim: Muslim Brothers Not Forced to Choose between the Front and the Declaration', *Akhbar al-Sharq*, 17 April 2006.

46. Bahiya Maradini, 'The Opposition Not Capable of Moving the Street', *Elaph*, 16 April 2006.

47. 'Brotherhood Leaders and Human Rights Activists Meet Civil Society Organisations in Turkey', *Akhbar al-Sharq*, 8 May 2006.

48. 'Delegation from the Foreign Relations Committee of the Muslim Brotherhood of Syria Visits Jumblaat', *Akhbar al-Sharq*, 1 May 2006.

49. 'Syrian Rights Activists Detained after Travel Abroad', *Human Rights Watch News*, 18 November 2005.

50. Syrian Human Rights Centre, 'Investigating Judge Issues New Accusation against Kamal al-Labwani', Press Release, 17 March 2006.

51. Syrian activists, interviews with author, Beirut, 30 June–1 July 2006.

52. 'Why the Beirut–Damascus Declaration Now', *Tishrin*, 17 May 2006.

53. 'Kilo and Issa Threatened to Three Years', *The Syria Monitor*, 13 May 2007.

54. Syrian activists, interviews with author, Beirut, 1 July 2006.

55. 'Syria: Four More Activists Sentenced to Prison', Human Rights Watch, *Human Rights News*, 17 May 2007.

56. 'EU Presidency Statement on the Sentencing of Intellectual Michel Kilo and Political Activist Mahmoud Issa in Syria', *SFCP Statements*, 14 May 2007.

57. 'Syria: More Activists Arrested Following Opposition Meeting', Human Rights Watch Press Release, 17 December 2007.

58. 'The Few Syrian Dissidents Remain Subject to a Ruthless Crackdown by the Authorities', *Le Monde*, 15 July 2008.

59. 'Syria Blocks 160 Websites: Rights Group', Agence France-Presse, 9 September 2008.

60. 25 July 2007 Regulation.

61. Nadim Houry, 'The Road to Damascus', *Guardian Unlimited*, 13 March 2007.
62. 'Sarkozy meets Assad in Syria', *International Herald Tribune*, 3 September 2008.
63. 'Israel Holds Peace Talks with Syria', *New York Times*, 22 May 2008.
64. Baker Calls Bush "Ridiculous" on Syria', Jewish and Israel News, 16 September 2008, <http://www.jta.org/cgi-bin/iowa/home/index.html>.
65. Ayman Abdel Nour, 'The View from Damascus', *Forbes Magazine*, 10 May 2008.
66. Yasin Hajj Salih, 'The Syrian Opposition', *al-Hayat*, 19 October 2008.

EIGHT

Partnership with the European Union: Hopes, risks and challenges for the Syrian economy

Anja Zorob

Syria belongs to the countries of the southern and eastern Mediterranean that, together with the members of the European Union (EU), launched in November 1995 the European–Mediterranean Partnership Initiative (EMP), also known as the Barcelona Process. Syria is the last of the Mediterranean Partner Countries (MPCs) that has not yet concluded a full partnership or Association Agreement (AA) with the EU. A Syrian–European Association Agreement was initialled in October 2004, but formal signature of the agreement remains blocked because of political reasons and the 'prerequisites' that Syria has been asked to fulfil before the European Council will give its final approval.

With President Bashar al-Asad's participation in the formal launch of the Union for the Mediterranean (UMed) in July 2008 in Paris and the thaw in Franco–Syrian relations, signature of the AA seems to be back on the agenda. Meanwhile, scepticism has gained ground among those concerned in Syria, who wonder whether it is worth the price to engage in this treaty. Apart from purely political considerations, such as the highly debated clause on weapons of mass destruction (WMD), the economic provisions of the draft Syrian–European AA go substantially beyond the ones found in the treaties with the other MPCs. While some experts argue that the agreement, with its far-reaching provisions to open up the Syrian economy, should be taken as a 'challenge' to push ahead with domestic reforms, others are convinced that it will be largely detrimental to the domestic economy.

Syrian–European Relations: Trade and economic co-operation

Relations between Syria and the EU continue to be governed by a Co-operation Agreement that was signed in 1977. In the framework of this agreement, Syrian industrial-goods exports to the EU are granted duty-free treatment on a non-reciprocal basis. For most of the time since the 1970s, the EU has been Syria's primary trading partner. At their peak, exports to the EU accounted for more than two-thirds of Syrian exports to the world as a whole, while imports from the EU accounted for between 30 and 40 per cent of Syria's total imports.

Figure 8.1: Syrian Trade with the EU and the World

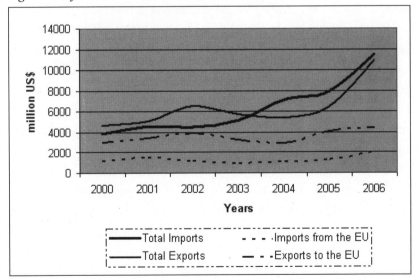

Source: Author's compilation based on data extracted from United Nations Comtrade database

Whereas trade with the rest of the world has witnessed a significant boost in recent years, as illustrated in Figure 8.1, Syrian exports to and imports from the EU have more or less stagnated. Accordingly, the share of imports from Europe in total Syrian imports dropped from 35 per cent at the beginning of the 2000s to below 20 per cent in 2006, marking the lowest share since the mid-1970s. Even in product categories such as machines, vehicles and equipment, Syrian importers are increasingly switching to suppliers from other parts of the world, in particular China and other south and east Asian countries.

Exports to the EU as a proportion of total Syrian exports decreased from 70 per cent in 2000–1 to less than 45 per cent in 2006. According to preliminary data released by the European Commission, the EU's share of total Syrian exports is now even lower, having fallen below 30 per cent in 2007.[1] In addition, exports to Europe predominantly consist of crude oil. Even in 2006, when the share of oil in total Syrian exports dropped below 45 per cent for the first time in more than a decade and a half, oil still accounted for 85 per cent of exports to the EU. Manufactured exports to Europe remain very small in volume. Even in textiles and clothing, Syria's market share in the EU stands at only 0.15 per cent, an extremely low figure compared with other MPCs like Morocco (3.35 per cent) and Tunisia (3.6 per cent). In other words, Syria has not been able to exploit the duty-free access granted by the 1977 Co-operation Agreement for industrial goods. Low competitiveness and the generally strong anti-export bias of the Syrian economy are the main factors responsible for this poor performance.

In contrast, the access of Syrian agricultural exports to European markets remains severely restricted. In the framework of the Co-operation Agreement, Syria has been granted significantly fewer concessions for agricultural products than most other MPCs. Accordingly, the share of the EU in total Syrian agricultural exports has not exceeded 10 to 13 per cent in recent years. In contrast, MPCs like Morocco and Tunisia are delivering more than half of their agricultural exports to the EU. Moreover, a large proportion of Syrian agricultural exports to the EU is made up of raw cotton. Syrian fruit, vegetables and live animals that enjoy high international competitiveness are primarily sold to other Arab countries.

Economic relations between Syria and the EU are not restricted to trade; the EU and its member states are currently Syria's largest donor.[2]

Nevertheless, as illustrated in Table 8.1, the amounts committed to Syria through the EU's principal financial instrument for implementation of the EMP over the period 1995–2006 were substantially lower than the amounts allocated to other Arab MPCs. Loans offered by the European Investment Bank (EIB) have, however, increased considerably in recent years. EIB loans to Syria were blocked for most of the 1990s and resumed only at the beginning of the current decade, after the Syrian government agreed to clear its accumulated debts with several EU members.

Table 8.1: Commitments in the Framework of MEDA[1] and ENPI[2] (€ million)

	Algeria	Egypt	Jordan	Lebanon	Morocco	Syria	Tunisia	WBG[3]
MEDA I (1995–99)	164	685	257	182	644	107	431	106
MEDA II (2000–6)	339	593	331	133	980	180	518	522
ENPI 2007–10	220	558	265	187	654	130	300	632
EIB Loans 2003–7 (million €)*	255	2,067	216	575	1,221	715	1,380	55
EU Member Countries Bilateral Assistance 2004–2006	709	809	179	153	1,205	204	378	849

1 Mesures d'accompagnement financières et techniques à la réforme des structures économiques et sociales dans le cadre du partenariat euro-méditerranéen.
2 Excluding funds for regional and cross-border programmes
3 West Bank and Gaza
* Finance contracts signed

Source: European Commission (2007b): *ENPI Regional Strategy Paper 2007–2013*; European Commission (2008): *Barcelona Process: Union for the Mediterranean*; European Investment Bank (2008), *Finance Contracts signed in the Mediterranean countries*.

Funds allocated to Syria through the new European Neighbourhood and Partnership Instrument (ENPI) are again significantly lower than those planned for the other MPCs. Although it is not yet a full member of the European Neighbourhood Policy (ENP), Syria is entitled to receive financial and technical assistance extended by the EU to its southern and eastern partners under the ENPI, which replaced the former MEDA programme at the beginning of 2007. According to the 2007–10 National Indicative Programme (NIP) and its recently revised edition for 2008–10, funds worth €130 million will be disbursed to provide technical assistance and policy advice for the support of economic, social and administrative reform. Besides not having signed the AA and therefore not yet being a full member of the ENP, several other factors are usually mentioned by the European Commission to explain the limited amount of assistance that has been offered to Syria. Most important among them is the low absorption capacity of the Syrian economy.[3]

Negotiating Partnership:
Hopes and expectations of a new treaty with the EU

Official negotiations on the Syrian–European AA got under way in Brussels in May 1998. After completing twelve rounds of negotiations, the two delegations agreed in late 2003 on a draft agreement, which was expected to be initialled before the end of the year. However, the process was blocked soon afterwards, because Great Britain, Germany and the Netherlands 'acting on behalf of Washington's agenda' requested a tightening of the clause dealing with WMD.[4] This draft AA was to be the first EU treaty to include such a clause. After a months-long tug-of-war about exact wording, the AA was finally initialled in October 2004, only to be put on hold shortly afterwards. Decisive in the subsequent hardening of the EU's position towards Syria was a further shift in the position of France following the assassination of former Lebanese Prime Minister Rafiq Hariri.[5] France had already been one of the major forces behind the adoption of United Nations Security Council Resolution 1559 in September 2004 which, among other things, called for the withdrawal of Syrian troops from Lebanon. Henceforth 'adequate' co-operation by the Syrian government with the international tribunal to investigate Hariri's murder was added to the list of 'prerequisites' to be fulfilled by Syria if it wished to gain the European Council's approval.

Most observers agree that it was from the beginning a political choice taken by the late Syrian President Hafiz al-Asad to join the Barcelona

Process. In addition to the likely perception on the part of the ruling elite that the 'opportunity costs' of staying out of the EMP would be too high, the EMP was likely viewed both as a mechanism to counter US–Israeli hegemony in the region and as part of the plan for a Middle Eastern Market.[6] However, the bilateral negotiations went on very slowly in the first years. Negotiations on the Syrian–European AA entered a critical stage only after American troops invaded Iraq in the spring of 2003, confronting the Syrian leadership with the threat of being the next target of US attack. Later in 2003, the Syrian Accountability and Lebanese Sovereignty Restoration Act (SALSA) was approved by the US Congress, providing President George W. Bush with the tools necessary to impose diplomatic and economic sanctions on Syria. To avert the risks and to find a strong international partner to support it against ever-increasing pressure from Washington, the Syrian delegation seems to have been pressed by its own leadership to complete negotiations in a very short period of time.[7] Consequently, they accepted provisions that were significantly more stringent than those in EU treaties with the other MPCs.

Beyond purely political motives, Syrian representatives and experts viewed the conclusion of an association agreement with the EU as an opportunity to improve the chances for economic growth and development through the channels of trade, investment and technology transfer. Partnership with the EU might well help the Syrian economy to integrate better with the world economy and serve as a stepping stone to multilateral trade liberalisation. Unlike most of the other MPCs, Syria is not a member of the World Trade Organisation (WTO). In 2001, the Syrian government applied for WTO membership and renewed its application twice in subsequent years, albeit without success. According to a senior WTO spokesman, it will probably take several years for Syria to become a viable candidate for accession, as a consensus must be reached among current WTO members before the negotiation process can be opened.

In the debate over the AA in the Syrian press, and in particular among Syrian economists, two different viewpoints have emerged. One highlighted the potential negative effects and risks of an agreement with the EU and thus preferred a more defensive or prudent approach to the negotiations. Another group interpreted the liberalisation of trade with the EU as a 'strategic choice' in the framework of the general process of economic reform.[8]

Even for the latter group, it is clear that – at least in the short to medium term – the Syrian economy will be confronted with high adjustment costs. However, such short-term losses would be more than compensated for by the longer-term benefits offered by the agreement with the EU, particularly in combination with a domestic programme of economic liberalisation and restructuring. The AA could well enhance efficiency through increased competition in the domestic market, improved market access of Syrian exports to the EU and, most importantly, greater capital investment, especially foreign direct investment (FDI). Syrian economists, intellectuals and political representatives alike expect the EU to increase financial and technical assistance significantly as soon as the agreement is signed.[9]

Finally, many in Syria see this agreement as an appropriate way to push the process of economic reform and liberalisation at home. The process of internal reform at the time the agreement was negotiated faced, and still faces, numerous obstacles, among them widespread popular opposition to economic liberalisation.[10] Since the autumn of 2004, voices warning against the agreement, or at least some of its key provisions, have been growing, asserting that its implementation threatens to destroy whole branches of the Syrian economy, in particular industry.

Structure and Contents of the Syrian–European Association Agreement

In its general structure the draft Syrian–European AA follows the agreements that have been concluded between the EU and the other MPCs. It consists of provisions for each of the three 'baskets' of the European–Mediterranean Partnership as agreed at the Barcelona conference of November 1995. In each of these baskets, and in particular the second basket involving Economic and Financial Partnership, the provisions of the Syrian–European AA are much broader in scope and depth than the provisions included in other AAs.[11]

The provisions of the first basket, or Political and Security Partnership, provide for the conduct of a regular dialogue on issues of mutual interest and for co-operation in different areas. Whereas the agreements with other MPCs only list 'respect for the principles of democracy and human rights', the Syrian–European AA calls for 'co-operation to counter the proliferation of WMD and their means of delivery', as well as for prosecuting the fight against terrorism as 'essential elements' of the treaty. Provisions for the third basket, Partnership in Social, Cultural and Human Affairs, are also quite elaborate, covering co-operation in areas such as culture and social development, justice, migration, the fight against organised crime and efforts to combat terrorism.

The basic element of the Economic and Financial Partnership is the gradual establishment of a free trade area (FTA) between Syria and the EU. The duty-free and quantitative restrictions-free access of Syrian industrial goods to the EU granted under the 1977 Co-operation Agreement is reaffirmed. In addition, and in contrast to the non-reciprocal commitments of the 1977 agreement, Syria must open its own market. For this purpose the Syrian administration will have to eliminate all import and export restrictions, including prohibitions, quotas and licensing requirements, immediately after the treaty comes into force. Customs duties and other surcharges applicable to the majority of industrial goods imports will be reduced to zero in a linear manner according to fixed schedules over a transitional twelve-year period while, on selected goods, such as those covered by the Information Technology Agreement, tariffs are to be abolished immediately.

The exchange of agricultural goods, processed agricultural products and fisheries products between Syria and the EU is to be liberalised in a progressive manner. Measured in terms of the pure number of goods, Syria is granted the largest number of concessions for agricultural goods among all MPCs.[12] However, only a part of these customs duties will be abolished completely and on agricultural products which the Syrian authorities define as 'strategic', annual tariff quotas (TRQs) or preferential duties will be set, in some cases limited to certain calendar periods. In return, Syria is offering the EU far-ranging access to its own agricultural market. Customs duties on the importation of agricultural goods, processed agricultural products and fisheries products will be dismantled to zero in a linear manner within twelve years. Annual tariff quotas at zero duty have been established for the EU's export of several kinds of fresh fruits. Besides quotas, wholesale services in 'strategic products' like wheat, tobacco and cotton will not be opened to foreign competition. Finally, agricultural trade between Syria and the EU will be bound by the principles of the WTO Agreement on the Application of Sanitary and Phytosanitary (SPS) measures.[13] In contrast to other MPCs, Syria has committed itself to the comprehensive reform and modernisation of customs procedures in line with EU and international standards. Furthermore, trade between the parties will be bound by the rules of the WTO Agreement on Technical Barriers to Trade. The use of EU standards and technical regulations in Syria will be encouraged with an aim to conclude agreements on conformity assessment.

With respect to investment and the liberalisation of services, Syria grants European investors national or most favoured nation (MFN) treatment. Aside from the EU treaty with Jordan, rights of establishment are mentioned only as a future goal in the other AAs. Excluded from the general right of establishment is the production of goods and services that had been reserved as state monopolies at the time the AA was negotiated. In other sectors, at least 25 per cent Syrian ownership is required.[14] In addition, the parties undertake to allow all payments for current transactions to be made in convertible currency and to ensure the free movement of capital, as well as free liquidation and repatriation of capital and profits. As regards competition rules, Syria has committed itself to taking into consideration EU rules when formulating its own laws. Moreover, and in contrast to the agreements concluded with the other MPCs, the parties will co-operate to enforce competition rules.

As far as government procurement is concerned, and again contrary to the other MPCs, the parties agreed to open procurement activities and to grant national treatment to the other party's goods, services and suppliers for a list of entities annexed to the agreement. With respect to intellectual, industrial and commercial property rights, the partners committed themselves to granting and ensuring their protection in accordance with the highest international standards, including the principles set by the WTO Agreement on Trade-Related Aspects of Intellectual Property Rights (TRIPS). For this purpose, Syria agreed to accede to a number of multilateral conventions. Finally, a detailed dispute-settlement mechanism is one of the features in which the Syrian–European AA goes beyond the rules stipulated in the agreements that have been concluded with the other MPCs.

Potential Benefits and Risks of the Syrian–European Association Agreement

Economic theory on trade and integration lists among the so-called static, that is, once-and-for-all, effects of a free trade area (FTA) or customs union (CU) the dynamics of trade creation, trade diversion and tariff revenue losses. Trade is 'created' whenever domestic production in one country is replaced by lower-cost imports from another, thereby increasing welfare by decreasing production costs, setting resources free for more efficient allocation and benefiting consumers with lower prices. The resources that are set free could possibly be reallocated to more competitive sectors. The problem is, however, that the chances for a reallocation of resources might not be readily available in a country like Syria. Such a process will take time and will depend crucially on the agreement's contributions in order to improve access to the EU market.

Applied to the case of the Syrian–European AA, this means that imports from the EU can be expected to rise with the implementation of free trade, putting pressure on the current account, diminishing government revenues and forcing domestic producers and other foreign suppliers out of the market. EU exports will expand specifically in those branches where production is still protected by high tariff and non-tariff barriers and where the Syrian economy does not enjoy a comparative advantage. In other words, many of Syria's import-substituting and capital-intensive public sector industries may come under strong pressure. The same may also be true of agricultural goods and among them in particular temperate-zone products, where production has been protected by a wall of quotas, tariffs and other regulations. The closure of a large number of Syrian enterprises in industry, agriculture and services will inevitably create high income and employment losses in the short to medium term.

Besides the potential loss of domestic production resulting from European imports, there is also a substantial risk of trade diversion. As a result of high tariffs remaining in place for other countries, Syrian importers would likely switch from more cost-efficient suppliers (such as China) to less cost-efficient European suppliers, thereby forgoing tariff revenues. The risk will probably apply in particular to goods for final consumption that are currently imported from other parts of the world. Syrian importers of machines and equipment in recent years have increasingly replaced European goods with ones from other regions of the world.

Finally, dismantling customs duties in trade with the EU will lead to losses of tariff revenues. The losses should be manageable, at least at first sight, since tax revenues from international trade are relatively low, amounting to around 7–9 per cent of budget revenues in recent years. In addition, there are several alternatives at hand to develop the domestic tax base, including the long-awaited introduction of a value added tax (VAT). More problematic is the general state of the government's budget, with a rising deficit despite steady cutbacks in investment expenditures as a result of declining oil exports and rising costs of government subsidies.

Losses of tariff revenue could be mitigated by the implementation of trade facilitation measures anchored in the Syrian–European AA, such as the simplification of customs procedures or the harmonisation of standards. Measures of this kind could lead to a reduction of transaction costs, not only in trade with the EU but also in trade with third countries. This could induce additional trade flows and thus enhance tariff revenues, besides saving costs in the public administration of foreign trade. Furthermore, the potential longer-term or dynamic effects of trade liberalisation with the EU might lead to intensified competition on the domestic market and help to break up monopolistic market structures, forcing Syrian firms to improve efficiency. In addition to the elimination of barriers in trade and investment, intensified competition should also result from the AA's call for the introduction of competition rules in line with the rules that prevail in the EU.[15]

Improving market access of Syrian exports to the EU, in other words trade-facilitating measures, seem to be the main benefit that the AA offers Syrian manufacturers. Better access to the EU should play a major role in encouraging Syrian manufacturers to switch from import-substituting to export-oriented production in the framework of an outward-oriented strategy of development. For agricultural products, the AA provides for an improvement in market access as well. Syrian experts and representatives hope that the extension of agricultural concessions will promote agricultural exports to the EU and thus heighten production and employment and attract foreign investment. In addition, increasing agricultural exports could help to contain a rising deficit in the trade and current account balances expected to result from trade liberalisation. To make effective use of the new concessions, however, Syrian farmers must work hard to fulfil other conditions required for successful access to the European markets: on-time delivery, rigorous standards and consistent quality.

Future market access of Syrian exports to the EU might be seriously constrained as a result of other aspects in the AA, among them the provision that both parties are allowed to resort to anti-dumping safeguards and countervailing measures. In addition, complex and restrictive rules of origin could seriously diminish the benefits of duty-free access for Syrian exports to the EU and indirectly also Syria's ability to attract FDI. Finally, trade facilitation and liberalisation of trade-related services will not only take time to materialise, they will also require additional funds and expertise which seem to be lacking in Syria, at least at the moment.

The improvement of market-access conditions or market enlargement plays a crucial role in stimulating investment. Investments are badly needed to restructure the Syrian economy and set up a competitive exports industry. Market-access related provisions in the AA provide only few incentives for market enlargement, at least in the short to medium term. However, the AA could contribute to improving conditions for greater FDI to Syria via cheaper imported inputs as a result of trade liberalisation with the EU. Moreover, the AA includes important measures for improving Syrian FDI policy, such as guaranteeing the unrestricted movement and repatriation of capital and profits. Granting rights of establishment to European companies may help to reduce uncertainties on the part of future investors. However, trade liberalisation with the EU risks the establishment of a so-called 'hub-and-spokes' pattern of investment, whereby future FDI will be attracted to the hub (the EU) at the expense of the Syrian spoke. The risk of this can be mitigated by free trade and deeper integration among the spokes. For this reason, it is vital for Syria to set up FTAs with the other MPCs. By doing so Syria can improve its ability to attract FDI and perhaps become a regional hub reaching out to neighbouring and Gulf countries. Syria should also accede to the Agadir Agreement and conclude FTAs with the other partners of the Pan-Euro-Med system.[16]

In the end, policies regarding trade and FDI are only two among many so-called 'host-country determinants' that influence the decisions of potential investors. The Syrian–European AA might offer another important benefit: its effect on locking-in reform and enhancing credibility. Credibility of reform is vital for investment, because without it investors are likely to stay away. Despite several shortcomings, the AA should be able to deliver an appropriate mechanism for signalling commitment and improving the credibility of the Syrian government. The detailed provisions of the AA send clear signals about the regime's motives and provide a credible means to increase the costs of 'bad policies'. Nevertheless, the agreement offers the possibility of anchoring the unilateral measures to deregulate foreign trade that have been enacted in recent years. On the other hand, the AA lacks provisions for improved market access and aid as 'rewards for good policy', which are important in order for a commitment mechanism to be able to alter future incentives.

What do the Syrians need to do and what does the EU have to offer in order to increase the benefits and lessen the costs of this agreement to the Syrian economy? It is crucial that the reform measures directly catalysed by the agreement be complemented with a wide range of other reforms and policy measures that cover macroeconomic management and structural adjustment in fields other than trade. In addition, to minimise the negative effects on production, income and employment, the Syrian administration could take steps to help local firms prepare themselves for EU competition.[17] Moreover, the Syrian administration could take steps to cope with income and employment losses through the establishment of social safety nets for affected income groups. The EU could contribute by expanding assistance to Syria. Programmes covered by the new NIP 2007–10 include a Trade Enhancement Programme, an Industrial Upgrading and Restructuring Programme focused on State-owned enterprises (SOEs) and a Social Protection Programme. These new programmes concentrate primarily on technical assistance and capacity-building, and should be accompanied by a significant expansion of financial assistance. By delivering more aid, the EU could support the Syrian administration in maintaining social protection systems, implementing measures of trade facilitation and improving conditions to attract FDI.

Future Outlook

Summing up the potential effects of the Syrian–European Association Agreement in the form that it was initialled in October 2004, one cannot but ask if it is worth the price for Syria to sign this document. From a purely economic point of view, the answer is clearly yes. The Syrian government and economy should accept this challenge. The Syrian economy is in urgent need of new resources to promote growth and development. The hope is that the AA, despite its many loopholes, risks and possible negative effects, will encourage policy-makers in Damascus to continue on the road to reform. And if the EU is serious about establishing a 'common space of shared prosperity around the Mediterranean Sea', it should be prepared to expand financial and technical assistance and to improve market access for Syria by implementing measures to expand financial and technical assistance, and improve market access for Syria by reducing barriers to imports of Syrian agricultural products and simplifying complicated rules of origin.

Notes

1. European Commission, *EU Bilateral Trade with the World 2008* <http://trade.ec.europa.eu/doclib/docs/2006/September/tradoc_113451.pdf>. European Commission (2008): *Barcelona Process: Union for the Mediterranean,* Communication from the Commission to the European and Council, COM (2008) 319 (Final), 20/05/2008. In general, sources for trade data such as the United Nations Comtrade database, IMF Direction of Trade Statistics database, data provided by EUROSTAT or the Syrian Central Bureau of Statistics (CBS) *Foreign Trade Statistics* differ greatly.
2. According to data from the Organisation for Economic Co-operation and Development (OECD)/Development Co-operation Directorate-Development Assistance Committee (DCD-DAC) , this is especially the case with regard to actually disbursed assistance in form of non-repayable grants.
3. European Commission, *European Neighbourhood and Partnership Instrument (ENPI): Regional Strategy Paper 2007–2013 and Regional Indicative Programme (2007–2010) for Euro-Mediterranean Partnership* <http://ec.europa.eu/world/enp/pdf/country/enpi_euromed_rsp_en.pdf>
4. Raymond Hinnebusch, 'Defying the Hegemon: Syria and the Iraq War', unpublished paper, 2005.
5. Jorg Michael Dostal, 'The European Union and Economic Reform in Syria', unpublished paper, 2008.
6. 'Abed Fadliya, 'The Near East and the Middle Eastern Market', in *Call for Middle Eastern Market and Its Economic Effects,* Damascus 1997 (Arabic); Raslan Khadur, 'The Economic Dimension of the Middle Eastern System', *Ma'lumat Duwwaliyyah,* nos. 27–8, 1995, pp. 31–6 (Arabic).

7. Samir Aita, 'The Political Economy of the Banking Sector in Syria', unpublished paper, 2008.

8. Aiman 'Abd al-Nur, *Syrian Views of an Association Agreement with the European Union*, EuroMeSCo Paper no. 14, Lisbon 2001.

9. Mtanious Habib, 'The Syrian Economy and the Conditions of the Euro-Mediterranean Partnership', unpublished paper, 2000 (Arabic); Nabil Sukkar, 'Economic Reforms and the Euro-Mediterranean Partnership', unpublished paper, 2000 (Arabic).

10. See Anja Zorob, 'The Syrian–European Association Agreement and its Potential Impact on Enhancing the Credibility of Reform', *Mediterranean Politics*, vol. 13, no. 1, 2008, pp. 1–21.

11. The following account is based on the text of the draft Syrian–European Association Agreement as published on the European Commission's official website.

12. Agricultural concessions granted to most of the other MPCs have been renegotiated and extended in the meantime. Lebanon was granted duty-free access for all of its agricultural exports except a list of goods for which quotas have been set.

13. See Anja Zorob, *Syrien im Spannungsfeld zwischen der Euro-Mediterranen Partnerschaft und der Grossen Arabischen Freihandelszone*, Saarbruecken 2006.

14. Ibid.; Samir Saifan, 'The Services Sector in the Syrian–European Association Agreement', unpublished paper, 2005.

15. In the spring of 2008, a competition law was issued after long years of being drafted. Syrian and foreign experts do not expect the law to be implemented in the near future.

16. See Anja Zorob, 'Intraregional Economic Integration: The Cases of GAFTA and MAFTA', in Cilja Harders and Matteo Legrenzi, eds. *Beyond Regionalism?*, Aldershot 2008, pp. 169–83.

17. In February 2007, a pilot programme called Industrial Modernisation and Upgrading Programme for the Syrian Arab Republic, sponsored by the United Nations Industrial Development Organisation and the Italian government, started to be implemented. It does not appear to be directly connected to the AA.

NINE

Demystifying Syrian Foreign Policy under Bashar al-Asad

Bassel F. Salloukh

Almost two decades ago Itamar Rabinovich noted that Syrian policy in Lebanon can be seen 'as a reflection of the regime's priorities and capabilities and as an instrument calculated to accomplish additional, far more ambitious, purposes'.[1] Syria's regional influence under Hafiz al-Asad was to a large measure due to Damascus's success in subduing Lebanon and deploying it in the service of Syria's geopolitical objectives, but especially the president's perennial quest to demonstrate to both Washington and Tel Aviv Syria's indispensability to any viable peace process.[2] The made-in-Lebanon Syrian regional 'empire'[3] also served to bolster the stability of the regime in Damascus. After all, both Hafiz and later Bashar al-Asad assumed that there is a causal connection between the weight of Syria's role in its immediate environment and the stability of the Ba'thi regime.[4] In this respect, Lebanon has served as both a tool to advance Syrian regional policy and an advance buffer against threats to regime stability.

Although the mantle of the presidency has shifted from father to son and the country's geopolitical environment has changed dramatically following the attacks of September 2001 and the United States' invasion and occupation of Iraq, Syria's Lebanon policy remains a valid prism through which to view its geopolitical objectives. The withdrawal of Syrian troops from Lebanon on 25 April 2005 paradoxically heightened Lebanon's utility to Syrian interests. Henceforth, the battle over post-Syria Lebanon is likely to determine the outcome of Syria's regional and international foreign policy contests.

Comparing Alternative Explanations

Studies of Syrian foreign policy under Bashar al-Asad posit a number of explanatory variables. Balance-of-power explanations underscore the geopolitical origins of the Syrian regime's alignment and foreign policy choices.[5] According to this view, state behaviour under Bashar is shaped by a set of external threats to Syria's security, especially US hegemony in the Middle East after the fall of Baghdad in April 2003 and the persistent Israeli menace. Syria's regional and international alignments, namely the rapprochements with Turkey, Jordan, Egypt and Iraq after 2000, along with the opening up to Europe until 2005, served to balance against these strategic threats. Similarly, the Syrian regime's quest to diversify its international linkages represented an attempt to mobilise non-Western coalitions counterbalance efforts by Washington and Paris to isolate Syria after the assassination of former Lebanese Prime Minister Rafiq Hariri on 14 February 2005.[6] Another variant of this type of systemic explanation locates Syria's foreign policy choices in the dynamics of its long-standing alliance game with Iran.[7]

Domestic-level arguments highlight sectarian, political economy, regime legitimacy and regime security variables. Sectarian arguments emphasise the 'Alawi identity of the regime, especially vis-à-vis Iran and Hizbullah. Proponents of this view contend that Syria's foreign policy under Bashar is driven by Shiʻi *politik*, the quest to assemble a 'Shiʻi crescent' gathering Damascus, Tehran and Hizbullah, to pursue their respective leaderships' sectarian interests.[8] Yet this argument neither explains Syria's alignment with the Sunni Palestinian movement HAMAS, nor does it account for the incompatible interests and policies implemented by Syria, Iran and Hizbullah in the wake of the occupation of Iraq and with regard to the peace process with Israel.[9]

Political economy explanations for Syria's foreign policy choices are often appended to realist arguments.[10] They connect state behaviour to attempts to diversify Syria's economic relations or to ameliorate the economy's structural crisis and offset demands for deeper economic liberalisation.[11] The 'opening to the East' – as Syrian officials label the policy of cultivating denser economic relations with China and India – makes available to the regime new technology and credit markets that are free of Western economic and political conditionality. Conversely, regime legitimacy explanations link what is presumed to be a rejection- ist, Arab nationalist ideology vis-à-vis Israel to the regime's quest for domestic legitimation in light of its minority sectarian social base.[12] Such ideological explanations fail the empirical test, however. Studies of Syria's positions regarding peace negotiations with Israel, both under Hafiz and Bashar, suggest that failure should be blamed on Israeli, rather than Syrian, inflexibility.[13] Moreover, the steady opening towards Iraq under Bashar was governed by balance-of-power and political economic considerations, not ideological ones.[14] Finally, and based on a critique of realism's preoccupation with external threats to state security,[15] the regime security perspective explains foreign policy choices in terms of the regime's evaluation of the impact that overlapping domestic and external threats might have on its survival.[16] Such arguments are implicit in a number of studies of Syrian state behaviour under Bashar, but they generally lack theoretical articulation.[17]

Perhaps the most popular explanation for Bashar's foreign policy choices, especially in Western and Arab policy and media circles, is the idiosyncratic variant that underscores the new Syrian leader's inexperience in foreign affairs and his consequent string of miscalculations, which incurred regional and international isolation and brought the Ba'thi regime to the brink of collapse.[18] Comparing Bashar's strategic and diplomatic skills to those of Hafiz, Dennis Ross argues that the former 'seems to have none of his father's guile and appears to have an extraordinary capacity for miscalculation'.[19] Similarly, Eyal Zisser blames the Syrian regime's domestic and international troubles in the wake of the US invasion of Iraq on 'Syria's own mistakes, rooted in the misreading and misinterpretation of the regional and inter- national, especially American, political scenes', as well as on Bashar's 'failure ... to step into his father's shoes and establish himself as a respected and authoritative leader both at home and abroad'.[20] Bashar's hostile opposi- tion to the US invasion of Iraq in his 27 March 2003 interview with the

Lebanese daily *al-Safir*, Syria's subsequent role in sabotaging the occupation of Iraq by funnelling fighters and military supplies across its borders, the failure to deliver on promises made to US Secretary of State Colin Powell in May 2003, the renewal of Emile Lahoud's presidential tenure in Lebanon in September 2004 and the ensuing confrontation with the US, France and the United Nations Security Council over United Nations Security Council Resolution 1559, which culminated in Hariri's assassination, are all presented as examples of the Syrian regime's gross miscalculations.

The miscalculations thesis is based on the neo-conservative assumption that states tend to bandwagon rather than balance when they face superior and highly mobile military forces like the ones made possible by the American army's Revolution in Military Affairs (RMA).[21] Regime-change advocates, whether in Washington or the Middle East, assumed that the overthrow of Saddam Hussein would frighten other so-called 'rogue states' into submission to American power. They foresaw a 'cascade of democratic dominos', or at least the spread of liberal democratic institutions, throughout the Middle East following the fall of Saddam's regime. This, it was expected, would end the menace of terrorism, alter the regional balance of power in favour of the US and Israel and secure American interests in a transformed Middle East.[22] Syria was expected to jump on the US bandwagon in a reconfigured regional order, assisting in, rather than resisting, the making of the prospective post-Saddam *pax Americana*.

As balancing theory predicts, however, threatened states rarely lend support in such a way, either because this makes the threatening state even stronger, or because conflicts of interest between the two states are often irreconcilable.[23] Rather, realists believe that states operate according to balancing logic and threatened states will pursue a range of different strategies in the face of resistance and opposition, including balancing, balking, binding, blackmail and delegitimation.[24] Faced with the prospect of US hegemony in the Middle East, and the threat this poses to Syria's geopolitical interests and regime security, Damascus has responded with a mix of classic balancing, asymmetric balancing and balking. Iraq and Lebanon emerged as the two principal arenas in which this balancing behaviour has been played out. The remainder of this chapter recreates the Syrian regime's security environment after the fall of Baghdad and the assassination of Hariri to offer an alternative explanation of its foreign policy choices, one based on balancing and regime security calculations rather than on Bashar al-Asad's presumed miscalculations.[25]

'*This is Not a Storm*'

The fall of Baghdad represented a dramatic event for the Syrian regime. In his 27 March 2003 interview with *al-Safir*, Bashar exaggerated Iraq's ability to withstand the US invasion. 'The United States and Britain will not be able to control all of Iraq,' he declared. 'There is now a very strong resistance by the army and the people in Iraq,' he continued, one that would dwarf the resistance that Israel encountered in Lebanon and the occupied Palestinian territories.[26] According to his interviewer, Bashar expected Saddam's regime to survive for six months and that the Iraqi army would inflict heavy casualties upon the invading troops.[27] This explains the unexpected silence with which Damascus received news of the fall of the Ba'thi regime in Baghdad. Yet after a short hiatus, Syria began balancing against the US occupation of Iraq.

Damascus interprets the invasion and occupation of Iraq as a direct threat to Syria's geopolitical interests and consequently to regime security. 'This is not a storm,' al-Asad contended in the aforementioned interview, 'for a storm passes,' and one can evade a storm by hiding. Rather, the invasion of Iraq is a US–Israeli 'plan', one that 'you cannot bow to'; it seeks to 'reorganise the region,' starting in Baghdad, in a manner that protects US and Israeli strategic interests. Whether the plan is to divide the region into sectarian states – the Israeli option, according to Bashar – or other types of grouping congenial to US interests, Damascus has interpreted the invasion and occupation of Iraq as a severe challenge. A stable, pro-American government in Iraq would tighten the chain of pro-Western states around Syria, leaving Damascus breathing space only in Lebanon. Alternatively, Iraq's vivisection along sectarian and ethnic lines would expose Syria's own Sunni–'Alawi cleavages and encourage its Kurdish community to demand greater political and socio-economic privileges. This would undercut the unity of the Syrian population and consequently the stability of the regime.[28] Moreover, the spectacular and sudden collapse of the Iraqi regime made Damascus fearful that a trigger-happy Bush administration might move against Syria.[29] After all, the post-September 2001 regime-change rhetoric emanating from Washington identified Syria as a priority target in the so-called 'war on terrorism'.[30] The fall of Baghdad left many capitals and commentators in the Arab world wondering who would be next, and in Damascus the genuine anxiety of the regime was palpable, not without cause.[31]

After the fall of Baghdad, neo-conservative hawks in the Bush administration gave voice to their desire to see 'regime change' occur in Damascus, a campaign culminating with Deputy Secretary of Defense Paul Wolfowitz's declaration that 'There will have to be change in Syria'[32] and a Pentagon memo to the White House entitled 'Roadmap for Syria', which outlined punitive options against a recalcitrant Syria.[33] Congress reintroduced the Syria Accountability and Lebanese Sovereignty Restoration Act on 12 April 2003, which empowered the US president to take punitive economic and diplomatic actions against Syria to 'halt Syrian support for terrorism, end its occupation of Lebanon, and stop its development of weapons of mass destruction'.[34] On 3 May 2003, Secretary of State Colin Powell visited Damascus and presented Bashar with a long list of demands with which Washington expected him to comply forthwith. The US demanded full co-operation from Damascus in the 'war on terrorism' and in Iraq – and hence strict monitoring of the Syrian–Iraqi border, a clampdown on money laundering, the repatriation of Iraqi funds from Syrian banks, an end to support for HAMAS and Islamic Jihad and the closure of their offices in Damascus and verification of Syria's arsenal of weapons of mass destruction (WMD). Powell's demands with regard to Lebanon included the withdrawal of all Syrian troops, an end to Syrian interference, the demobilisation and disarmament of Hizbullah and the dismantling of its rocket batteries in southern Lebanon, and the deployment of the Lebanese Army over all Lebanese territory, including the border with Israel.[35]

The Syrian regime responded with an offer to reach an understanding with Washington on a number of common interests. Brigadier General Bahjat Sulaiman's astonishing article in *al-Safir* best represents this line of thinking. Sulaiman, then chief of the General Intelligence Directorate's (GID) internal branch and a powerful figure inside the security establishment, suggested obliquely that Syria would help control Hizbullah, Palestinian armed groups and *jihadi* Salafis in Lebanon, would address the issue of Palestinian offices in Damascus and would contribute to the stabilisation of Iraq in exchange for US guarantees regarding the security of the regime and Syria's reintegration into the peace process. Sulaiman's article was not without threats, however. Failing to reach a deal and insisting instead on targeting regime stability or Syrian control over Lebanon, the article suggested, could unleash against Israel and US regional interests a number of Islamist groups that had hitherto been checked by Syrian intelligence networks, namely Hizbullah, HAMAS and Islamic Jihad.[36]

By the summer of 2003, Syria concluded that Washington was unwilling to bargain with Damascus over Powell's conditions; it instead expected unconditional compliance.[37] This meant that the US was determined to emasculate Syria regionally, and consequently undermine, if not change, the regime. After all, Damascus assumed that compliance with Powell's conditions, especially against what the US administration considered terrorism in Iraq and Lebanon, would change Syria's regional role and alliances substantially, threatening the stability of the regime.[38] Maurice Gourdault-Montagne, French President Jacques Chirac's presidential adviser, paid Damascus a secret visit in November 2003, carrying a message from the leaders of France, Germany and Russia. The emissary advised Bashar to accommodate the new US-dominated regional environment. The Syrian president remained obstinate, however.[39] In the Syrian regime's geopolitical calculations, bandwagoning is not an option; it would threaten rather than protect regime survival. Consequently, Syrian–American confrontation in Iraq escalated.

Bashar calculated that protecting the regime entailed sabotaging the US occupation of Iraq and turning the country into another Vietnam.[40] The substantial Syrian intelligence co-operation with the Central Intelligence Agency against al-Qa'ida cells in Europe and the Middle East, aimed at mending relations between the two states and paving the way for co-operation on regional issues, was suspended after the fall of Baghdad.[41] Syrian intelligence agencies' expertise in penetrating radical Islamist cells in the suburbs of European capitals was then retooled and placed at the service of the asymmetric campaign against US troops in Iraq.[42] On this interpretation, funnelling foreign fighters and weapons across the Syrian–Iraqi border was neither a miscalculation nor a puzzling choice. Rather, it constituted Syria's response to the combined threats posed by the US-led occupation of Iraq. Not unlike other Arab regimes that feared the regional consequences of a democratic, stable, pro-Western regime in Baghdad, Damascus sabotaged the occupation with a mix of classical and asymmetric balancing in order to protect its regional interests and regime security. Lebanon would soon become a second front in the battle to protect the Syrian regime.

'A War by Stages'

Syria's almost total control over Lebanon since 1990 not only advanced the regime's regional interests, especially vis-à-vis the peace process, but also provided a secure source of much-needed rents to finance the regime's neo-patrimonial networks and offset pressure for economic reform. The invasion and occupation of Iraq heightened Lebanon's value to Syria. By the end of 2003, however, Damascus's hold over Lebanon was no longer secure.[43] Troubles in Lebanon climaxed as Lahoud's tenure as president came to an end. A growing chorus of heavyweight Lebanese politicians, including the Druze leader Walid Jumblatt and Rafiq Hariri, opposed the renewal of Lahoud's term. On 1 September 2004 the Maronite Church weighed in, publicly opposing a renewal of Lahoud's tenure. Even Syrian Vice President 'Abd al-Halim Khaddam advised Bashar against renewing Lahoud's presidency, urging him to select one of Syria's other Maronite allies to avoid international retribution.[44]

On 2 September, Security Council Resolution 1559 was promulgated. It declared support 'for a free and fair electoral process in Lebanon's upcoming presidential election, conducted according to Lebanese constitutional rules and devised without foreign interference or influence'. The resolution also called on 'all remaining foreign forces to withdraw from Lebanon' and mandated the 'disbanding and disarmament of all Lebanese and non-Lebanese militias' in the country.[45] Snubbing the international community, Damascus instructed its Lebanese allies to pass a constitutional amendment that renewed Lahoud's tenure for another three years. Hariri, who had earlier vowed not to renew Lahoud's term, was strong-armed by Damascus into supporting the decision.[46] The constitutional amendment was passed in parliament on 3 September 2004.

Was this another example of Bashar's miscalculations? Or was the decision governed by balancing and regime-security considerations? A reconstruction of Syria's security environment and decision-making calculus on the eve of Resolution 1559's promulgation offers an answer.

As late as August 2004, Bashar stood against renewing Lahoud's term.[47] Khaddam claims that on 18 August he was reassured by Bashar that Lahoud's tenure would not be extended.[48] In fact, the regime sent signals to pro-Syrian Maronite politician Jean Obeid, then minister of foreign and expatriate affairs, that he had been selected to succeed Lahoud.[49] Only when the regime in Damascus became convinced, in late August, that Resolution 1559 was going to be promulgated did Bashar decide to renew Lahoud's tenure.[50] Unlike the Syrian Accountability Act, which was considered more a nuisance than a threat,[51] 1559 ended the post-Iraq guessing game in Arab capitals: Damascus concluded that the US and the European Union, the latter represented by Chirac's France, had set their sights on the Syrian regime.[52] Resolution 1559 signified a US–French convergence directed against Syria, which was reached on 6 June 2004, on the occasion of the sixtieth anniversary of the Allied landings at Normandy.[53] It signalled to Damascus the beginning of a concerted international effort to evict Syria from Lebanon, thereby threatening its regional position and consequently the survival of the regime. Lebanon would now be used as a beachhead against Syria to undermine the latter's geopolitical interests, namely, its control over Lebanon, influence with Hizbullah, alliance with Iran and spoiler role in the peace process through HAMAS and Islamic Jihad. A beleaguered Syria would then be forced to accept the US-dominated regional order, offer assistance to the US occupation in Iraq and end its obstructionist role in the peace process.

The timing of Resolution 1559 coincided with the emergence of what from Damascus looked to be a perilous alliance among Syria's adversaries in Lebanon, one that included for the first time the Maronite Church, represented by Patriarch Mar Nasrallah Butrus Sfeir, the Druze of Jumblatt and, albeit behind the scenes, Hariri.[54] Bashar and his principal lieutenants in Lebanon were already suspicious of Hariri's growing threat to Syria's position in Lebanon. From their perspective, he had consolidated the Sunni community in Lebanon behind his leadership in the 2000 parliamentary elections and had, moreover, made suspicious inroads into the Syrian regime's inner circle, co-opting high-ranking Sunni insiders such as Khaddam and long-serving Chief of Staff General Hikmat al-Shihabi and befriending Syria's intelligence prefect in Lebanon until October 2002, Major General Ghazi Kan'an.[55] Damascus suspected that Hariri was involved in the making of 1559 because of his personal connection with Chirac and because the resolution was tailor-made to address his demands, as well as those of Washington and Paris. Hariri wanted free presidential elections to ensure the election of anyone but Lahoud; Paris wanted the withdrawal of Syrian troops from Lebanon; and Washington wanted Hizbullah's disarmament and demobilisation.[56]

Bashar described Resolution 1559 as another 'stage' in an ongoing 'war by stages' against Syria's regional role, one that predated the invasion of Iraq.[57] Its aim was not to protect Lebanon's sovereignty, he argued; it was rather a tool used by the US and France to shift Lebanon from one geopolitical camp to another and compel Syria to disarm Hizbullah in exchange for a staged Syrian withdrawal from Lebanon.[58] After all, the international community had led the Syrian regime to believe that a partial withdrawal would have been acceptable.[59] From this perspective, renewing Lahoud's term was part of a strategy to ensure the regime's survival at a moment of great regional transformation, and to do so from Damascus's first line of defence: Lebanon.[60] Lahoud's pro-Syrian loyalties were unquestionable and Damascus reasoned that only he could maintain the pro-Syria orientation of the Lebanese army in the event of a Syrian withdrawal.[61] Khaddam suggests that Bashar's advisers and Lebanese allies persuaded him that only a trusted military commander of Lahoud's calibre could block future investigations of the Syrian regime's activities over the preceding fifteen years.[62] The renewal of Lahoud's term was followed by the formation on 26 October 2004 of a thoroughly pro-Syrian cabinet under the premiership of the trusted 'Umar Karami. This 'made in Syria' cabinet, as it was called by US Deputy Secretary of State Richard Armitage,[63] was tasked with preparing for a full-blown confrontation with the international community. It did not have long to wait.

Surviving the Regime's Darkest Hours

The regime in Damascus experienced its darkest hours in the aftermath of Rafiq Hariri's assassination. Some of its members were convinced that it was indeed passing through its dying days.[64] The popular mood in Damascus was of a regime that had committed a deadly mistake and was on its way out.[65] A chorus of voices predicted imminent collapse, given its inability to withstand international and regional retribution.[66] Two versions have been advanced to explain the motives behind Hariri's assassination. One view, propounded by the 14 March Alliance in Lebanon and adopted by its regional and international allies, suggests that Damascus eliminated Hariri because of the threat he posed not only to its position in Lebanon but also to the security of the Syrian regime.[67] The assassination was meant to neutralise an overlapping external and domestic threat to regime security: he was organising a powerful cross-sectarian Lebanese alliance, including Hizbullah, which aimed at extricating Lebanon from Syria's grip.[68] Advocates of this view note that the Syrian regime's campaign to eliminate and terrorise its rivals in Lebanon commenced only after the promulgation of Resolution 1559.[69] This underscores how serious a threat to regime survival Damascus considered 1559 to be. The withdrawal from Lebanon following Hariri's assassination and the domestic consolidation at home, by eliminating potential alternatives to the regime, in particular Kan'an,[70] and carrying out a clampdown against dissidents, underlined the regime's determination to eradicate real or potential threats. Any miscalculation involved the regime's failure to organise its withdrawal from Lebanon immediately after the fall of Baghdad.[71] Otherwise, its foreign policy choice adheres to balancing and regime-security predictions.

An alternative explanation advanced by many of Syria's Lebanese allies suggests that Bashar was preparing to redeploy some 14,000 Syrian troops out of Beirut and its environs to the Biqa' Valley shortly after the renewal of Lahoud's term. Redeployment – the preferred euphemism for withdrawal used by the Syrian regime – had been broached by Bashar as early as 2001 and was communicated to a number of Lebanese politicians. Syria had also received guarantees that a partial withdrawal in compliance with Resolution 1559 would be received favourably by the international community.[72] On this view, the decision to withdraw fully, rather than partially, from Lebanon was a response to Hariri's assassination. The consequent domestic consolidation was meant to insulate the regime from threats emanating from Lebanon, and also from challenges arising from inside the party (Khaddam), the army (al-Shihabi) and the security apparatus (Kan'an).[73]

Be that as it may, Syria's troop withdrawal opened a new phase in its relations with Lebanon. In addition to Iraq, the West Bank and the Gaza Strip, Lebanon was now a principal arena in a grand geopolitical battle that pitted the US, France and the so-called 'moderate' Arab states led by Saudi Arabia against Syria, Iran, Hizbullah, HAMAS and Islamic Jihad. In much the same way that Washington was bent on using Lebanon to isolate the Syrian regime, Damascus was determined to use Lebanon to abort the new regional order and choreograph its reintegration into the regional and international arena. It did so by spoiling any political settlement in Lebanon that jeopardised its own interests. Damascus thus deployed a mix of asymmetric balancing strategy and balking in the struggle over Lebanon.

Syria outsourced its Lebanon policy to allied local actors, principally Hizbullah. The alliance between Hizbullah and Nabih Birri's AMAL was engineered by Damascus to guarantee political cover as Hizbullah waged Syria's political battles in Lebanon.[74] Hizbullah consequently spearheaded the effort to block Lebanon's transformation into a pawn serving Washington and the 'moderate' Arab states in the confrontation with Syria and Iran. The signing of the Memorandum of Understanding with Michel 'Awn's Free Patriotic Movement on 6 February 2006 created a balance with the 14 March Alliance. It insisted on the depoliticisation of the international investigation into Hariri's assassination, demanded a veto over domestic and foreign policy decisions in a national unity government and marked a refusal to supply the parliamentary quorum necessary for any presidential candidate who might be insensitive to Syria's interests.[75]

Damascus was especially apprehensive of Lebanon's role as a beachhead to destabilise the regime. US demands for a change in the Syrian government's policies were taken as camouflage for more sinister intentions.[76] Syria's exit from Lebanon had emboldened its rivals to seek regime change more forcefully.[77] Damascus accused Riyad of engineering contacts between Jumblatt (who was now calling openly for regime change in Syria),[78] Khaddam and the Muslim Brothers; it also accused Saudi Arabia of supporting Rif'at al-Asad's anti-regime campaign inside and outside the country, of financing Islamist groups inside Syria, of instigating anti-regime sentiments in the armed forces and of inviting foreign intervention against Syria.[79] The clampdown on Syrian dissidents in March 2006, and then again following the publication of the 12 May 2006 Beirut–Damascus manifesto, signalled the regime's intolerance to domestic dissent, and its apprehensions lest the Syrian opposition succeed in building bridges with anti-Syrian forces in Lebanon.[80] Dormant anti-Lebanese sentiments, animated by a slanderous anti-regime campaign and an anti-Syrian discourse by leaders of the 14 March Alliance that bordered on racism, enabled the regime to rally substantial sectors of the population and evade sectarian suspicions created by Hariri's assassination.[81]

Syria's policy in Lebanon collided with a US–Saudi decision to deny its Lebanese allies a political victory. Damascus considered Riyad's acquiescence in the July 2006 Israeli war against Hizbullah, and its refusal to offer overflight rights to Iranian supply planes, to be part of a co-ordinated effort to defeat Hizbullah and subsequently encircle Syria with hostile regimes.[82] Riyad also rallied substantial sectors of the Sunni political and religious establishment in Lebanon in an attempt to neutralise Hizbullah's political and military weight and derail Syria's Lebanon policy. Hizbullah's military operations on 8 May 2008 ended the political stand-off in Beirut, but at the expense of aggravating Sunni–Shi'i tensions. Although the Syrian regime facilitated Qatar's mediation to reach a swift resolution of the crisis, for fear of sectarian conflict spilling over into Syria,[83] Riyad responded with dangerous liaisons along the Lebanese–Syrian border. The emergence of pro-Hariri armed Salafi groups in northern Lebanon coupled with Sunni–'Alawi skirmishes in Tripoli served to spotlight the Syrian regime's sectarian vulnerabilities and remind it of the proximity of explosive sectarian conflicts.[84]

Conclusion

The 21 May 2008 Doha Accord that ended the political stand-off in Lebanon in a manner favourable to Syria's allies, followed by the 25 May 2008 election of army commander General Michel Sulaiman, a figure sensitive to Syria's security interests in Lebanon,[85] and the subsequent formation on 11 July 2008 of a national unity government in which the opposition acquired veto power, closed a difficult chapter in Syrian foreign policy. To be sure, these developments have injured the regime. Israel's attack against an alleged nuclear facility in northeast Syria on 6 September 2007,[86] mysterious assassinations inside the lion's den[87] and rumours of an aborted coup in Damascus in February 2008[88] have bruised the country's deterrent posture and raised questions about the kind of arrangement Syria has accepted in exchange for regime security and a partial reintegration into international and regional politics.

Nevertheless, the image of a confident President Bashar al-Asad attending the Union for the Mediterranean summit in Paris on 13 July 2008, hosting French President Nicolas Sarkozy on 3 August 2008 and then gathering in Damascus the leaders of France, Qatar and Turkey on 4 September 2008 underscored the dramatic close to Syria's regional and international isolation. The summits appear to confirm Syria's central role in Lebanon and other regional affairs. Jumblatt's expressed hope for an ignominious collapse of the Ba'thi regime have proved whimsical;[89] the 'moderate' Arab states' efforts to ostracise Syria and draw it away from Iran have exacerbated intra-Arab tensions without delivering Damascus to the fold. A foreign policy based on classical balancing, asymmetric balancing and balking has enabled Syria to resist US threats to its geopolitical interests and protect the security of the regime. With US policies being bludgeoned in Iraq, Lebanon and the occupied Palestinian territories, Bashar found he could afford to signal accommodation towards a future US administration: Syria has once again increased its co-operation with US forces to secure the border with Iraq and declared its readiness to engage in direct talks with Israel provided there is US–French sponsorship for the implementation of a prospective agreement.[90] Syria's Lebanon policy played a central role in this rehabilitation and perhaps Damascus learned belatedly that its Lebanese proxies can be far better assets than the heavy-handed tactics deployed by its own army and intelligence services. Bashar can take solace that, against all expectations, the Ba'thi regime has survived and overcome challenges that, for the ruler of Damascus, must have felt like more than enough for a lifetime.

Notes

1. See Itamar Rabinovich, 'The Changing Prism: Syrian Policy in Lebanon As a Mirror, an Issue and an Instrument' in Moshe Ma'oz and Avner Yaniv, eds. *Syria Under Assad*, London 1986, p. 179.
2. For a discussion see Bassel Salloukh, 'Syria and Lebanon: A Brotherhood Transformed', *Middle East Report*, no. 236, 2005, pp. 14–21.
3. The label is Jihad al-Zain's. Interview in Beirut, 10 August 2008.
4. Interview with Karim Pakraduni, Beirut, 7 August 2008.

5. See Volker Perthes, 'Syrian Regional Policy under Bashar al-Asad: Realignment or Economic Rationalization?', *Middle East Report*, no. 220, 2001, pp. 36–41; Raymond Hinnebusch, 'Globalization and Generational Change: Syrian Foreign Policy between Regional Conflict and European Partnership', *Review of International Affairs*, vol. 3, no. 2, 2003, pp. 190–208; Flynt Leverett, *Inheriting Syria*, Washington, DC 2005, pp. 99–146; Volker Perthes, 'The Syrian Solution', *Foreign Affairs*, vol. 85, no. 6, 2006, pp. 33–40; Daniel L. Byman, 'Syria and Iran: What's Behind the Enduring Alliance?', <http://www.brookings.edu/opinions/2006/0719middleeast_byman. aspx>; Moshe Ma'oz, *The 'Shi'i Crescent': Myth and Reality*, Washington, DC 2007. For the Syrian regime's own realist explanation of its foreign policy choices see Sami Klib, 'Suriya Hadi'a 'ala Hazar ba'd al-I'sar', *al-Safir*, 6 and 7 April 2006. The two-part article is an interview with General Muhammad Nasif, once a formidable figure in Syria's General Intelligence and, since April 2006, adviser to Vice President Faruq al-Shar'.

6. See Steven Heydemann, *Upgrading Authoritarianism in the Arab World*, Washington, DC 2007, pp. 23–4.

7. See Fred H. Lawson, 'Syria's Relations with Iran: Managing the Dilemmas of Alliance', *Middle East Journal*, vol. 61, no. 1, 2007, pp. 29–47.

8. See Jordanian King 'Abdallah's comments to the *Washington Post*, 8 December 2004. See also Rachel Bronson, 'Syria: Hanging Together or Hanging Separately', *Washington Quarterly*, vol. 23, no. 4, 2000, pp. 91–105.

9. For a discussion see Amal Saad-Ghorayeb, 'Questioning the Shia Crescent', *al-Ahram Weekly*, 19–25 April 2007; Ma'oz, *The 'Shi'i Crescent'*.

10. As, for example, Perthes, 'Syrian Regional Policy Under Bashar al-Asad' and Hinnebusch,, 'Globalization and Generational Change' where political economy arguments are advanced alongside balance-of-power ones.

11. See Heydemann, *Upgrading Authoritarianism in the Arab World*, pp. 23–4 and the press coverage of Bashar's trip to India in *al-Safir*, 18–19 June 2008.

12. See Marius Deeb, *Syria's Terrorist War on Lebanon and the Peace Process*, London 2003.

13. See Jerome Slater, 'Lost Opportunities for Peace in the Arab–Israeli Conflict: Israel and Syria, 1948–2001', *International Security*, vol. 27, no. 1, 2002, pp. 79–106 and Jihad al-Zain, 'Thalath Asatir Hawl al-Nizam al-Suri', *al-Nahar*, 5 May 2008.

14. See Perthes, 'Syrian Regional Policy Under Bashar al-Asad', p. 40 and Hinnebusch, 'Globalization and Generational Change', p. 200.

15. The *locus classicus* of this critique is Barry Buzan, *People, States and Fear: An Agenda for International Security Studies in the Post-Cold War Era* second edition, Boulder, Colo. 1991; Brian L. Job, ed. *The Insecurity Dilemma*, Boulder, Colo. 1992 and Mohammed Ayoob, *The Third World Security*

Predicament: State Making, Regional Conflict, and the International System, Boulder, Colo. 1995.

16. For a theoretical argument applied to the Iraqi case see F. Gregory Gause, III, 'Iraq's Decisions to Go to War, 1980 and 1990', *Middle East Journal*, vol. 56, no. 1, 2002, pp. 47–70.

17. See Garry C. Gambill, 'The American–Syrian Crisis and the End of Constructive Engagement', *Middle East Intelligence Bulletin*, vol. 5, no. 4, 2003 and Gambill's 'The Lion in Winter: Bashar Assad's Self-Destruction', *Mideast Monitor*, vol. 1, no. 1, 2004.

18. See Max Abrahms, 'When Rogues Defy Reason: Bashar's Syria', *Middle East Quarterly*, vol. 10, 2003; Eyal Zisser, 'Syria and the United States: Bad Habits Die Hard', *Middle East Quarterly*, vol. 10, no. 3, 2003, pp. 29–37; Ziad K. Abdelnour, 'The US–Syrian Crisis: Why Diplomacy Failed', *Middle East Intelligence Bulletin*, vol. 5, no. 10, 2003; 'Abdullah Bouhabib, 'Akhta' Suriya al-Istratijiya fil-'Ilaqa ma' Washington', *al-Hayat*, 11 April 2005; Michel Kilu, 'Suriya fi Aswa' Ahwaliha Munzu Istaqalat!', *al-Nahar*, 9 May 2005; William Harris, 'Bashar al-Assad's Lebanon Gamble', *Middle East Quarterly*, vol. 12, no. 3, 2005; Dennis Ross, 'U.S. Policy toward a Weak Assad', *Washington Quarterly* vol. 28, no. 3, 2005, pp. 87–98; David W. Lesch, *The New Lion of Damascus*, New Haven 2005, p. 189; Eyal Zisser, 'Bashar al-Assad: In or Out of the New World Order?', *Washington Quarterly*, vol. 28, no. 3, 2005, pp. 115–31; Nicholas Blanford, *Killing Mr Lebanon*, London 2006, especially p. 103; Eyal Zisser, *Commanding Syria*, London 2007, pp. 125–97.

19. Ross, 'U.S. Policy', p. 89.

20. Zisser, 'Syria, the United States, and Iraq'.

21. See John Mearsheimer, 'Hans Morgenthau and the Iraq War: Realism versus Neo-Conservatism', 21 April 2005, <http://www.openDemocracy.net>.

22. John J. Mearsheimer and Stephen M. Walt, *The Israel Lobby and U.S. Foreign Policy*, New York 2007, p. 55. See also *Boston Globe*, 10 September 2002 and *The New Yorker*, 17 February 2003.

23. See Stephen M. Walt, *Taming American Power: The Global Response to U.S. Primacy*, New York 2006, pp. 183–7.

24. See the excellent discussion in ibid., chap. 3.

25. Omnibalancing was not a viable option for the Syrian regime. The principal threat to the Syrian regime was from other states, not internal actors, and bandwagoning with the external threat would not have necessarily eliminated any possible domestic threat. For a discussion of omnibalancing see Steven R. David, 'Explaining Third World Alignment', *World Politics*, vol. 43, no. 2, 1991, pp. 233–56.

26. See the text of the interview in *al-Safir*, 27 March 2003.

27. Interview with Talal Salman, Beirut, 7 August 2008.

28. See Bashar al-Asad's interview in *al-Hayat*, 7 October 2003 and Klib, 'Suriya Hadi'a 'ala Hazar ba'd al-I'sar'.

29. Interview with Karim Pakraduni.

30. Charles Krauthammer, 'The War: A Road Map', *Washington Post*, 28 September 2001; Tom Barry, 'On the Road to Damascus? Neo-Cons Target Syria', *Counterpunch*, 8 March 2004 and Mearsheimer and Walt, *The Israel Lobby*, pp. 263–79.

31. Interviews with Jihad al-Zain and Talal Salman.

32. Quoted in Ed Vulliamy, 'Syria Could be Next, Warns Washington', *Observer*, 13 April 2003. See also Toby Harnden, 'Syria Now Top US Target for "Regime Change"', *Telegraph*, 8 April 2003 and Patrick Seale, 'Reflections on Why the US and Israel are Threatening Syria', *Daily Star*, 18 April 2003.

33. See Eli J. Lake, 'Few Good Men', *New Republic*, 26 May 2003, pp. 14–16.

34. See the text at: <http://www.fas.org/asmp/resources/govern/108th/pl_108_175.pdf>. The Act was signed into law by President Bush on 12 December 2003.

35. See Nqoula Nasif, 'Ma Taquluh Washington wa Dimashq 'an Muhadathat Burns', *al-Nahar*, 14 September 2004 and Randa Haydar, 'Ma Wara' al-Matalib al-Amirkiya min Dimashq', *al-Nahar*, 5 May 2003.

36. See Bahjat Sulaiman, 'Suriya wa-l-Tahdidat al-Amerkiya', *al-Safir*, 15 May 2003. Sulaiman wanted to publish the article under a pseudonym to ensure regime deniability but the newspaper refused to publish it unless it carried his name.

37. The timing coincides with a press conference by then Syrian Foreign Minister Faruq al-Shar', in which he substantially escalated the Syrian rhetoric against the US. See his comments in *al-Hayat*, 28 July 2003.

38. See Michel Kilu, 'Suriya Tuwajeh 1559 Bi'aqliyat al-Harb al-Barida', *al-Nahar*, 11 November 2004.

39. See David Ignatius, 'Bush's New Ally: France?', *Washington Post*, 1 February 2006.

40. Interviews with Karim Pakraduni and Talal Salman. See also the analysis in Jihad al-Zain, 'Al-Ra'is al-Asad ma' CNN: al-Kalimat-al-Mafatih', *al-Nahar*, 14 October 2005; Bashar al-Asad's interview with CNN on 12 October 2005; and Sami Klib, 'Al-Asad min al-Difa' ila al-Istratijiya', *al-Safir*, 16 July 2008.

41. Seymour M. Hersh, 'The Syrian Bet', *The New Yorker*, 28 July 2003.

42. Saudi journalists describe how the Saudi government reached agreement with its Syrian counterpart to repatriate Saudi nationals trying to slip to Iraq through Syria. To test Syrian intentions, the Saudis sent a group of intelligence officers posing as foreign fighters to Syria. Instead of repatriating

them, Syrian authorities helped the Saudis cross over to Iraq. Interviews with Saudi journalists in Dubai and Beirut, June 2006.

43. For a comprehensive analysis see Bassel F. Salloukh, 'Opposition under Authoritarianism: The Case of Lebanon under Syria', unpublished paper, 2007.

44. See 'Abd al-Halim Khaddam's interview with al-'Arabiyyah satellite channel reproduced in *al-Nahar*, 31 December 2005.

45. The text is at: <http://www.un.org/News/Press/docs/2004/sc8181.doc. htm> .

46. For accounts of the infamous Hariri–Bashar meeting of 26 August 2004, where Bashar is quoted as saying to Hariri 'I am Lahoud and Lahoud is me. If your friend Chirac wants me out of Lebanon, I would sooner break Lebanon on your head and the head of Chirac than break my word', see George Bkasini, *Al-Tariq ila al-Istiqlal: Khams Sanawat ma' Rafiq Hariri*, Beirut 2008, pp. 180–4 and Blanford, *Killing Mr Lebanon*, pp. 100–3. Both accounts of the meeting are based on interviews with individuals sympathetic to Hariri's version. The Syrian regime has denied this version of events.

47. Interview with Talal Salman.

48. See Blanford, *Killing Mr Lebanon*, p. 99.

49. Consequently, Obeid was conspicuously absent from the 28 August 2004 cabinet meeting that requested from parliament a constitutional amendment permitting the renewal of Lahoud's tenure and from the subsequent parliamentary session of 3 September 2004.

50. Interview with Talal Salman.

51. See Bashar's interview in *al-Hayat*, 7 October 2003.

52. Interview with Jihad al-Zain.

53. In a joint press conference after the Chirac–Bush summit at the Élysée Palace on 5 June 2004, Bush declared that 'The United States and France ... agree that the people of Lebanon should be free to determine their own future, without foreign interference or domination.' Chirac also noted that 'we have expressed renewed conviction and belief that Lebanon has to be ensured that its independence and sovereignty are guaranteed.' See the text of the joint press conference at: <http://www.whitehouse.gov/ news/releases/2004/06/20040605-6.html> .

54. For an account of the behind-the-scenes deliberations between representatives of the three sides, see Bkasini, *Al-Tariq ila al-Istiqlal*, pp. 169–77. The consequent Memorandum of Understanding between Patriarch Sfeir, Jumblatt and Hariri called for disarming Hizbullah and de-linking the party from its popular Shi'i base in an attempt to undermine its ability to negotiate a solution to its weapons arsenal. The first objective would be achieved by convincing Israel to withdraw from the Shib'a Farms in

exchange for a Security Council resolution deploying UN troops in the farms pending a settlement of the Syrian–Israeli conflict. The second objective entailed proactive populist socio-economic state policies aimed at replacing Hizbullah's own social services network and thus delegitimising the party inside the Shi'i community. See the text of the memorandum in Bkasini, *Al-Tariq ila al-Istiqlal*, pp. 174–7. This version of events contradicts the one supplied by Hizbullah Secretary General Hasan Nasrallah, who disclosed that in meetings with Hariri before the latter's assassination, Hariri pledged to safeguard Hizbullah's weapons arsenal until a comprehensive settlement of the Arab–Israeli conflict was reached. See Nasrallah's comments during the session with Michel 'Awn hosted by Jean 'Aziz on OTV station, 6 February 2008 and Jean 'Aziz, 'Azmat Thiqa? Bal Sira' man Yabqa Hayan', *al-Akhbar*, 16 February 2008. Blanford's account confirms Nasrallah's version, but adds a caveat: that the Hariri–Nasrallah compromise included a pledge by Hizbullah to 'act wisely and not resort to actions that seriously jeopardise [sic] the national good'. See Blanford, *Killing Mr Lebanon*, p. 191.

55. See Khaddam's interview reproduced in *al-Nahar*, 31 December 2005 and Blanford, *Killing Mr Lebanon*, p. 88.

56. See Blanford, *Killing Mr Lebanon*, p. 103; Ibrahim Hamidi, 'Suriya fil-Mashhad al-Faransi', *al-Hayat*, 22 February 2006. In fact, Hariri's biographer confirms the Syrian regime's suspicions of a Hariri hand in the making of 1559. He reveals that three days after the Normandy summit, Hariri called him, declaring the 'commencement of [Lebanon's] independence', that during the Normandy summit Chirac succeeded in eliciting Bush's support for the twin objectives of blocking the extension of Lahoud's term and pressuring Damascus to withdraw its troops from Lebanon. See Bkasini, *Al-Tariq ila al-Istiqlal*, pp. 168–9. Both Harris, 'Bashar al-Assad's Lebanon Gamble' and Zisser, 'Syria, the United States, and Iraq', make similar allusions.

57. See Bashar's speech reproduced in *al-Safir*, 11 November 2005.

58. Ibid.

59. Interview with Karim Pakraduni. See also Bashar's speech reproduced in *al-Safir*, 11 November 2005; Hamidi, 'Suriya fil-Mashhad al-Faransi'.

60. Which explains Bashar's comments to a Regional Command meeting of the Ba'th Party in early 2005. Khaddam quotes Bashar commenting at the meeting that when the decision to renew Lahoud's tenure was taken, he assumed that his decision was correct by a 50 per cent ratio; after the promulgation of Resolution 1559, Bashar became 100 per cent convinced that he had taken the right decision. See Bkasini, *Al-Tariq ila al-Istiqlal*, p. 219.

61. Interview with Karim Pakraduni.

62. See the interview with 'Abd al-Halim Khaddam in *al-Sharq al-Awsat*, 6 January 2006.

63. See his comments in *al-Hayat*, 27 October 2004.

64. Comments by Paul Salem at the workshop entitled 'Al-'Ilaqat al-Lubnaniya-al-Suriya: Hal min Majal Li-'Ilaqat Sahiha?' organised by the Issam Fares Center for Lebanon, Beirut, 15 June 2008 and the author's conversation with Salem, Beirut, 26 August 2008.

65. Interview with Talal Salman.

66. See, for example, Michael Young, 'A Perfect Storm of Syrian Irrelevance', *Daily Star*, 15 September 2005; Eli Lake, 'Policy on Syria Moves Toward Regime Change', *New York Sun*, 8 June 2005; and Ross, 'U.S. Policy toward a Weak Assad'.

67. See, for example, Bkasini, *Al-Tariq ila al-Istiqlal*; Blanford, *Killing Mr Lebanon*; Marwan Iskandar, *Rafiq Hariri and the Fate of Lebanon*, Beirut 2006; and Hasan Sabra, 'Dahiyat al-Haqudin', *al-Shira'*, 12 February 2006.

68. See Alexandre Adler, 'Pourquoi a-t-on tué Rafic Hariri?', *Le Figaro*, 16 February 2005. Jean 'Aziz also suggests that in his discussions with Nasrallah in early 2005, Hariri suggested that the two men could join forces to resolve not just local but regional problems as well. See 'Aziz, 'Azmat Thiqa?'

69. With the assassination attempt against Marwan Himadah on 1 October 2004. Evidence gathered by Lebanese Military Intelligence suggests that the assassination of George Hawi on 21 June 2005 may have been the work of an Israeli-affiliated intelligence network in Lebanon. See *al-Safir*, 6 May 2008.

70. On 12 October 2005, Syrian authorities announced that Kan'an, then interior minister, had committed suicide in Damascus.

71. Hence the difference between Hafiz and Bashar. See Jihad al-Zain, 'Al-Talaqi al-Sa'udi-al-Suri 'ala al-Iraq', *al-Nahar*, 22 September 2005 and al-Zain, 'Al-Ra'is al-Asad ma' CNN'.

72. Including Lahoud and Hariri. Interview with Karim Pakraduni. See also Blanford, *Killing Mr Lebanon*, p. 199.

73. Interview with Karim Pakraduni.

74. Interview with Karim Pakraduni.

75. For a detailed analysis see Bassel F. Salloukh, 'Democracy in Lebanon: The Primacy of the Sectarian System' in Nathan Brown and Emad El-Din Shahin, eds. *The Struggle for Democracy in the Middle East*, London forthcoming.

76. Interview with Karim Pakraduni.

77. See Jean 'Aziz, 'Limaza kana al-Asad Yadhak li-Nikat al-Lubnaniyin?', *al-Akhbar*, 1 July 2008.

78. See David Ignatius, 'Mob War in the Mideast', *Washington Post*, 4 January 2006. Interestingly, Jumblatt would later claim that he had called for regime change during his visit to the US in March 2006, but that Secretary of State Condoleezza Rice informed him that the Syrian regime should change its behaviour. See Jumblatt's off-the-record comments quoted in *al-Akhbar*, 11 August 2008.

79. Interviews with Karim Pakraduni and Talal Salman; Nqoula Nasif, 'Lahoud la Yastaqil ila li-'Awn', *al-Nahar*, 30 October 2005; Khudur Talib, 'Munawashat Sa'udiya-Suriya 'ala Khat al-Tamas al-Lubnani', *al-Safir*, 6 February 2008; and the anonymous article entitled 'Al-Asad Yattahem al-Sa'udiya bil-Ta'amur 'ala Nizameh', *al-Akhbar*, 28 May 2008.

80. See Joshua Landis and Joe Pace, 'The Syrian Opposition', *Washington Quarterly*, vol. 30, no. 1, 2006–7, p. 61.

81. Interview with Talal Salman.

82. See Nqoula Nasif, 'Dimashq-al-Riyad: Al-'Inaq Nusf al-Tariq wal-Iraq wa Lubnan Nusfaha al-Akhar', *al-Akhbar*, 3 March 2007.

83. Interview with Karim Pakraduni.

84. See Nadir Fawaz, "Arqala Sa'udiya lil-Dawha Istad'at Inzar Hizbullah', *al-Akhbar*, 24 June 2008.

85. Damascus was behind Sulaiman's appointment as army commander during Lahoud's tenure. Lahoud's candidate for the post, General As'ad Ghanim, was overruled by Damascus. See Nqoula Nasif, 'Imtihan al-Mu'asasa al-'Askariya: Tasyis al-Jaysh am Ta'yin Qa'id Musayas', *al-Akhbar*, 23 August 2008.

86. See David E. Sanger and Mark Mazzetti, 'Israel Struck Syrian Nuclear Project, Analysts Say', *New York Times*, 14 October 2007.

87. Namely, Hizbullah commander 'Imad Mughniyyah in Damascus on 12 February 2008 and General Muhammad Sulaiman in Tartus on 2 August 2008. For details see *Sunday Times*, 17 February 2008; *Guardian*, 5 August 2008; and *al-Sharq al-Awsat*, 5 August 2008.

88. By Head of Military Intelligence (and Bashar's brother-in-law) 'Asif Shawkat. See *Haaretz*, 10 June 2008, quoting from the *Die Welt*, 7 June 2008; 'The Mysterious Downfall of Asif Shawkat', *Mideast Monitor*, vol. 3, no. 2, 2008. Reports suggesting Shawkat's demotion inside the Syrian intelligence establishment may have proved premature. Interviews with journalists in Beirut, August 2008.

89. Walid Jumblatt, 'The Struggle for Freedom and Democracy in Lebanon', Washington Institute for Near East Policy, 19 October 2007.

90. Michael Bergman, 'Realism Must Rule in Engaging Syria', *Boston Globe*, 23 July 2008; James Denselow, 'The Axis of Pragmatism', *Guardian*, 27 July 2008; David Ignatius, 'A Syrian–Israeli Breakthrough?', *Washington Post*, 27 August 2008; and *al-Safir*, 28 August 2008.

The Beginning of a Beautiful Friendship: Syrian–Turkish relations since 1998

Fred H. Lawson

Syria's relations with Turkey have improved dramatically over the past decade. In October 1998, it looked possible that the two countries would resort to brute force in their dealings with one another. Ankara ordered some 10,000 troops to the Syrian border and the chief of the Turkish general staff told reporters that 'the current situation is that of an undeclared war'.[1] Damascus responded by reaffirming its 'keenness for good, neighbourly relations with Turkey' but nevertheless deployed thirty-six of its 120 Scud-C surface-to-surface missiles to forward positions close to the Turkish frontier.[2] Knowledgeable observers expressed little surprise at the crisis, in light of long-standing tensions and mutual mistrust that reflected ongoing disagreements over the distribution of Euphrates River water and persistent Turkish allegations that the Syrian authorities were providing material and moral support for the radical Kurdistan Workers' Party (Partiya Karkerana Kurdistan or PKK).[3]

By the autumn of 2008, a recurrence of this sort of military confrontation had become almost impossible to imagine. The Turkish government had hired a German company that spring to remove hundreds of land mines from key districts along the border. The head of the chamber of commerce in the Turkish town of Nusaybin told the press that 'as soon as the mine clearance is done, construction will begin on a new border crossing for our people and goods'.[4] In July, the governor of the northern Syrian metropolis of Aleppo announced that eighteen large-scale investment projects had been approved by the Syria–Turkey Inter-Regional Co-operation Programme, on top of the forty-two that were already underway. The projects had been chosen, according to the selection committee, 'on the basis of their priority and contribution to bilateral co-operation, economic development and employment, as well as the likelihood of long-term success'.[5]

Such a marked shift in Syrian–Turkish relations seems hard to explain.[6] Meliha Altunisik and Ozlem Tur report that the initial rapprochement occurred as a result of 'instructions from President [Hafiz al-]Asad to reach an agreement with the Turkish side', but offer no explanation for why the Syrian leader took this important decision.[7] Altunisik and Tur situate the steady expansion of strategic and economic ties between the two countries in the context of growing threats to Syria from the United States after September 2001 and the heightened potential for Kurdish independence after March 2003.[8] The crucial question of why increased US pressure on one of Turkey's long-time adversaries pulled Damascus and Ankara closer together, rather than driving the two governments farther apart, is posed but left unanswered.[9]

Other analysts point to a combination of economic and military factors to account for the change. Mustafa Aydin and Damla Aras observe that the warming of relations took place after Ankara 'opted for an export-led growth policy over its long favoured import-substitution policy'.[10] But they also note that it was senior Turkish commanders, not manufacturers and traders, who supervised the overall campaign to mend fences with Syria.[11] Only after Damascus agreed to sever all connections with the PKK was a variety of measures adopted to encourage commercial expansion, including a transportation agreement designed to boost rail, sea and air links and a memorandum of understanding signed that reinvigorated the long-dormant Joint Economic Committee. A notable increase in bilateral trade and investment occurred shortly thereafter.[12]

No one doubts that closer collaboration on security matters and greater economic interaction work to the benefit of Syria and Turkey alike. Yet the potential gains from mutual co-operation had been present long before the 1998 crisis and could well have remained unrealised for many years thereafter. What prompted Damascus to pursue a sustained rapprochement with Ankara beginning in the late 1990s was a convergence of strategic trends that raised the cost of conflict with Turkey, while at the same time diminishing the danger to Syria of taking steps to improve relations with its powerful northern neighbour.[13] Subsequent trends in bilateral relations illustrate similar dynamics: whenever Turkey has found it difficult to exploit Syrian overtures, co-operation has flourished, but whenever Turkey gains the capacity to take advantage of Syria, co-operation flags.

Damascus's Initial Warming to Ankara

Rather than stand firm in the face of Turkish belligerence, the Syrian government agreed in October 1998 to expel the PKK's historic leader, Abdullah Ocalan, from Damascus and set up an integrated surveillance network to prevent Kurdish militants from infiltrating into southern Anatolia. By early 1999, PKK training facilities on Syrian and Lebanese territory had been shut down as well. A Joint Security Committee made up of senior commanders from the Syrian and Turkish armed forces started to meet on a regular basis to discuss a wide range of tactical problems and strategic issues.[14] Delegations of high-ranking army officers paid a succession of visits between the two capitals as 1999 opened.[15]

At the same time, Turkish officials invited Damascus to dispatch an economic mission to Ankara to discuss opportunities for commercial and industrial co-operation. Syria's deputy prime minister for economic affairs, Salim Yasin, accepted the invitation and travelled to the Turkish capital in mid-March 1999. The communiqué issued at the end of the trip promised that the two countries 'will exert all possible efforts to raise and diversify [bilateral] trade. [To that end,] they agreed to exchange visits by mercantile and economic delegations to review the potential of establishing a private council for businessmen in both countries.'[16] The document also declared that the two governments would draw up a protocol that would eliminate double taxation on goods produced in one country but distributed and sold in the other.[17]

More important, the energetic governor of Aleppo, Muhammad Mustafa Miru, hosted a delegation headed by the governor of the adjacent Turkish province of Killis. The meeting generated plans 'to open [trade] exhibitions between the two countries, to arrange sports and cultural activities [and] to benefit from the experience of the Killis organized industrial region to set up an organized industrial region in Aleppo'.[18] The two governors also agreed to permit families with members living on both sides of the border to visit one another on major religious holidays without first securing entry and exit visas.

Such initiatives remained limited due to lingering political friction, which continued to simmer just beneath the surface. At the June 1999 meeting of the Joint Security Committee, Turkish representatives formally requested that Lebanon be incorporated into the security arrangements that had been drawn up between Turkey and Syria. Syrian representatives riposted by arguing that whether or not Lebanon took part in the arrangements was a matter that 'concerns Lebanon, which is a sovereign country', and thereby required face-to-face negotiations between Ankara and Beirut.[19] The Syrians then demanded that several members of the Muslim Brothers who had escaped to Turkey in the 1980s be extradited to Syria in exchange for handing over suspected PKK activists who were thought to be residing in Syria. They also asked for written proof that the PKK enjoyed ready access to bank accounts in Syria, and asserted that since 'Syrian banks are government-owned and transparent', it was highly unlikely that any such accounts existed.

Early March 2000 brought a renewed thaw in Syrian–Turkish relations. Governor Miru of Aleppo assumed the premiership in Damascus and immediately welcomed a team of senior officials from Turkey's foreign ministry to the Syrian capital to lay the groundwork for official talks between the two countries' foreign ministers.[20] Two months later, Turkey's minister of state for economic affairs led a contingent of some 100 Turkish industrialists to Damascus for the reconvening of the moribund Joint Economic Committee; the delegation met with Syria's ministers of finance, agriculture and energy, and informed their hosts that Turkey intended to raise the level of trade with Syria to one billion US dollars per year.[21] The good feelings that were engendered by the visit were undermined in late summer, when Turkish officials drastically reduced the southward flow of the Euphrates River, without notifying Syrian authorities in advance.[22] But the two states' foreign ministers reconciled during the Organisation of the

Islamic Conference summit in Doha that November, telling reporters that a comprehensive memorandum of understanding was being drafted to chart a course towards future co-operation.[23] At the same time, Vice President 'Abd al-Halim Khaddam arrived in Ankara with a letter from President Bashar al-Asad, promising that the two countries would 'turn over a new leaf' in their dealings with one another.[24]

Syria's minister of petroleum and natural resources travelled to Ankara in mid-January 2001 to confer with senior Turkish oil officials. The meeting produced an agreement that encouraged private Turkish oil companies to explore for oil and natural gas inside Syria and work with Syrian public sector companies to increase the efficiency of oil and gas production and transportation.[25] A delegation led by the chief of the political section of the general staff of the Syrian armed forces followed a week later and toured a number of military facilities and defence plants around Ankara and Istanbul.[26] The visit was reciprocated by a group of senior Turkish officers who met with the Syrian defence minister in Damascus in mid-April.[27] Such discussions culminated in the signing on 10 September 2001 of a bilateral security pact by the two ministers of the interior, aimed at 'combating crime and criminals, organized crime and terrorism'.[28] The agreement pledged the two governments to exchange information, share investigative techniques and explore 'new developments, particularly in the field of forensic security'. A separate agreement laid the groundwork for the routine repatriation of 'illegal immigrants' between the two countries.

Bilateral military agreements proved more elusive. The Syrian general in charge of strategic planning paid a call to Ankara in January 2001, which was reciprocated by Turkey's chief of military plans and principles at the end of April. Discussions at these meetings were reported to concern whether or not the two armed forces might embark on a series of joint training exercises in the near future. According to the *Turkish Daily News*, the Turkish general staff favoured carrying out such manoeuvres, but insisted that the authorities in Damascus in return relinquish all claim to the province of Hatay (Iskandarun).[29] This the Ba'thi regime adamantly refused to do.

Damascus's pursuit of better relations with Ankara from the autumn of 1998 to the end of 2001 grew out of a conjunction of developments that sharply increased the cost of armed conflict with Turkey. In the first place, the consolidation of the Turkish–Israeli alignment left Syria vulnerable to a co-ordinated military assault on the part of its two principal adversaries.[30] The chances that such an attack might be carried out increased in January 1998, when American warships provided logistical support for Turkish and Israeli naval units as part of the Reliant Mermaid exercises in the eastern Mediterranean.[31] Plans to engage in further joint manoeuvres were made public that July, as the two countries' prime ministers met to announce the formation of 'an Israeli–Turkish axis'.[32] Subsequent Reliant Mermaid exercises took place in December 1999 and January 2001; further combined naval and air manoeuvres were carried out in April and June 2001. These operations led one well-informed observer to remark that 'the current level of [Turkish–Israeli] military co-operation has created an infrastructure for common military action in the future.'[33]

Furthermore, Turkey and Israel concluded a succession of agreements to supply Israeli-made weapons systems and technical expertise to the Turkish armed forces beginning in the late 1990s. Such arrangements not only dramatically improved the capabilities and readiness of Turkey's front-line armoured divisions and fighter-bomber squadrons, but also raised the level of interoperability between the two countries' military establishments. In the spring of 2002, for instance, Ankara contracted with Israel Military Industries to install guns and armament on its M-60 A1/3 tanks that were identical to those found on the upgraded Israeli version.[34] As a result of deals like these, the battle-worthiness of the Syrian armed forces declined markedly compared with the combined effectiveness of the Turkish and Israeli militaries.[35]

Moreover, Syria found itself increasingly dependent on water supplies that originated inside Turkish territory. Severe drought made the Euphrates River particularly vital to the cities and farms of northeastern Syria in the spring of 1999, and the authorities in Ankara took no steps to allay fears that they might divert water from both the Euphrates and the nearby Khabur River in order to sustain agricultural and industrial production in southeastern Turkey. At the same time, it had become common practice for Turkish administrators to draw off clear water to irrigate farmland north of the border and then channel the chemical-ridden run-off downstream.[36] In addition, the managers of the high dams that Turkey had constructed across the Euphrates and its major tributaries tended to discharge water from the reservoirs only at times when Turkish enterprises needed electrical power, and to keep the floodgates closed whenever Turkish demand for electricity dropped. Under these circumstances, it became more and more difficult for Syrian officials to predict when sufficient water might be available for farming, urban sanitation and power generation. Suspicions about Ankara's intentions regarding the future disposition of water resources escalated when it became public knowledge that Turkish officials were negotiating a deal to ship fresh water to Israel from the Mediterranean port of Antalya.[37]

Even as the chances that Syria might prevail – or even hold its own – in a military confrontation with Turkey diminished almost to zero, however, Damascus found itself less vulnerable than before to any attempt on Ankara's part to take advantage of Syrian overtures. Public opinion in Turkey throughout the late 1990s overwhelmingly opposed military collaboration with Israel and expressed considerable sympathy for the Palestinian cause.[38] Pro-Palestinian attitudes began to be articulated more clearly among the Turkish population following the outbreak of the al-Aqsa uprising in September 2000. In the same vein, polls showed a high level of disapproval among the Turkish public for Israeli efforts to retain exclusive control of Jerusalem. President Ahmet Necdet Sezer responded to these sentiments by instructing Turkey's representatives to the United Nations to vote in favour of an October 2000 resolution that condemned Israel for the use of excessive force against civilians in the Occupied Territories. Under these circumstances, the likelihood that Ankara would take steps to collaborate with Israel to exploit Syrian overtures dropped off markedly.

Meanwhile, the Turkish government was grappling with a pronounced resurgence of ethnic activism at home, particularly among the country's heterogeneous Alevi population. Alevi activism had been officially encouraged in the mid-1990s, largely as a counterweight to the Islamist movement.[39] During the years of quasi-Islamist Welfare Party rule, the Alevi community split into three broad factions: one avowedly anti-Islamist, and therefore supportive of the fundamental principles of Kemalism; one resolutely socialist and, by extension, sympathetic to Kurdish demands for political and social justice; and one more accommodationist, and willing to work with Sunni activists to transform the political system.[40] The first faction welcomed the June 1997 ousting of the Welfare Party-led government and quickly allied itself to the successor government headed by Mesut Yilmaz of the Motherland Party. The second and third, by contrast, kept their distance from the new ruling coalition, thereby forcing it to take steps to appease their adherents. Not only were state monies earmarked for the first time to fund Alevi community projects, but the government also declared that Alevis and Sunnis were equal partners in the body politic.[41] Given the historical ties between various Alevi groups in Anatolia and Hatay and the 'Alawi community of northwestern Syria, the authorities in Damascus found themselves in a position to influence a sensitive aspect of Turkey's internal affairs if Ankara attempted to take advantage of Syrian overtures.

In the wider strategic arena, Ankara embarked on a campaign to construct good working relations with the newly independent republics of the Caucasus shortly after the disintegration of the Soviet Union.[42] This initiative from the outset confronted a notable obstacle: long-standing animosity and mistrust between Turkey and Armenia. Partly in response to Turkey's effort to build bridges to Georgia and Azerbaijan, the government in Yerevan forged links with Syria. President Levon Ter-Petrossian's first official overseas mission was in fact to Aleppo, whose sizeable Armenian population accorded him an enthusiastic welcome. Manufactured goods from Aleppo, particularly textiles, confections and other sorts of processed food, found ready buyers in Armenian markets. Co-operation between Armenia and Syria accompanied a reinvigoration of economic and military partnerships between these two countries and the Russian Federation.[43] So by the close of the 1990s, it had become possible for Syrian officials to interfere with the progress of Turkey's drive to boost relations with its eastern neighbours, if Ankara bit the hand that Damascus extended.

Finally, Turkey grew more deeply entangled in the intricacies of Kurdish affairs in northern Iraq as the 1990s came to an end. The Turkish government's attempts to mediate between the Kurdistan Democratic Party (KDP) and the Patriotic Union of Kurdistan (PUK) collapsed on the very eve of the October 1998 crisis.[44] Irritated by Washington's decision to step in and broker an agreement that jeopardised long-standing Turkish interests, Ankara encouraged the Ba'thi regime in Baghdad to reassert a modicum of control over the Kurdish provinces.[45] When this strategy proved unviable, the Turkish government carried out large-scale military incursions into northern Iraq in April–May 1999 and April–May 2000. These offensives brought Turkey and its KDP client face to face with Iran and its PUK ally and put Ankara and Tehran in a situation in which 'neither [wanted] to upset the sphere of interests that they share in northern Iraq'.[46]

Damascus could therefore exercise considerable leverage in its dealings with Ankara in the period immediately following the 1998 crisis. Syria found itself at a decided strategic disadvantage relative to Turkey and recognised that it would suffer almost certain defeat in any future military confrontation with its powerful neighbour. Nevertheless, the government in Damascus benefited from changing circumstances that limited the amount and severity of the damage it would suffer if it made overtures to Turkey and such overtures ended up being rebuffed or exploited. Syrian officials therefore took the risk of lowering their guard and adopting a conciliatory posture toward the country's long-time northern adversary.

Accelerated Rapprochement

Connections between Damascus and Ankara strengthened substantially during the late winter and spring of 2002. A pair of agreements to carry out joint exercises and collaborate in military training missions was drafted that February.[47] Four months later, the chief of the Syrian general staff, General Hasan al-Turkmani, led a team of senior officers to the Turkish capital to sign the two agreements. The Syrian commanders went on to discuss with their hosts a variety of 'means of developing and boosting bilateral cooperation in the military field, including training and defence industries'.[48] During a subsequent meeting in Damascus, the two sides explored the possibility of collaborating in the production of military equipment and even broached the thorny question of whether Turkey might sell weapons to Syria.[49]

At the same time, economic initiatives started to proliferate. Syria's minister of construction and housing journeyed to Ankara in March to sign a protocol whereby Turkish companies became eligible to be awarded government contracts for major infrastructural projects inside Syria.[50] Five months later, the Syrian minister of irrigation toured southeastern Turkey, inspecting the massive Southeastern Anatolia Project (GAP) and a new industrial zone outside Gaziantep.[51] He told reporters that a Turkish businessperson from that city had recently set up a factory in Syria and that a number of other Turkish companies had won bids to renovate and upgrade existing public sector plants.

Gathering war clouds in the Gulf at the beginning of 2003 accompanied unprecedented levels of Syrian–Turkish co-operation. Foreign Minister Abdullah Gul was welcomed to Damascus in early January, where he met with President al-Asad and Prime Minister Miru on the first stop of a whirlwind tour of Arab capitals. Informed observers asserted that Gul undertook the tour in order to determine whether or not Arab governments would back Ankara if it decided to resist United States' pressure to join the military campaign against Iraq.[52] By stopping first in Syria, the Arab state that had been the most outspoken in condemning the use of military force to overturn the Ba'thi regime in Baghdad, the Turkish foreign minister sent an unmistakable signal to Washington, while buttressing the resolve of critics of the US-led war effort throughout the Arab world.[53] Syria effectively co-sponsored the late January meeting in Istanbul of Middle Eastern foreign ministers that stood opposed to the war and volunteered to host a follow-up gathering.[54]

Immediately after Foreign Minister Faruq al-Shar' had publicly decried the dangers of using military force in Iraq, officials in Damascus welcomed a delegation of influential Turkish commercial and industrial representatives. At almost the same time, the president of Damascus University hosted a team of Turkish university administrators, who initialled a cluster of scientific and cultural protocols. The sixth meeting of the Joint Economic Committee convened in July with the goal of forging a free trade area between the two countries; as the prelude to such an arrangement, the body proposed a handful of border trade centres to encourage trade between northern Syria and southern Turkey.[55] These developments culminated in Prime Minister Miru's visit to Ankara, the first by a sitting Syrian premier since 1986.[56] Miru looked on as Minister of Economy and Foreign Trade Ghassan al-Rifa'i signed a memorandum of understanding that covered a wide range of issues related to economic affairs and natural resources.[57] More importantly, at least to Damascus, the two prime ministers announced that talks concerning water distribution would be undertaken in the near future.[58] At the close of his visit, Miru invited Turkish businesspeople to trade and invest more heavily in Syria and reiterated the special privileges that had been accorded to Turkish enterprises to facilitate such activities.[59]

As 2003 drew to a close, security matters returned to the fore. The commander in chief of Turkey's gendarmerie led a delegation of security officers to Damascus to confer with Syria's interior minister in early December. The latter then travelled to Ankara to confirm the discussions with Turkey's interior minister. Even as the two interior ministers were touring the International Academy for Combating Drugs and Organised Crime and several other 'security and gendarmerie organisations', President al-Asad spoke out from Athens to say that he looked forward to cultivating better relations with Turkey. He then announced that Damascus had extradited 'twenty-two suspected terrorists' to Turkey for prosecution.[60]

Prime Minister Miru's historic trip to Ankara was eclipsed in early January 2004, when President al-Asad made the first official visit to Turkey by a Syrian head of state. Besides taking part in a number of ceremonial functions, al-Asad met with the Turkish president, prime minister, foreign minister, head of the parliamentary defence committee, chief of the general staff and other senior officials.[61] High on the agendas of the meetings stood the question of how best to deal with Kurdish autonomy in northern Iraq, the prospects for Syrian and Turkish partnership with the European Union, plans to encourage mutual tourism and the future of the Arab–Israeli conflict. The summit resulted in agreements to create a Syrian consulate in Gaziantep, to begin removing land mines along the frontier and to construct a network of commercial centres in towns along the border. As a remarkable concession to his hosts, President al-Asad put his signature on documents that explicitly referred to Turkey in its present boundaries, thereby implicitly abandoning Syria's long-standing claim to the province of Hatay (Iskandarun). The shift in policy was underscored by a proposal to open a Syrian commercial office in the provincial capital of Antioch.

Immediately after al-Asad's visit, a group of 300 Turkish manufacturers took part in an industrial equipment exposition in Damascus and came away with contracts worth some $250 million.[62] The Joint Economic Committee in early March 2004 discussed the possibility of setting up a bilateral free trade zone, as well as a joint agricultural area in the provinces along the border.[63] Newly appointed Syrian Prime Minister Muhammad Naji' al-'Utri welcomed Turkey's finance minister to Damascus at the end of the month to pursue these projects and to inaugurate official co-operation in the banking sector.[64] Negotiations on agriculture resulted in a June proto-col to work together on vegetable cultivation, soil and water conservation and farm education.[65] The year ended with the signing of a draft free trade pact, along with intimations from Turkish Prime Minister Recep Tayyip Erdogan that Syria might be permitted to draw additional water from the Tigris River.[66]

Marked improvement in the relations between Damascus and Ankara starting in early 2002 prompted Israel to carry out a variety of initiatives designed to drive a wedge between Syria and Turkey and thereby re-energise the Turkish–Israeli alignment. Most salient was a sharp rise in hostility directed towards Syria. February 2001 saw the election of Ariel Sharon to the premiership in Israel. The Sharon government stepped up military operations in south Lebanon and in April 2001 Israeli aircraft attacked a Syrian radar post in retaliation for activities undertaken by the Lebanese Islamist organisation Hizbullah along the Israel–Lebanon border. Despite these provocations, Damascus signalled that it was interested in resuming bilateral talks. Such signals were persistently rebuffed, to the growing irrita-tion of President Bashar al-Asad, who in turn escalated his government's anti-Israel rhetoric. More important, al-Asad revived the demand that any peace agreement between Syria and Israel must be predicated on a just resolution of the Israeli–Palestinian conflict. This demand led Washing-ton to exclude Syria from the initial stages of the so-called 'road map to peace', which was drawn up by the United States, the United Nations, the European Union and Russia during the autumn of 2002.

Israel's insistence that the Syrian authorities expel all representatives of radical Palestinian organisations from the country kept tensions high throughout 2003–4. In September 2004, Israel uncharacteristically claimed responsibility for the killing of an influential member of the Palestinian Islamist group HAMAS outside his house in Damascus. The assassination effectively derailed overtures that Syria had been making to the Sharon government through the good offices of the former US ambassador to Israel, Martin Indyk. Rather than pulling Syria away from Turkey, however, heightened Israeli belligerence pushed the two former adversaries closer together. Prime Minister al-'Utri met with Prime Minister Erdogan in July 2004 and publicly expressed his government's gratitude for Turk-ish statements of concern regarding Israel's treatment of the Palestinians and the detrimental impact that US economic sanctions were having on the Syrian economy.[67] The Turkish prime minister's refusal to accept an invitation to visit Israel that autumn was applauded by the leadership in Damascus, as was Erdogan's September meeting with Palestinian Prime Minister Ahmad Qurai. When Foreign Minister Gul did at last travel to Israel in early January 2005, he carried with him a conciliatory message from President al-Asad to the Israeli leadership.[68]

It is likely that Turkey's decision to strengthen ties with Syria, even at the risk of undermining its alignment with Israel, was prompted at least in part by the Israeli government's deepening involvement in northern Iraq. Israeli commandos and intelligence agents had provided covert assistance to Kurdish militias throughout the 1990s and such activities surged as local resistance to the US occupation escalated during the last quarter of 2003.[69] Ankara lodged repeated complaints with the Israeli government, charging that these missions laid the foundation for full Kurdish autonomy. The warnings were dismissed out of hand on the grounds that 'the training and the purchase of property [were] not official but done by private persons'.[70] Turkish officials riposted by publicly criticising Israeli policy towards the Palestinians, and in May 2004 recalled Turkey's ambassador to Israel 'for consultations on how to revive the Middle East peace process'.[71] At the same time, the government in Ankara began 'freezing Israeli firms out of future contracts for military hardware such as helicopters and unmanned aerial vehicles'.[72] As Turkey's strategic partnership with Israel turned sour during 2003–4, relations with Syria steadily improved.

Rapprochement Cools Off

Israel's refusal to acknowledge President al-Asad's overtures in the winter of 2004–5 ushered in a period of stagnation in Syrian–Turkish relations. Turkish President Sezer sent a dramatic signal to Washington in April 2005 by paying an official visit to Damascus despite US warnings to cancel the trip.[73] But no new bilateral agreements resulted from the visit. That same month, some fifty-five Syrian textile and food enterprises engaged in marathon talks with eighty-seven Turkish companies, but the negotiations led to no more than a half-dozen new contracts to export Syrian products to Turkey and purchase Turkish industrial machinery.[74] Although Syria's deputy prime minister for economic affairs, 'Abdullah al-Dardari, told reporters in October that the two governments had agreed to work together in the area of oil exploration and production, he also remarked to reporters that serious obstacles stood in the way of new investments. Moreover, the draft bilateral free trade agreement remained unratified.[75]

Political relations took an equally chilly turn. Foreign Minister Gul pointedly admonished his Syrian counterpart, saying that: 'The international community has concrete expectations from you [regarding the February 2005 assassination of the former Lebanese prime minister, Rafiq Hariri]. We, as a friendly country, advise you to heed the international community's warning. You should take solid steps to prove that you take them into account. Otherwise, you will be unable to find any support to defend you.'[76] More ominously, Foreign Minister Walid Mu'allim met with his Armenian counterpart in Damascus in early April 2006 to discuss a number of regional issues, including the prospects for Syria's relations with Turkey.[77] The government in Yerevan had long complained that Ankara's imposition of sanctions on Armenia to force it to give up its claim to Nagorno-Karabakh damaged not only the country's domestic economy but also the prospects for expanded commercial relations between Armenia and Syria.[78]

In May 2006, a newly organised Syrian Islamist opposition party, the Movement for Justice and Construction (Harakah al-'Adalah wal-Bina), intimated that it enjoyed loose ties to Turkey's ruling Justice and Development Party (Adalet ve Kalkinma Partisi or AKP).[79] Shortly thereafter, the Turkish government welcomed Lebanese Prime Minister Fuad al-Sanyurah to Ankara and concluded a bilateral protocol on educational and technical exchange.[80] And in a less than tactful moment, Prime Minister Erdogan commented that he had sent a special envoy to President al-Asad to ensure that escalating tensions in the region would be defused without resorting to what he called 'an emotional approach. We have to try', he went on, 'to reach a [stable] point through a reasonable approach' instead.[81] A month later, Erdogan presided over the groundbreaking ceremony for a massive new dam across one of the major tributaries of the Tigris River.[82] Relations reached a nadir of sorts in August 2006, when Ankara proposed to deploy a contingent of Turkish troops to southern Lebanon to secure the area in the aftermath of the Israeli invasion that summer.[83]

Cooler relations between Damascus and Ankara during the course of 2005 accompanied a marked reinvigoration of Turkey's partnership with Israel. Prime Minister Erdogan travelled to Jerusalem that May and announced the conclusion of seventeen new agreements to engage in collaborative military projects. The premier punctuated the trip by publicly shaking hands with Prime Minister Sharon and inviting him to visit the Turkish capital.[84] The commanders of Turkey's air force and navy undertook separate missions to Israel in December and Israel's chief of the general staff arrived in Ankara to confer with his Turkish counterpart at the end of the year. After a brief interruption caused by the AKP government's positive response to HAMAS's victory in the January parliamentary elections in Palestine, several new bilateral economic agreements were signed in the spring of 2006. A Turkish construction company was awarded the contract to construct a new $360 million electricity generating plant in Israel that October.[85] The resuscitation of the Turkish–Israeli axis left Damascus once again vulnerable to some sort of joint offensive and thereby undermined the Syrian government's willingness to pursue further co-operation with Ankara.

Meanwhile, Turkey significantly reduced its involvement in the Kurdish-controlled areas of northern Iraq. Turkish restraint derived in the first place from deference to the United States, whose government warned that military operations against the PKK would precipitate violence across the region. In addition, the authorities in Ankara appear to have expected US military commanders to take steps to uproot the PKK from its Iraqi strongholds, perhaps with the assistance of the mainstream Kurdish militias. Only after Iranian troops carried out military operations in northeastern Iraq did the Turkish high command order a resumption of air and artillery strikes against PKK targets.[86] By this time, Kurdish unrest had erupted inside Syria, making it much harder for the Ba'thi regime in Damascus to manipulate Kurdish discontent as a retaliatory weapon against Turkey.

Taking advantage of its strengthened position, Ankara exerted pressure on Syria to remain on the sidelines as tensions between Israel and the Palestinians heated up during the summer of 2006. In early July, Prime Minister Erdogan dispatched a senior adviser to Damascus to urge President al-Asad to refrain from taking part in the escalating crisis.[87] President al-Asad in turn appealed to Erdogan to restrain Israel when it became apparent that the Israel Defense Forces were about to advance across the border into Lebanon.[88] Turkish efforts to keep Syria from intervening in the fighting continued into August.[89] When it looked as if Damascus might be working with Tehran to supply weapons to Hizbullah, Ankara resorted to firmer measures: on at least four different occasions Turkish warplanes forced aircraft suspected of carrying armaments to land at Diyarbakir to be searched.[90] Such bullying put a damper on co-operation between the two governments.

Resumption of Momentum

Not until the last weeks of 2006 did Syrian–Turkish rapprochement regain momentum. At the close of the Joint Economic Committee meeting in late November, Deputy Prime Minister al-Dardari and Turkey's Deputy Prime Minister Abdullatif Sener signed a collection of agreements aimed at boosting bilateral trade and investment. The agreements also initiated co-operation between the Central Bank of Syria and Turkey's Banking Supervisory Commission.[91] A week later, Prime Minister al-'Utri convened the inaugural congress of Syrian–Turkish Local Authorities, noting that, 'The aims of this conference constitute a progressive step and specific move for further cementing the ever-growing relations of co-operation between Syria and Turkey in economic, commercial, cultural and social domains'.[92] More important, Syria's interior minister, General Bassam 'Abd al-Majid, was simultaneously conferring with his Turkish counterpart on a wide range of security issues. The two ministers agreed to set up joint co-ordination committees to implement the anti-terrorism protocols that had previously been signed. Furthermore, the Turkish team invited Syrian cadets to enrol in Turkey's well-equipped police academies.[93]

At the beginning of February 2007, Foreign Minister Walid al-Mu'allim travelled to Ankara as part of a drive 'to revive tripartite co-ordination' among Syria, Turkey and Iran.[94] His agenda included the promotion of economic relations with the coming into force of the bilateral free trade agreement on 1 January, developments in Iraq and 'the situation in the Palestinian territories'. To facilitate his mission, the Turkish government announced that it 'has decided to lessen its role in Lebanon after its attempts in the period following the Israeli aggression, because of its realisation that the Lebanese issue is too complicated and because it is aware that there is a rejection among certain Lebanese factions for such a role'. In early April, Minister of Defence al-Turkmani and Chief of the General Staff 'Ali Habib welcomed the commander of the Turkish air force to Damascus; the generals reviewed ways to enhance bilateral military co-operation.[95] Meanwhile, in Aleppo, President al-Asad met with Prime Minister Erdogan to co-ordinate energy production and oil transportation policies. The two leaders capped the summit by attending a football match between Syria's al-Ittihad and Turkey's Fenerbahce, with al-Asad telling reporters that he planned to cheer for Fenerbahce and Erdogan had promised to root for al-Ittihad. Residents of Hatay who wished to attend the match were permitted to cross the border without passports, 'thanks to co-ordination by the foreign and interior ministries of the two countries'.[96]

President al-Asad paid a return visit to Ankara in mid-October 2007, 'placing yet another brick in the edifice of special relations between the two countries'.[97] Turkish officials let it be known that they intended to help their guest to 'understand' the reasons behind any future military incursion into northern Iraq.[98] While he was in the Turkish capital, al-Asad signed a broad-ranging memorandum of understanding, according to whose terms the two governments pledged to promote investments and expand joint projects in border districts, improve transportation links, accelerate Turkish technical assistance to Syrian financial institutions and rehabilitate the obsolete oil pipeline between Killis and Homs, the site of Syria's primary oil refinery.[99] Syria's new minister of economy and trade, 'Amr Husni Lutfi, attended the first meeting of the Syrian–Turkish Partnership Council in Mersin in mid-November and announced plans to open a free trade zone 'in one of Syria's main industrial centres for Turkish investors'.[100] He also announced that an additional commercial passageway would shortly be opened at al-Qamishli.

The thorny question of water distribution at last received concerted attention as 2008 opened. The water and environment ministers of Syria, Turkey and Iraq gathered in Damascus in January and agreed to set up technical committees to investigate the 'most rational' and sustainable means to exploit regional water resources.[101] In the wake of the conference, the Syrian ministry of agriculture released plans to bring 50,000 hectares of newly reclaimed land into production in al-Hasakah province, using water drawn from the Tigris River.[102] Brighter prospects for co-operation over water set the stage for a joint economic forum in Damascus, in which some 700 Syrian and Turkish businesspeople discussed items of mutual interest.[103] Meanwhile, across town, Syria's finance minister, Muhammad al-Husain, was discussing strategies to increase efficiency at the border crossings with Turkey's minister of state for foreign trade, Kursad Tuzman.[104] Two weeks later, the Syrian government revised its official maps so as to remove the district around Iskandarun from Syrian territory.[105] In June, Syrian Minister of Petroleum Sufyah al-Alaw attended the Third Turkish–Arab Economic Forum in Istanbul and announced that the two governments planned to form a joint company to explore for oil in Syria; he went on to remark that 'in the future we could found joint nuclear power plants for electricity production'.[106] And in July the Syria–Turkey Inter-Regional Co-operation Programme launched eighteen additional development projects in the contiguous provinces of Aleppo, Killis, Gaziantep and Onkobinar Gate.[107]

President al-Asad's return to Ankara in early August 2008 underscored the accelerating pace of Syrian–Turkish co-operation. The Syrian president was reported to have brought with him a confidential report detailing Iran's nuclear research programme, as well as thoughts on how best to deal with current trends in Iraq and Palestine.[108] He was followed to the Turkish capital by Deputy Prime Minister al-Dardari, who initialled an agreement to build a jointly run pipeline to transport natural gas, and by Minister of the Interior 'Abd al-Majid, who worked with Turkish officials to formulate common policies on a variety of internal and border security matters.[109]

Closer relations between Damascus and Ankara took shape in the context of clear signs that Turkey intended to resume direct intervention in northern Iraq. As 2007 opened, Prime Minister Erdogan called US-led efforts to collaborate in suppressing radical Kurdish organisations 'a failure' and hinted that he would order the Turkish armed forces to supply arms to the Turkmen population of Kirkuk and Mawsil if the situation continued to deteriorate.[110] Turkish troops took up forward positions along the border at the end of May and chased Kurdish guerrillas back into Iraqi territory on several occasions. Commanders on the ground were reported to be pushing the government to authorise more extensive operations.[111] The potential for a large-scale offensive remained high throughout the summer and autumn, despite the signing of a Turkish–Iraqi security pact in late September that pointedly omitted a provision which would have allowed Turkish troops to engage in 'hot pursuit' of Kurdish fighters.[112] Matters came to a head in mid-October, when Turkish forces launched artillery and aerial assaults against PKK positions. The offensive continued into the spring of 2008.[113]

To a greater extent than was the case in earlier incursions, however, the military operations that Turkey undertook in 2007–8 jeopardised its own economic interests. Trade with the Kurdish provinces of northern Iraq totalled some $3 billion in 2006 and was expected to exceed $5 billion in 2007; Turkish construction companies carried out the great majority of infrastructure projects around Erbil, Dohuk and Sulaimaniyyah.[114] Ties to northern Iraq were particularly important for economic expansion in Turkey's impoverished southeastern region, which exported significant quantities of manufactured goods, agricultural products and unskilled labour to Kurdish districts across the border.

In addition, Turkey's AKP-led government confronted severe challenges at home. Opposition parties disrupted parliamentary proceedings in April 2007 and attempted to block the election of the AKP foreign minister, Abdullah Gul, to the presidency. The country's senior military commanders then charged that the party was seeking to undercut the secular foundation of the political system by nominating an Islamist to be head of state.[115] The Constitutional Court took the hint and invalidated the presidential balloting.[116] AKP candidates prevailed in parliamentary elections that July, but the wide margin of victory that the party enjoyed led secularist forces to worry that the ensuing government would implement policies that reflected religious principles.[117] Such fears heightened after the new parliament elected Gul to the presidency, prompting the general staff to issue a statement warning that 'our nation has been watching the behaviour of centres of evil who systematically try to corrode the secular nature' of the Kemalist order.[118] The crisis of governance simmered into early 2008, as clandestine ultra-nationalist groups carried out a campaign of violence against prominent Islamists and liberals and the parliament enacted laws that encouraged Islamist practices.[119] Burgeoning economic difficulties increased the country's overall vulnerability.[120]

Meanwhile, Turkey faced growing problems in the Caucasus. Relations between Ankara's primary regional allies, Georgia and Azerbaijan, and the Russian Federation deteriorated dramatically during the last quarter of

2006. At the end of the year, Moscow imposed significant economic sanctions on both countries in an attempt to derail the Baku-Tbilisi-Ceyhan (BTC) pipeline project.[121] Russia then stepped up its efforts to improve the infrastructure of Armenia, paying special attention to new oil facilities that linked Russia and Armenia directly to Iran.[122] The AKP government attempted to parry Russian moves by offering additional technical and military assistance to Georgia and Azerbaijan.[123] By the fall of 2007, the BTC pipeline had become a pivotal security concern for the Turkish authorities, both with respect to developments in the Caucasus and in connection with military operations in northern Iraq.[124] Any interruption in the flow of BTC oil had the potential to exacerbate the difficulties that Turkey's domestic economy was already experiencing. Consequently, Ankara was in no position to manipulate commercial and financial connections with Syria to its own advantage in 2007–8 and co-operation between the two countries flourished.

Conclusion

Syria's relations with Turkey have improved dramatically over the past decade. The use of armed force between the two countries, which appeared to be a distinct possibility in the autumn of 1998, seems highly unlikely today. Instead, economic transactions are flourishing, governmental co-operation is expanding, military and security connections are strengthening and even the tricky problem of water distribution has begun to look manageable. These improvements in bilateral relations have resulted partly from Damascus's recognition that it is in no position to mount an attack on its powerful northern neighbour, particularly in light of Turkey's strategic partnership with Israel. But they also reflect broader, and more recognisable, dynamics in the anarchic regional arena. Whenever Syria has good reason to expect that Turkey will take advantage of any overtures it might make, the leadership in Damascus has refrained from offering accommodations or concessions to Ankara. By the same token, whenever Turkey finds itself too vulnerable or preoccupied to be able to exploit Syrian overtures, Damascus has ventured to leave itself open to Ankara, not only economically but with regard to security matters as well. In this way, as in so many others, Syrian foreign policy is shaped by calculations that are common to all states and can thus be understood without presuming that the country's leaders act in ways that are idiosyncratic, prone to miscalculation or out of touch with the contemporary world.

Notes

1. *New York Times*, 2 October 1998.
2. Associated Press, 4 October 1998.
3. Henri J. Barkey, 'Reluctant Neighbors: Reflections on Turkish–Arab Relations,' *Beirut Review*, no. 7, 1994; Robert Olson, 'The Kurdish Question and Turkey's Foreign Policy, 1991–1995: From the Gulf War to the Incursion into Iraq', *Journal of South Asian and Middle Eastern Studies*, vol. 19, 1995; Muhammad Muslih, 'Syria and Turkey: Uneasy Relations' in Henri J. Barkey, ed. *Reluctant Neighbor: Turkey's Role in the Middle East*, Washington, DC 1996; Murhaf Jouejati, 'Water Politics as High Politics: The Case of Turkey and Syria' in Barkey, ed. *Reluctant Neighbor*; Serdar Guner, 'The Turkish–Syrian War of Attrition: The Water Dispute', *Studies in Conflict and Terrorism*, vol. 20, 1997; Robert Olson, 'Turkey–Syria Relations since the Gulf War: Kurds and Water', *Middle East Policy*, vol. 5, 1997; Serdar Guner, 'Signalling in the Turkish–Syrian Water Conflict', *Conflict Management and Peace Science*, vol. 16, 1998; Robert Olson, 'Turkey–Syria Relations, 1997 to 2000: Kurds, Water, Israel and "Undeclared War"', *Orient*, vol. 42, 2001; Nilufer Narli, 'Major Points of Dispute in Turkish–Arab Relations', *III. Congrès International du Dialogue Turco-Arab*, Istanbul 2003; and Ozden Zeynep Oktav, 'Water Dispute and Kurdish Separatism in Turkish-Syrian Relations', *The Turkish Yearbook*, vol. 34, 2003.
4. Reuters, 4 July 2008.
5. *Syria Today*, 20 July 2008.
6. Continued hostility was predicted by Alan Makovsky and Michael Eisenstadt, 'Turkish–Syrian Relations: A Crisis Delayed?', *Policywatch* (Washington Institute for Near East Policy), no. 345, 1998; Kemal Kirisci, 'Turkey and the Muslim Middle East' in Alan Makovsky and Sabri Sayari, eds. *Turkey's New World*, Washington, DC 2000, pp. 46–7; O. Zeynep Oktav Alantar, 'The October 1998 Crisis: A Change of Turkish Foreign Policy towards Syria?', *Cahiers d'Etudes sur la Méditerranée orientale et le monde turco-iranien*, no. 31, 2001; Bulent Aras and Hasan Koni, 'Turkish–Syrian Relations Revisited', *Arab Studies Quarterly*, vol. 24, 2002; Erik L. Knudsen, 'Syria, Turkey and the Changing Power Configuration in the Middle East' in Tareq Y. Ismael and Mustafa Aydin, eds. *Turkey's Foreign Policy in the 21st Century*, Aldershot 2003.
7. Meliha Benli Altunisik and Ozlem Tur, 'From Distant Neighbors to

Partners? Changing Syrian–Turkish Relations', *Security Dialogue*, vol. 37, 2006, p. 238.

8. Ibid., pp. 239–41.

9. Ibid., pp. 243–5. Improved relations are similarly described, but left unexplained, in Bulent Aras and Rabia Karakaya Polat, 'From Conflict to Cooperation: Desecuritization of Turkey's Relations with Syria and Iran', *Security Dialogue*, vol. 39, 2008. See also Ozden Zeynep Oktav, 'The Limits of Change: Turkey, Iran, Syria' in Nursin Atesoblu Guney, ed. *Contentious Issues of Security and the Future of Turkey*, Aldershot 2007, pp. 91–4.

10. Mustafa Aydin and Damla Aras, 'Political Conditionality of Economic Relations between Paternalist States: Turkey's Interaction with Iran, Iraq and Syria', *Arab Studies Quarterly*, vol. 27, 2005, p. 23.

11. Ibid., p. 26 and p. 39, n. 25. See also Alain Gresh, 'Turkish–Israeli–Syrian Relations and their Impact on the Middle East', *Middle East Journal*, vol. 52, 1998, pp. 190–1.

12. Aydin and Aras, 'Political Conditionality', pp. 33–5.

13. Robert Jervis, 'Co-operation Under the Security Dilemma', *World Politics*, vol. 30, 1978.

14. Altunisik and Tur, 'From Distant Neighbors to Partners?' p. 238.

15. Deutsche Presse-Agentur, 24 February 1999; *al-Hayat*, 27 February 1999.

16. Deutsche Presse-Agentur, 24 March 1999.

17. Syrian Arab Republic Radio, 24 March 1999 (British Broadcasting Corporation [BBC] Summary of World Broadcasts [SWB]).

18. Anatolia News Agency, 14 June 1999 (SWB).

19. *al-Hayat*, 30 June 1999.

20. Deutsche Presse-Agentur, 6 March 2000.

21. Middle East News Line, 9 May 2000.

22. Deutsche Presse-Agentur, 28 September 2000.

23. *Daily Star* (Beirut), 13 November 2000.

24. Malik Mufti, 'Turkish–Syrian Rapprochement: Causes and Consequences', *Policywatch*, no. 630, 2002.

25. Anatolia News Agency, 15 January 2001 (SWB).

26. Anatolia News Agency, 23 January 2001 (SWB).

27. Syrian Arab Television, 18 April 2001 (BBC Monitoring Middle East [MME]).

28. Syrian Arab News Agency (SANA), 10 September 2001 (MME); *Turkish Daily News*, 16 September 2001.

29. *Turkish Daily News*, 12 September 2001.

30. George Gruen, 'Dynamic Prospects in Turkish–Israeli Relations', *Israel Affairs*, vol. 1, 1995; Alain Gresh, 'Turkish–Israeli–Syrian Relations and their Impact on the Middle East', *Middle East Journal*, vol. 52, 1998; Amikam

Nachmani, 'The Remarkable Turkish–Israeli Tie', *Middle East Quarterly*, June 1998; Neill Lochery, 'Israel and Turkey: Deepening Ties and Strategic Implications, 1995–98', *Israel Affairs*, vol. 5, 1998; Marios L. Evriviades, 'The Turkish–Israeli Axis', *Orient*, vol. 39, 1998; Meliha Altunisik, 'The Turkish–Israeli Rapprochement in the Post-Cold War Era', *Middle Eastern Studies*, vol. 36, 2000; Raphael Israeli, 'The Turkish–Israeli Odd Couple', *Orbis*, vol. 45, 2001; Ofra Bengio and Gencer Ozcan, 'Old Grievances, New Fears: Arab Perceptions of Turkey and its Alignment with Israel', *Middle Eastern Studies*, vol. 37, 2001; Philip Robins, *Suits and Uniforms: Turkish Foreign Policy since the Cold War*, London 2003, chap. 7; Joshua Walker, 'Turkey and Israel's Relationship in the Middle East', *Mediterranean Quarterly*, vol. 17, 2006.

31. Robins, *Suits and Uniforms*, p. 65.

32. Altunisik, 'The Turkish–Israeli Rapprochement', p. 185.

33. Efraim Inbar, *The Israeli–Turkish Entente*, London 2001, p. 28.

34. Ibid., p. 23.

35. See Anthony H. Cordesman, *Arab–Israeli Military Forces in an Era of Asymmetric Wars*, Westport, Conn. 2006.

36. Patrick Seale, 'Turkey and Syria: The War Over Water', *Middle East International*, 4 June 1999.

37. Jolyon Naegele, 'Turkey: Demirel's Israeli Trip Spotlights Turkish–Syrian Relations', Radio Free Europe/Radio Liberty (RFE/RL), 15 July 1999; Patrick Seale, 'Where Do They Go from Here?', *Middle East International*, 24 December 1999; *Turkish Daily News*, 7 August 2002.

38. Gokhan Bacik, 'The Limits of an Alliance: Turkish–Israeli Relations Revisited', *Arab Studies Quarterly*, vol. 23, 2001, pp. 58–60.

39. Martin van Bruinessen, 'Kurds, Turks and the Alevi Revival in Turkey', *Middle East Report*, July–September 1996; Bedriye Poyraz, 'The Turkish State and Alevis: Changing Parameters of an Uneasy Relationship', *Middle Eastern Studies*, vol. 41, 2005.

40. Tahire Erman and Emrah Goker, 'Alevi Politics in Contemporary Turkey', *Middle Eastern Studies*, vol. 36, 2000.

41. Poyraz, p. 515.

42. Gareth M. Winrow, 'Turkish Policy toward Central Asia and the Transcaucasus' in Makovsky and Sayari, eds. *Turkey's New World*; Paul B. Henze, 'Turkey's Caucasian Initiatives', *Orbis*, vol. 45, 2001; Nasuh Uslu, 'The Russian, Caucasian and Central Asian Aspects of Turkish Foreign Policy in the Post Cold War Period', *Alternatives*, vol. 2, 2003; Robins, *Suits and Uniforms*, chap. 8; and Mustafa Aydin, 'Foucault's Pendulum: Turkey in Central Asia and the Caucasus', *Turkish Studies*, vol. 5, 2004.

43. Uslu, 'Russian, Caucasian and Central Asian Aspects', p. 170.

44. Robins, *Suits and Uniforms*, pp. 340–1.

45. Robert Olson, *Turkey's Relations with Iran, Syria, Israel and Russia, 1991–2000*, Costa Mesa, Calif. 2001, p. 99.

46. Ibid., p. 101.

47. *al-Hayat*, 1 March 2002.

48. Syrian Arab Republic Radio, 19 June 2002 (MME); *al-Hayah*, 1 March 2002 and Altunsik and Tur, 'From Distant Neighbors to Partners?', p. 240, n. 24.

49. *Christian Science Monitor*, 26 June 2002.

50. Anatolia News Agency, 14 March 2002 (BBC Monitoring Europe [ME]).

51. Anatolia News Agency, 24 August 2002 (ME).

52. BBC, 4 January 2003.

53. *al-Quds al-'Arabi*, 13 January 2003.

54. Jean-Christophe Peuch, 'Turkey: Istanbul Meeting Urges Iraq to Cooperate', RFE/RL, 24 January 2003.

55. Anatolia News Agency, 28 July 2003 (ME).

56. *al-Hayat*, 5 August 2003.

57. Anatolia News Agency, 29 July 2003 (MME).

58. Anatolia News Agency, 30 July 2003 (ME).

59. Syrian Arab Republic Radio, 30 July 2003 (MME).

60. Syrian Arab News Agency (SANA), 8 December 2003 (MME) and *Turkish Daily News*, 18 December 2003.

61. *al-Hayat*, 6 January 2004 and *Tishrin*, 6 January 2004.

62. *Middle East*, February 2004.

63. SANA, 6 March 2004 (MME).

64. Agence France Presse, 26 March 2004.

65. Anatolia News Agency, 24 June 2004 (ME).

66. SANA, 22 December 2004 (MME); Bulent Aras, 'After the Threats, Syria and Turkey are Fast Friends', *Daily Star* (Beirut), 4 January 2005.

67. Anatolia News Agency, 13 July 2004 (ME).

68. Jean-Christophe Peuch, 'In Israel, Turkish Foreign Minister Seeks Mideast Peace Role for Turkey', RFE/RL, 4 January 2005.

69. Gawdat Bahgat, 'Iraq and Israel', *Journal of South Asian and Middle Eastern Studies*, vol. 19, 2003; Seymour M. Hersh, 'Plan B', *The New Yorker*, 28 June 2004; Mustafa Kibaroglu, 'Clash of Interest Over Northern Iraq Drives Turkish–Israeli Alliance to a Crossroads', *Middle East Journal*, vol. 59, 2005 and BBC, 20 September 2006.

70. Hersh, 'Plan B'.

71. *Jerusalem Post*, 27 May 2004.

72. 'Israel's Shifting Geopolitical Security Concerns Threaten Its Relationship with Turkey', PINR Report, 3 September 2004.

73. Agence France Presse, 14 April 2005; Philip Robins, 'Turkish Foreign Policy since 2002', *International Affairs*, vol. 83, 2007, p. 296.

74. *The Syria Report*, second quarter 2005.

75. Anatolia News Agency, 6 October 2005 (ME); ArabicNews.com, 8 October 2005.

76. *Milliyet*, 23 July 2005 (ME); United Press International, 12 January 2006.

77. Noyan Tapan News Agency, 10 April 2006 (BBC Monitoring Trans-Caucasus Unit).

78. Arminfo (Yerevan), 5 March 2002 (BBC Monitoring Trans-Caucasus Unit).

79. *al-Quds al-'Arabi*, 10 May 2006 (MME).

80. Anatolia News Agency, 7 June 2006 (ME).

81. Turkish TRT 2 Television, 3 July 2006 (ME).

82. Anatolia News Agency, 5 August 2006 (ME).

83. Anatolia News Agency, 16 August 2006 (ME).

84. Robins, 'Turkish Foreign Policy', p. 300; Robert Olson, 'Turkey's Policies toward Kurdistan–Iraq and Iraq: Nationalism, Capitalism and State Formation', *Mediterranean Quarterly*, vol. 17, 2006, p. 60.

85. *Turkish Daily News*, 13 October 2005.

86. Associated Press, 10 May 2006; *Christian Science Monitor*, 29 August 2006.

87. Anatolia News Agency, 4 July 2006; *Jerusalem Post*, 7 July 2006.

88. SANA, 19 July 2006; Anatolia News Agency, 19 July 2006.

89. SANA, 4 August 2006.

90. *Hurriyet*, 19 August 2006.

91. SANA, 30 November 2006 (MME).

92. SANA, 9 December 2006 (MME).

93. SANA, 10 December 2006 (MME).

94. *al-Hayat*, 31 January 2007.

95. SANA, 3 April 2007.

96. *Turkish Weekly*, 4 April 2007.

97. *Tishrin*, 16 October 2007.

98. *al-Hayat*, 17 October 1007.

99. *al-Thawrah*, 17 October 2007.

100. Oxford Business Group, 'Syria: Turkish Delight', 19 November 2007.

101. SANA, 11 January 2008.

102. *al-Hayat*, 12 March 2008.

103. Xinhua, 27 April 2008.

104. SANA, 28 April 2008.

105. Syria Media Report, 23 May 2008 <www.iwpr.net>.

106. Gareth Jenkins, 'Syria Proposes Nuclear Cooperation with Turkey', *Eurasia Daily Monitor*, 16 June 2008.
107. *Syria Today*, 16 July 2008.
108. SANA, 6 August 2008.
109. SANA, 20 August 2008.
110. *Financial Times*, 31 January 2007.
111. *Daily Star* (Beirut), 31 May 2007; *Guardian*, 1 June 2007; Yigal Schleifer, 'Turkish Military Presses for Offensive against Militant Bases in Iraq', <www.Eurasianet.org>, 5 June 2007; *Christian Science Monitor*, 8 June 2007; *Guardian*, 30 June 2007; and Associated Press, 9 July 2007.
112. BBC, 28 September 2007.
113. Associated Press, 10 October 2007; *Guardian*, 22 October 2007; *Washington Post*, 24 October 2007; *New York Times*, 29 October 2007; *al-Ahram Weekly*, 6–12 December 2007; *Washington Post*, 27 December 2007; Reuters, 11 January 2008; *Washington Post*, 5 February 2008; Agence France Presse, 20 March 2008; and *Guardian*, 2 May 2008.
114. Nicholas Birch, 'A Turkish Raid into Iraq Could Have Significant Economic Ramifications for Ankara', <www.Eurasianet.org>, 17 October 2007.
115. Nicholas Birch, 'Turkey Grapples with Constitutional Crisis surrounding Presidential Vote', <www.Eurasianet.org>, 27 April 2007 and Yigal Schleifer, 'Turkey's Constitutional Crisis Deepens', <www.Eurasianet.org>, 30 April 2007.
116. Nicholas Birch, 'Turkey: High Court Invalidates Presidential Vote', <www.Eurasianet.org>, 1 May 2007.
117. Breffni O'Rouke, 'Turkey: Governing Party could be Emboldened by New Mandate', RRE/RL, 23 July 2007.
118. Jeffrey Donovan, 'Turkey: Conservative Muslim Elected President', RFE/RL, 29 August 2007.
119. Nicholas Birch, 'Turkey: Conspiracy Investigation Revives Concern about the "Deep State"', <www.Eurasianet.org>, 11 February 2008 and 'Can Turkey's Regime Crisis be Defused?', Turkey Analyst, 22 February 2008.
120. Yigal Schleifer, 'Turkey: More Woes for Government, as Economy Loses Steam', <www.Eurasianet.org>, 18 April 2008.
121. Alexandros Petersen and Taleh Ziyadov, 'Azerbaijan and Georgia: Playing Russian Roulette with Moscow', Central Asia-Caucasus Analyst, 10 January 2007.
122. Haroutiun Khachatrian, 'Russia and Iran May Restore Rail Corridor through Armenia', Central Asia–Caucasus Analyst, 16 May 2007.
123. Ertan Efegil, 'Turkish AK Party's Central Asia and Caucasus Policies: Critiques and Suggestions', *Caucasian Review of International Affairs*, vol. 2, 2008.
124. Reuters, 17 October 2007.

Notes on Contributors

Myriam Ababsa is a social geographer based in Jordan. Her PhD defended at Tours University in 2004 was entitled 'Idéologies et territoires dans un front pionnier du monde arabe: Raqqa et le Projet de l'Euphrate en Jazîra syrienne'. She was awarded the Special Mention of the Best Doctoral Dissertation Prize from the Syrian Studies Association for it in 2006. Her research focus is now on Jordan; she is preparing a social and economic atlas of Jordan at the French Institute for the Near East (IFPO). Her book, *Amman de pierre et de paix* (Paris, 2007), appeared in the 'Les villes en mouvement' series published by Editions Autrement.

Souhail Belhadj completed his PhD at Sciences-Po Paris on political leadership within Syrian authoritarianism. He graduated from Sciences-Po Paris in 2001, specialising in political history (his master thesis addressed the issue of the management of religious circles by Tunisia's nationalists between 1945 and 1955). He has done extensive field research in Syria, including high-level interviews. His publications include 'Démocratie, famille et procédure: ethnométhodologie d'un débat parlementaire syrien', with Baudouin Dupret and Jean-Noël Ferrié, *Revue européenne de sciences sociales*, vol. 45 no 139, 2007 and 'Y a-t-il de vraies transformations politiques internes en Syrie?', with Eberhard Kienle in B. Dupret, Z. Ghazzal, Y. Courbage and M. Al-Dbiyat. eds, *La Syrie au présent: reflets d'une société*, 2007.

Baudouin Dupret was educated in law, Arabic, Islamic sciences and political and social sciences. He is a senior research fellow affiliated to the French National Centre for Scientific Research (CNRS). He was based for several years in Cairo and in Damascus. He currently belongs to the Institut des

Sciences Sociales du Politique (ISP-Cachan, Paris, France) and teaches in Brussels, Louovain-la-Neuve and Paris. He is the author of *Au nom de quel droit. Répertoires juridiques et référence religieuse dans la société égyptienne musulmane contemporaine* (Paris, 2000), *Le Jugement en action. Ethnométhodologie du droit, de la morale et de la justice en Egypte* (Geneva, 2006) and *Droit et sciences sociales* (Paris, 2006). He has co-edited several volumes in the field of the sociology and anthropology of law in the Middle East, for example *Legal Pluralism in the Arab World* (New York, 1999), *Standing Trial: Law and the Person in the Modern Middle East* (London, 2004) and *Narratives of Truth in Islamic Law* (London, 2007). He has also co-edited a work on present-day Syria: *La Syrie au present: reflets d'une société* (Arles: Actes Sud, 2007).

Diana V. Galbraith obtained her Bachelor's Degree in International Relations from Mills College in Oakland, California. She has also studied at Pomona College, Harvard University and Stanford University. She plans a career in international affairs and translated this essay while she was working in Ohio on the presidential campaign of President Barak Obama.

Julie Gauthier holds a doctorate from the Ecole des hautes etudes en sciences sociales in Paris. She is the author of 'Syrie: le facteur kurde,' *Outre-Terre* no. 14 (2006).

Zohair Ghazzal is Professor of Historical and Social Sciences at Loyola University, Chicago and Fellow at the Institute for Advanced Study at Princeton. He published *The Political Economy of Damascus in the Nineteenth Century* (in French, 1993), and *The Grammars of Adjudication: The Economics of Judicial Decision Making in Fin-de-siècle Ottoman Beirut and Damascus* (Beirut, 2007) and co-directed with Baudouin Dupret *La Syrie au présent: reflets d'une société* (Paris, 2007). He is now completing a book on Syria's criminal system entitled 'The Ideal of Punishment' and working on forms of life in contemporary urban settings in Greater Syria.

Bassam Haddad is Director of the Middle East Studies Program at George Mason University and Visiting Professor at Georgetown University. He serves as Founding Editor of the *Arab Studies Journal* (www.

arabstudiesjournal.org), a peer-reviewed research publication and also serves on the Editorial Committee of Middle East Report (http://www.merip. org/). He is co-producer/director of the award-winning documentary film, *About Baghdad* (www.aboutbaghdad.com) and director of a film series on *Arabs and Terrorism* (www.arabsandterrorism.com). He is currently working on a book on Syria's political economy, provisionally titled *The Political Economy of Regime Security: State–Business Networks in Syria* and has recently directed a new film series on Arab/Muslim immigrants in Europe, titled *The 'Other' Threat* (www.TheOtherThreat.com).

Salwa Ismail is Reader in Comparative Politics of the Middle East in the Department of Politics and International Studies, School of Oriental and African Studies, University of London. She researches and writes on everyday life, politics and forms of governance in the Arab world and also on Islamist movements and on modern Arab and Islamic political thought. She is the author of *Political Life in Cairo's New Quarters: Encountering the Everyday State* (Minneapolis, 2006) and *Rethinking Islamist Politics: Culture, the State and Islamism* (London, 2003 and 2006). Her publications include articles in *PS: Political Science and Politics* (2008), *Muslim World Journal of Human Rights* (2007), *Government and Opposition* (2004), *Historical Reflections* (2004) and *Comparative Studies in Society and History* (2000).

Joshua Landis is Co-Director of the Center for Middle East Studies and Assistant Professor at the University of Oklahoma. He writes the blog 'Syria Comment', which is read by over 2,000 readers a day, amongst whom are officials in Washington, London and Damascus. He is a frequent analyst on television and radio, having appeared on PBS, CNN, BBC and al-Jazeera. He travels regularly to Syria and Lebanon. His recently published articles on Syria focus on Islamic education, the political opposition and Syria's role in the 1948 Palestine War. His book, *Democracy in Syria*, will be published by Palgrave Macmillan in the near future.

Fred H. Lawson is Rice Professor of Government at Mills College. He is the author of *Why Syria Goes to War* (Ithaca, New York, 1996), *Constructing International Relations in the Arab World* (Stanford, Calif., 2006) and other studies of political economy and foreign policy in the contemporary Middle East. In 1992–3, he was Fulbright Lecturer in International Relations at the University of Aleppo.

Joe Pace has spent ten months in Syria researching civil society, the opposition and Islamism. After obtaining his B.A. from Harvard University, he spent a year in Egypt working with Human Rights Watch. He is currently enrolled in Yale Law School where he is specialising in international humanitarian law and the protection of civil liberties in the war on terror.

Thomas Pierret is an Aspirant at the FNRS (Belgium) and a doctoral student in political science at Sciences-Po, Paris and the University of Louvain. A fluent Arabic speaker, he conducted prolonged fieldwork in Syria for a doctoral thesis on the country's *'ulama*. His paper shows in particular how age-old structures such as mosque-based study groups and Sufi networks have been developed in order to attract middle-class professionals. His general research interests revolve around Islamic social movements, forms of religious authority, the role of tradition, the Sufi–Salafi divide and the relations between Muslim religious forces and authoritarian regimes.

Bassel F. Salloukh is Assistant Professor of Political Science at the Lebanese American University (Beirut) and Senior Non-Resident Research Fellow at the Interuniversity Consortium for Arab and Middle Eastern Studies (ICAMES) in Montréal, Canada. He is co-author of *Mapping the Political Landscape: An Introduction to Political Science*, 2nd edition, (Toronto, 2007) and co-editor of *Persistent Permeability: Regionalism, Localism, and Globalization in the Middle East* (London, 2004). His recent publications appeared in the *International Journal of Middle East Studies*, the *Canadian Journal of Political Science* and *Middle East Report*. He serves as consultant to a number of international organisations and is an expert commentator for media outlets in North America, Europe and the Middle East.

Anja Zorob is Senior Research Fellow at the Institute of Development Research and Development Policy at the University of Bochum in Germany. Her main research areas are economics and politics of the Middle East and North Africa and economic development and regional integration with special focus on Euro-Mediterranean and intra-Arab relations. Her recent publications include 'The Syrian–European Association Agreement and Its Potential Impact on Enhancing Credibility of Reform', *Mediterranean Politics*, vol. 13, no. 1, 2008, pp. 1–21 and 'Intraregional Economic Integration: The Cases of GAFTA and MAFTA', in Cilja Harders and Matteo Legrenzi, eds *Beyond Regionalism? Regional Cooperation, Regionalism and Regionalisation in the Middle East*, (Aldershot, 2008), pp. 169–83.

Bibliography

Ababsa, Myriam, 'Les Mausolées Invisibles: Raqqa – Ville de Pélérinage Chiite ou Pole Etatique en Jazira Syrienne?', *Les Annales de Géographie*, no. 622, 2001.

—— 'Privatisation in Syria: state farms and the case of the Euphrates Project', RSCAS Working Papers, no. 1, 2005.

Abboud, Samer and Ferdinand Arslanian, *Syria's Economy and the Transition Paradigm*, Boulder, Colo., Lynne Rienner Publishers, 2008.

Altunisik, Meliha Benli and Ozlem Tur, 'From Distant Neighbors to Partners? Changing Syrian–Turkish Relations', *Security Dialogue*, vol. 37, 2006.

Aoyama, Hiroyuki, *History Does Not Repeat Itself (or Does It?): the political changes in Syria after Hafiz al-Asad's death*, Tokyo, Institute of Developing Economies, Japan External Trade Organisation, 2001.

Aras, Bulent and Hasan Koni, 'Turkish–Syrian Relations Revisited', *Arab Studies Quarterly*, vol. 24, 2002.

Aras, Bulent and Rabia Karakaya Polat, 'From Conflict to Cooperation: desecuritization of Turkey's relations with Syria and Iraq', *Security Dialogue*, vol. 39, 2008.

Bahout, Joseph, *Les Entrepreneurs Syriens: économie, affaires et politique*, Beirut, Centre d'études et de recherches sur le Moyen-Orient contemporain, 1994.

Batatu, Hanna, 'Some Observations on the Social Roots of Syria's Ruling, Military Group and the Causes for its Dominance', *Middle East Journal*, vol. 35, 1981.

—— 'Syria's Muslim Brethren', *MERIP Reports*, no. 110, 1982.

—— *Syria's Peasantry, The Descendants of its Lesser Rural Notables and their Politics*, Princeton, Princeton University Press, 1999.

Becker, Carmen, 'Strategies of Power Consolidation in Syria under Bashar al-Asad', *Arab Studies Journal*, vol. 13, no. 2, 2005–06.

Berger, M. S., 'The Legal System of Family Law in Syria', *Bulletin d'Etudes Orientales*, vol. 49, 1997.

Böttcher, Annabelle, *Syrische Religionspolitik unter Asad*, Freiburg, Arnold-Bergstrasser-Institut, 1998.

Bolbol, Ali A., 'The Syrian Economy: an assessment of its Microeconomic and financial development, 1974–1999', *Journal of Development and Economic Policies*, vol. 4, no. 2, 2002.

Calzoni, Irene, 'Shiite Mausoleums in Syria with Particular Reference to Sayyida Zaynab's Mausoleum', in Biancamaria Scarcia Amoretti, ed., *La Shi'a nell-Impero Ottomano*, Rome, Academia Nazionale dei Lincei, 1993.

Cobban, Helena, *The Israeli–Syrian Peace Talks, 1991–1996 and Beyond*, Washington, D.C., United States Institute of Peace Press, 2000.

Cooke, Miriam, *Dissident Syria*, Durham, N.C., Duke University Press, 2007.

Droz-Vincent, Phillipe, 'Syrie: "la nouvelle génération" au pouvoir', *Maghreb/Mashrek*, no. 173, 2001.

—— Phillipe, 'Succession en Syrie', *Les Cahiers de l'Orient*, 2001.

Dupret, Baudouin, Zouhair Ghazzal, Youssef Courbage and Mohammed al-Dbiyat, eds, *La Syrie au présent: reflets d'une société*, Arles, Sindbad-Actes Sud, 2007.

Gauthier, Julie, 'Syrie: le facteur Kurde', *Outre-Terre*, vol. 14, no. 1, 2006.

Geoffroy, Eric, 'Soufisme, réformisme et pouvoir en Syrie contemporaine', *Egypte/Monde Arabe*, vol. 29, 1997.

George, Alan, *Syria: Neither Bread nor Freedom*, London, Zed Press, 2003.

Ghadbian, Najib, 'The New Asad: Dynamics of Continuity and Change in Syria', *Middle East Journal*, vol. 55, no. 4, 2001.

Gonnella, J., *Islamische Heiligenverehrung im Urbanen Kontext am Beispiel vom Aleppo*, Berlin, Klaus Schwarz, 1995.

Goodarzi, Jubin M., *Syria and Iran: diplomatic alliance and power politics in the Middle East*, London, I.B. Tauris, 2006.

Gresh, Alain, 'Turkish–Israeli–Syrian Relations and their Impact on the Middle East', *Middle East Journal*, vol. 52, no. 2, 1998.

Haddad, Bassam, 'The Formation and Development of Economic Networks in Syria' Steven Heydemann, ed., *Networks of Privilege in the Middle East*, New York, Palgrave Press, 2004.

—— 'Syria's Curious Dilemma', *Middle East Report*, no. 236, 2005.

Heck, P., 'Religious Renewal in Syria: the case of Muhammad al-Habash', *Islam and Christian–Muslim Relations*, vol. 15, 2004.

Hinnebusch, Raymond A., *Syria: revolution from above*, London and New York, Routledge, 2001.

—— 'Globalization and Generational Change: Syrian foreign policy between regional conflict and European partnership', *Review of International Affairs*, vol. 3, no. 2, 2003.

—— and Soren Schmidt, *The State and the Political Economy of Reform in Syria*, Boulder, Colo., Lynne Rienner Publishers, 2008.

Hopfinger, Hans and Marc Boeckler, 'Step by Step to an Open Economic System: Syria sets course for liberalization', *British Journal of Middle Eastern Studies*, vol. 23, no. 2, 1996.

Joya, Angela, 'Syria's Transition, 1970–2005: from centralization of the state to market economy', *Research in Political Economy*, vol. 24, 2007.

Kienle, Eberhard, 'Entre jama'a et classe: le pouvoir politique en Syrie contemporaine', *Revue du monde musulman et de la Méditerranée*, vol. 59–60, 1991.

—— ed., *Contemporary Syria: liberalization between cold war and cold peace*, London, British Academic Press, 1994.

Landis, Joshua and Joe Pace, 'The Syrian Opposition', *Washington Quarterly*, vol. 30, no. 1, 2006–07.

Lawson, Fred H., 'Political–Economic Trends in Ba'thi Syria: a reinterpretation', *Orient*, vol. 29, 1988.

—— *Why Syria Goes to War: thirty years of confrontation*, Ithaca, N.Y., Cornell University Press, 1996.

—— 'Syria's Relations with Iran: managing the dilemmas of alliance', *Middle East Journal*, vol. 61, no. 1, 2007.

Lesch, David W., *The New Lion of Damascus: Bashar al-Asad and Modern Syria*, New Haven, Conn., Yale University Press, 2005.

Leverett, Flynt, *Inheriting Syria: Bashar's Trial by Fire*, Washington, D.C., The Brookings Institution, 2005.

Lobmeyer, Hans Guenter, *Opposition und Widerstand in Syrien*, Hamburg, Deutsches Orient-Institut, 1995.

—— 'Islamic Ideology and Secular Discourse: the Islamists of Syria', *Orient*, vol. 32, 1991.

Longuenesse, Elisabeth, 'The Class Nature of the State in Syria', *MERIP Reports*, no. 77, 1979.

Marschall, Christin, 'Syria–Iran: a strategic alliance', *Orient*, vol. 33, 1992.

Mervin, Sabrina, 'Sayyida Zaynab: bainlieu de Damas ou nouvelle ville sainte chiite?', *Cahiers d'études sur la Méditerranée orientale et le monde Turco-Iranien*, vol. 22, 1996.

—— *Un reformisme Chiite*, Paris, Institut Français du Proche Orient, 2005.

Muslih, Muhammad, 'Asad's Foreign Policy Strategy', *Critique*, no. 13, 1998.

Olson, Robert, 'Turkey–Syria Relations since the Gulf War: Kurds and water', *Middle East Policy*, vol. 5, 1997.

—— 'Turkey–Syria Relations, 1997 to 2000: Kurds, water, Israel and "undeclared war"', *Orient*, vol. 42, no. 1, 2001.

Perthes, Volker, 'The Syrian Private Industrial and Commercial Sectors and the State', *International Journal of Middle East Studies*, vol. 24, no. 1, 1992.

—— *The Political Economy of Syria under Asad*, London, I.B. Tauris, 1995.

—— ed., *Scenarios for Syria: Socio-Economic and Political Choices*, Baden-Baden, Nomos Verlagsgesellschaft, 1998.

—— 'The Political Economy of the Syrian Succession', *Survival*, vol. 43, 2001.

—— *Syria under Bashar al-Asad: Modernization and the Limits of Change*, London, Oxford University Press for IISS, 2004.

Petran, Tabitha, *Syria*, London, Earnest, 1972.

Picard, Elizabeth, 'Ouverture économique et renforcement de l'armée en Syrie', *Oriente Moderno*, vol. 59, 1979.

—— 'La Politique de la Syrie au Liban', *Maghreb/Mashrek*, no. 116, 1987.

Pinto, Paulo G., 'Pilgrimage, Commodities, and Religious Objectification: the making of transnational Shiism between Iran and Syria', *Comparative Studies of South Asia, Africa and the Middle East*, vol. 27, no. 1, 2007.

Rabil, Robert G., *Embattled Neighbors: Syria, Israel and Lebanon*, Boulder, Colo., Lynee Rienner Press, 2003.

Rabo, Annika, *A Shop of One's Own: Independence and Reputation among Traders in Aleppo*, London, I.B. Tauris, 2005.

Sadowski, Yahya M., 'Patronage and the Ba'th: corruption and control in contemporary Syria', *Arab Studies Quarterly*, vol. 9, 1987.

Salamandra, Christa, *A New Old Damascus: Authenticity and Distinction in Urban Syria*, Bloomington, In., Indiana University Press, 2004.

Salloukh, Bassel, 'Syria and Lebanon: a brotherhood transformed', *Middle East Report*, no. 236, 2005.

Schmidt, Soren, 'State and Market in Syria: the politics of economic liberalization', in Dietrich Jung, ed., *Democratization and Development: New Political Strategies for the Middle East*, New York, Palgrave Press, 2006.

Slater, Jerome, 'Lost Opportunities for Peace in the Arab–Israeli Conflict: Israel and Syria, 1948–2001', *International Security*, vol. 27, no. 1, 2002.

Staudigl, Robert, *Die Türkei, Israel und Syrien zwischen Kooperation und Konflikt*, Munich, Herbert Utz, 2004.

Sunayama, Sonoko, *Syria and Saudi Arabia: Collaboration and Conflicts in the Oil Era*, London, I.B. Tauris, 2007.

Talhami, Ghada Hashem, *Syria and the Palestinians: The Clash of Nationalisms*, Gainesville, Fl., University Press of Florida, 2001.

Tejel, Jordi, *Syria's Kurds: History, Politics and Society*, London, Routledge, 2008.

Van Dam, Nikolaos, 'Middle Eastern Political Cliches: "Takriti" and "Sunni Rule" in Iraq; "Alawi Rule" in Syria — A Critical Appraisal', *Orient*, vol. 21, 1980.

—— *The Struggle for Power in Syria: Politics and Society under Asad and the Ba'th Party*, London, I. B. Tauris, 1996.

Weismann, Itzchak, 'Sa'id Hawwa: the making of a radical Muslim thinker in modern Syria', *Middle Eastern Studies*, vol. 29, 1993.

Wieland, Carsten, *Syria: Ballots or Bullets? Democracy, Islamism, and Secularism in the Levant*, Seattle, Cune Press, 2006.

Wilson, Mary C., *The Modern History of Syria*, Cambridge, Cambridge University Press, 2009.

Winckler, Onn, 'Hafiz al-Asad's Socioeconomic Legacy', *Orient*, vol. 42, no. 3, 2001.

Zisser, Eyal, 'A False Spring in Damascus', *Orient*, vol. 44, no. 1, 2003.

—— 'Bashar al-Asad and His Regime; between continuity and change', *Orient*, vol. 45, no. 2, 2004.

—— *Commanding Syria: Bashar Al-Asad and the First Years in Power*, London, I.B. Tauris, 2007.

Zorob, Anja, *Syrian im Spannungsfeld zwischen der Euro-Mediterreanen Partnerschaft und der Grossen Arabischen Freihandelszone*, Saarbrücken, Verlag für Entwicklungspolitik, 2006.

—— 'Reform without Adjustment: the Syrian style of economic opening', in Henner Fuertig, ed., *The Arab Authoritarian Regime between Reform and Persistence*, Newcastle, Cambridge Scholars Publishers, 2007.

—— 'The Syrian–European Association Agreement and its Potential Impact on Enhancing the Credibility of Reform', *Mediterranean Politics*, vol. 13, no. 1, 2008.

Index

SOAS MIDDLE EAST ISSUES

Published by
SAQI
in association with
The London Middle East Institute (LMEI)
School of Oriental and African Studies (SOAS)
University of London

SOAS Middle East Issues is an authoritative, internationally refereed series of in-depth analyses of contemporary political, economic and social issues in the region stretching from Morocco to Iran.

The series takes no editorial stand on issues and requires material published to be sound and presented without bias. All opinions expressed are those of the authors and not necessarily those of the editorial board of SOAS Middle East Issues or the London Middle East Institute.

The London Middle East Institute (LMEI) of SOAS is a charitable, tax-exempt organisation whose purpose is to promote knowledge of all aspects of the Middle East, both among the general public and to those with special interests in the region. Drawing on the expertise of over seventy SOAS academic Middle East specialists, accessing the substantial library and other resources of SOAS and interacting with over 300 individual and corporate affiliates, the LMEI since its founding in 2002 has sponsored conferences, seminars and exhibitions, conducted training programmes; and undertaken consultancies for public and private sector clients. The LMEI publishes a monthly magazine – *The Middle East in London* – and with Saqi it publishes four books annually in the SOAS Middle East Issues series. For further information please visit the Institute at www.lmei.soas.ac.uk.